Philology of the Flesh

Philology of the Flesh

John T. Hamilton

The University of Chicago Press
Chicago and London

The University of Chicago Press, Chicago 60637
The University of Chicago Press, Ltd., London

Published 2018
Printed in the United States of America

27 26 25 24 23 22 21 20 19 18   1 2 3 4 5

ISBN-13: 978-0-226-57282-6 (cloth)
ISBN-13: 978-0-226-57296-3 (e-book)
DOI: https://doi.org/10.7208/chicago/9780226572963.001.0001

Library of Congress Cataloging-in-Publication Data

Names: Hamilton, John T., author.
Title: Philology of the flesh / John T. Hamilton.
Description: Chicago ; London : The University of Chicago Press, 2018. | Includes bibliographical references and index.
Identifiers: LCCN 2017056781 | ISBN 9780226572826 (cloth : alk. paper) | ISBN 9780226572963 (e-book)
Subjects: LCSH: Incarnation—History of doctrines. | Philology—Religious aspects. Classification: LCC BT220 .H227 2018 | DDC 232/.1—dc23
LC record available at https://lccn.loc.gov/2017056781

♾ This paper meets the requirements of ANSI/NISO Z39.48-1992 (Permanence of Paper).

Contents

Author's Note

Citations from primary texts are provided in the original languages and generally set in the footnotes. Unless otherwise noted, the translations are mine. For the secondary scholarship, I have consulted available English translations, which have been slightly modified when relevant.

La chair est triste, hélas! et j'ai lu tous les livres.
—STÉPHANE MALLARMÉ, *Brise marine*

1

Elliptical Prolegomena

In recounting the necromantic experience of unpacking his library, Walter Benjamin offers some insights into the collector's affection for the books acquired.[1] Emphasis consistently falls on the nonfunctional, nonutilitarian value of the collection, focusing on the manner by which the bibliophile attends to the rebirth of each volume and how he thereby assumes responsibility for its singular fate. The editions, which are carefully exhumed from the crates, are not simply to be read, but rather to be adored and cherished, held and preserved. Next to nothing is said about the printed content. Even though the texts continue to represent meaningful thoughts and experiences, even though each work still refers to imagined and historical worlds beyond the page, the collector's passion adheres to the physical medium. Certainly the

1. Walter Benjamin, "Ich packe meine Bibliothek aus: Eine Rede über das Sammeln" [1931], in Benjamin, *Denkbilder* (Frankfurt a. M.: Suhrkamp, 1994), 88–96 ["Unpacking my Library: A Talk about Collecting," Harry Zohn, trans., in Benjamin, *Selected Writings, Volume 2, 1927–1934*, Michael Jennings, ed. (Cambridge: Harvard University Press, 1999), 486–93].

books can still communicate a detachable message, but the love described here is more concerned with how they communicate themselves. For the bibliophile, the message is never distinct from the medium because the message always remains incarnate in the medium.

In the course of this brief essay, Benjamin singles out one specimen in particular: an illustrated edition of Honoré de Balzac's 1831 novel, *La Peau de chagrin*, printed in Paris at the Place de la Bourse in 1838. Benjamin purchased the attractive book some fifteen years earlier at the Rümann auction in Berlin at considerable cost to the student's limited budget. Days before the item went up for bidding, the young man fell in love with this deluxe edition, which inspired in him "the ardent wish to hold on to it forever" (93/490). What instigated the bibliophile's loving affection (*philia*) for this book (*biblion*) was not merely what the pages conveyed: his passion was not primarily concerned with the novel's plot or with whatever information its descriptions might provide, but rather for the book itself, for this unique exemplar. When one reads solely for the message, the means for transmitting that message become dispensable as soon as its ideational content has been received. The physical, fleshly qualities of the volume—its form and appearance, its shape and feel, its aroma and heft, as well as the concrete conditions of its acquisition—are hastily superseded once the verbal content has passed from the page to the mind of the reader. In contrast, what caught Benjamin's eye and nourished his affection was not the novel's usefulness, but rather the book's potential to stand as a source of ceaseless enjoyment, as a fount of inexhaustible friendship—*philia*.

Strikingly, although Benjamin does not once mention the plot of Balzac's novel, the book's narrative can serve to illuminate the bibliophile's loving attachment, albeit negatively. For Benjamin's description of this youthful book buying adventure contrasts with the experience of Balzac's protagonist, Raphael de Valentin, a young man contemplating suicide, who unexpectedly happens upon the *peau de chagrin*: a piece of untanned leather tucked away in the upper floors of a bizarre antiquarian's shop. The coarse skin bears a magical inscription, which, although described as Sanskrit, is clearly written in Arabic. It was only in the illustrated 1838 edition—the one that Benjamin purchased in Berlin—that Balzac included the "original text" in addition to the French translation. The mysterious lines inform the reader that the one who possesses this talisman will be granted every wish; yet with every wish fulfilled, the skin itself, along with the owner's life, will diminish irreparably. Despite the warning, Raphael falls in love not with the skin itself but rather with what it can accomplish for him. And so, as Balzac's novel unfolds, every desire is indeed granted. Raphael comes to possess uncountable riches and property. He lords over worldly objects, which are discarded almost as soon as they are acquired. His life is one, grand *carnivale*—a "farewell to the flesh"—a steady adieu both to the uncanny shagreen and to his own vitality. The skin and Raphael's own life quickly diminish with every gratification. Thus, the grainy leather becomes a source of "grief" and "sorrow" (*chagrin*). In stark contrast to Benjamin's desire to hold on to his precious tome forever, Raphael's insatiable will causes his inscribed possession to evanesce at an alarming rate. By using this text, he uses it up.

It is not gratuitous that Raphael discovers the unusual *peau de chagrin* hanging opposite a glowing picture of the Christ, the Word Incarnate, painted by his namesake, the Italian master Raphael. Before alighting upon the magical skin, the young man spent some time surveying the shop's array of exotic objects and pondering how these "fantastic images" had been "resurrected" into the eternity of art.[2] As the melancholic Raphael reflects, these pieces are "fantastic" insofar as they have conquered time; their finitude has been exchanged for a kind of infinitude or deathlessness. These curiosities only reinforce the protagonist's resolution to take his own life, for they show that death is the prerequisite for immortality. The painting of Christ is different. Locked away in a mahogany cabinet, it is open to view only upon special request. For this reason, the shop's owner must be called in. This older man is equally fantastic, cropping up suddenly "as if he had stepped out of a nearby sarcophagus" (77/43). The allusion to a sarcophagus—an enclosure designed "to eat" (*phagein*) the "flesh" (*sarx, sarkos*)—already points to this figure's discarnate appearance: his "scrawny or fleshless [*décharné*] arm," his "colorless lips," his "pale and hollow cheeks" (77–78/44). When the strange man opens the cabinet's panel to reveal the portrait of Christ, Raphael's disposition changes radically:

> At the sight of this immortal creation he forgot the fantastic objects he had studied in the shop and the wayward visions he had seen in slumber. He became human again [*redevint homme*], saw that the old man was merely a

2. Honoré de Balzac, *La Peau de chagrin* [1831], in *La Comédie humaine*, vol. 10: *Etudes philosophiques*, Pierre-Georges Castex, ed. (Paris: Gallimard, 1979), 78–79 [Balzac, *The Wild Ass's Skin*, Herbert Hunt, trans. (London: Penguin, 1977), 45].

> creature of flesh [*une créature de chair*], fully alive and in no way phantasmagorical. He began to live in the real world.[3]

Unlike the other antiquities, which represent eternal death, the painting of the Savior displays eternal life. It alerts the young man to the life around him, including the fleshliness of his otherwise fleshless guide. The dejected protagonist, who shares his name with the divine Italian artist, thereby returns to life. While indulging in the sight of the luminous incarnation, he "became human again" (*redevint homme*), just as the divine Word (*logos*) once became man. At least at this point, Raphael is a *philologist of the flesh*: someone who exhibits *philia* for the word made flesh, for the *logos ensarkos.*

This redemptive philology, however, does not last. The sallow antiquarian coldly disrupts the epiphany by remarking on the price paid to acquire the painting. As a consequence, the young man immediately relapses into melancholy; for he now learns that everything is exchangeable, that everything is a commodity, even the sacred portrait of the Word Incarnate. Once he catches sight of Raphael's disillusionment, once he notices the young man plunging back into misery, the old dealer realizes that he has found a worthy subject for the frightening power of the mysterious shagreen. He instructs Raphael to turn his back to the painting of Christ and instead read the portentous inscription on the rough leather: an act of reading that will be of substantial use-value, capable of granting every wish, under the fatal proviso that with every accomplishment both the text and the life of the reader grow shorter and shorter. From this moment forward, the novel becomes a story of precipitous *excarnation*. Complete gratification will spell the complete loss of life.

Reading can be exhausting. The multiple and complex efforts expended to scan page after page, gathering the many visual marks and understanding their significance, require considerable amounts of mental and physical energy. However habituated, the manner by which a reader produces meaning is a laborious process. Every letter calls for attentiveness, even if only at a subconscious level, as the syllables come to form each word and as the words compose broader syntactic

3. Balzac, *La Peau de chagrin*: "À l'aspect de cette immortelle création, il oublia les fantaisies du magasin, les caprices de son sommeil, redevint homme, reconnut dans le vieillard une créature de chair, bien vivante, nullement fantasmagorique, et revécut dans le monde réel" (79) [*The Wild Ass's Skin*, 46].

units. The reader then proceeds from the order of the sentence all the way to the work as a whole—that is, to the reconstruction of a verbal corpus that ultimately relates to other, similarly reconstructed works. These textual bodies, the personal libraries stored in the mind of each individual reader, result from years of continuous diligence and the cultivation of memory. One must become ever more deeply familiar with language and languages, including the infinite variations and refinements in meaning, historical, cultural, social, and individual. Such industry cannot be performed without extensive strain on the reader's stamina: the strain on the eyes, the discomfort of remaining still, the struggle to keep distraction at bay.

The exertion devoted to creating bodies of sense therefore depletes the reader's own mind and body. The page takes on life by drawing on the life force of the reading subject. This economy of transferred energy was already discerned in the biblical Book of Ecclesiastes: "Of making many books there is no end, and much study is wearisome to the flesh" (Eccl. 12:12 [NKJV]). It is an observation that persists across the ages, motivating for example the opening line of Stéphane Mallarmé's *Brise marine* ("Sea Breeze" [1866]), cited in the epigraph above: "The flesh is sad, alas! And I've read all the books."[4] Mallarmé's early poem pronounces the desire to flee the ennui of the book-cluttered desk for the open expanse of the sea despite the risk of shipwreck. Life is said to begin when the book is put to the side, when the word becomes deed. This theme spans the ages and becomes absolutely central to pictorial representations of the Christian Annunciation, which almost invariably depict the Virgin Mary with a volume folded down upon her lap as the angel Gabriel announces that she bears the Son of God in her womb.[5] The fleshly labor expended by the reader to bring the scriptural word to life corresponds to the labor pains of giving birth to the Word made flesh.

Reading can be exhausting not only because it drains the physical and mental resources of the reader, but also because the method of transforming the materiality of the letter into a signifying corpus requires converting the inscribed marks into vehicles of meaning. Reading in this general sense means *looking through* rather than *looking at* the visual information on the page. Looking through the text means that the fleshly aspects of the word must finally yield

4. Stéphane Mallarmé, "Brise marine," in *Œuvres complètes*, 2 vols. (Bibliothèque de la Pléiade), Bertrand Marchal, ed. (Paris: Gallimard, 1998), 1: 15.

5. On this iconographic motif, see Laura Saetveit Miles, "The Origin and Development of the Virgin Mary's Book at the Annunciation," *Speculum* 89 (2014), 632–69.

to an acknowledgment of the ideational content that these inked or pixelated markings serve to represent. Cognitive operations, which begin by recognizing marks as verbal bearers of meaning and end by determining what these terms aim to transmit, calls for a degree of *decarnalization,* as the flesh of the text is organized into a corporate vessel of ideas, thoughts, and expression. At some point, the fleshly qualities of the word—its physical properties, its appearance and sound, but also its coloring, the way it visually and audibly rhymes with other words within and across particular languages, in brief, *how* a textual component communicates—at some point, these carnal characteristics must be rendered transparent, made to work for *what* is being transmitted. In this regard, reading entails incorporating every word into a *body of sense,* into a mediating container, one that is capable of delivering the represented *content* with minimal delays, compromises, or damage. To tarry with the flesh of the text itself would jeopardize the word's transparency and thus threaten the delivery of meaning. The carnal seductions of the discourse would prevent readers from receiving the message intended, holding them back from arriving at the destination of meaning. Through the power and will of the subject alone, the reading process can move on. Failing to do so would amount to a feeling of *discontent.*

Readers have long benefitted from the fruits of philology, which ostensibly prepares a text to serve as a source of unobstructed transmission. Yet insofar as philology denotes a loving affection for the word—a *philia* for the *logos*—the scope and quality of this intimacy may be variously understood. On the one hand, there is a *philology of the body,* which features methods of dematerialization and decarnalization as sketched out above—methods that are committed to the immaterial idea and therefore strive to free meaning from base mediation. Conventionally, the philologist of the body, like a good textual critic, works on the printed corpus in order to render it more readable, more transparent: collating variants, achieving consistency, clarifying obscurities, resolving textual cruxes, removing anachronisms, and so forth. Like a well-trained, disciplined body, the emended text promises to deliver its message with minimal hindrances or complications. That is to say, the philology of the body perfects the written material as an instrument that facilitates the passage from page to mind. The general reader who takes advantage of these efforts is thus able to move through a text with fewer impediments, invited to abstract its sense and ultimately discard the material transmission itself. For having arrived at the idea, having reached this destination, the vehicle of sense is no longer needed. Its role has been accomplished. Its mission is completed in the referential transmission.

Texts, however, have never been exclusively reducible to merely instrumental functions. A book may be regarded as a body, but that does not mean it is exclusively a vessel of ideational transport. To think of the body beyond its vehicular status is to recall the flesh that constitutes the corpus. The flesh that exceeds the boundaries of the body transgresses corporeal limitations, resisting *incorporation* into some meaningful or useful system of sense. For this reason the flesh is frequently linked to the sin of lust or *luxuria*. On the other hand, then, in contrast to the philology of the body, there is a *philology of the flesh*. Whereas the former attends to the book's instrumental capacity, the philology of the flesh exhibits a love that never wants to part with the word's material manifestation. It effectively denies the separateness of *logos* and its physical form, often taking the verbal form itself as content. In the philology of the flesh, meaning is not merely a detachable kernel of sense *embodied* within the book's binding—like a soul awaiting liberation from its somatic prison—but rather a nondetachable presence *incarnate* in the very word. For the philologist of the flesh, clutching on to whatever is perceived as *de luxe*, the word's materiality matters.

What should already be apparent is that the philology of the flesh points directly to the Christian doctrine of Incarnation, which holds that the divine *logos* became *flesh* at a particular historical moment. From the outset, it bears noting that this fundamental dogmatic claim, explicitly pronounced in the Prologue to the Gospel of John, is decidedly not exhausted by its theological import. Indeed, the theme of incarnation has always spoken as much to the nature of language as to the nature of God and humankind, promising to shed some light onto the formulation, communication, and reception of any verbal message. Whereas metaphors of the body imply the separability of form and content, metaphors of the flesh suggest their inseparability—an inseparability that is exemplified by the Incarnation. The present study takes seriously the ramifications of these incarnational metaphors, considering and assessing what they might illustrate in regard to human expression, including their relationship to the cultural and historical contexts in which language circulates.

By pressing the notion of philology as the love for the *logos*, the readings below investigate the breadth, depth, and limits of verbal styles that are irreducible to mere information. They question the viability of approaches to reading that restrict themselves to vehicular criteria that invariably diminish the formal qualities of what is verbally transmitted. That is not to say, however, that the philology of the flesh abandons reading or even the acquisition of sense. Quite to the contrary, it suggests that reading must resolutely attend to the flesh of language, that it must not neglect the primacy of the medium, even or precisely when that medium exceeds what it ostensibly aims to mediate.

The basic problem pertains to the figuration of Jesus Christ, whose singular nature is said to consist in the hypostatic union of divine and human natures. As the Word made flesh, Christ is "the way, the truth and the life" (John 14:6 [NKJV])—that is, his *truth* is expressed both as the *way* and as the *life*, both as *referent* and as *reference, representation* and *revelation*. Christ presents himself both as the *vehicular sign* of life—which precisely as a *sign* points beyond itself ("No one comes to the Father except through Me" [John 14:6; NKJV])—and as the *living principle* in itself: simultaneously both path and destination. The conjunction of Christ's fleshly presence and its capacity to refer beyond itself corresponds very closely to the doubled aspect of poetic utterance, which generally maintains some tension between language's designative function and all the material and formal features that disrupt designation.[6]

The chapters below aim to think through, but also to think with, the profundity of these fleshly disruptions or intrusions. By attending to a highly selective—and in no way comprehensive—number of interventions from the fifteenth century to the present day, the readings offered here attempt to outline divergent approaches to the word-as-flesh, approaches that interrogate the tendency to overlook linguistic difference. Philologies of the flesh stall the reduction of verbal expression to semantic or designative functions alone, and thus refuse to rest content with instrumentalizing discourse. The philologist of the flesh takes note of the noise that accompanies informational transmission and slows down the drive toward verbal transparency. By attending to this noise, by exercising these pauses, my readings strive to reveal how our relationships to each other, to the world, and to ourselves remain intimately tied to how we relate to the concrete languages in which we think and live.

What is the *word* that philology loves? The noun *logos* is derived from the verb *legein*, which in the Homeric epics means *to gather, to enumerate, to select*, and consequently, in Attic Greek, *to speak*. The verb's root is related to the Latin *legere*, which also primarily denotes *to gather, to collect*, and thus, *to read out a select pas-*

6. Kimberly Johnson identifies precisely this "dynamic interaction of referentiality and materiality" as operative in the devotional lyric of the English seventeenth century, which persistently turns to incarnational metaphors: Johnson, *Made Flesh: Sacrament and Poetics in Post-Reformation England* (Philadelphia: University of Pennsylvania Press, 2014), 22.

sage or simply *to read*, as in the modern Romance verbs for reading (*leggere, lire, leer*) and also in the German *lesen*, which can also denote *picking* or *gleaning*. The semantic network that informs the Greek term *logos* thus covers a broad array of significations: any kind of account or computational reckoning; a measure or proportional relation; an explanation, an argument, a plea, or a discourse; a narrative, discussion, or saying; a rule of conduct; a reason or the general capacity for reasoning and for thinking; and finally any verbal expression or phrase, which affirms a close connection between the mind of the speaker and what is spoken.

Although in ancient Greek *logos* is rarely used to denote a single word, in the Hebrew tradition, the Septuagint translators consistently employ the term to refer to the Word of the Lord (*logos kyriou*) as the divine source for the commandments and truths revealed in the holy books. Here, the *logos* is the powerful word of Creation itself. The idea of God's Word as a supreme, transcendent origin is reaffirmed by the Christian tradition established by the Gospel of John: "In the beginning was the *logos*"—the word, through which "all things were made" (John 1:1–3 [KJV]).

This divine, creative beginning should guarantee the truth of the material, written signs that outwardly represent the *logos*. All the same, there remains a threat of corruption—sometimes implicit, sometimes explicit—whenever God's word must rely on the mediating technology of written signifiers. And it is this compromising danger that the Christian Incarnation aims to address; for the very idea of the Word made flesh promises to reveal the truth to the world in full presence without mediation. Writing alone may be misleading, unclear, or ambivalent. Christ's presence in the world aims to correct the possible misunderstandings of scripture. It establishes and maintains the valorization of interiorized meaning over the technical means for conveying that meaning externally. The Christian doctrine of Incarnation—that the divine Logos "became flesh and dwelt among us" (John 1:14 [KJV])—would appear to consolidate all logocentrist claims, insofar as it is the Word present in the flesh, a full presence without the need for technical mediation, the perfect conjunction of an immanent, material signifier and its transcendental, spiritual signified. In the Gospels, the performative efficacy of Christ's words, their miraculous capacity to heal, attests to this sheer power of presence.

On the basis of this power of presence, one finds a perennial set of literary aspirations throughout European history, from medieval texts and post-Reformation poetics to the modern novel—a long and complex tradition that has consistently turned to the Christian Incarnation as a model for verifying literary representation. The operative conceit consists in seeing the text as a real and present body in the flesh. Modern theatrical representations have long hinged on an ideal of exemplification, which assesses the actors' accomplishments on the basis of their capacity to incarnate their roles. A similar ideal is discernible across the history of prose fiction. Throughout his magisterial study on mimesis, Erich Auerbach posits the Incarnation and Passion of Christ as the central paradigms that motivate and allow us to evaluate "the representation of reality in Western Literature."[7]

It is therefore perfectly understandable that the critique of logocentrism—including the critique of origin and authorial intention—frequently adopts an *anti-carnist* position. The formidable presence of the word incarnate would appear to override *différance* altogether, glossing over any gap between meaning and its verbal transmission. Roberto Esposito draws attention to a prevalent "antipathy or allergy to the vocabulary of the flesh," which he detects in thinkers as diverse as Jean-François Lyotard, Gilles Deleuze, and Jean-Luc Nancy. In Esposito's estimation, this line of thought aims to deconstruct the closed circuit of the corporeal signifier and the spiritual signified, which is presumably modeled on the Christian Incarnation. Indeed, for poststructuralist critics, the purported relationship without gap, whereby the living body becomes the absolute sign of its own interiority, robs the body of its own corporeality.

Referring explicitly to Nancy's deconstructive reading of the Christian Eucharist in *Corpus*, Esposito explains:

> This dialectic set in motion by the carnalization of the body results in its infinite disincorporation. Reduced to signifying only its own organic figure and turned toward its own interiority as toward the primary and ultimate essence of itself, the body ends up losing the exteriority, multiplicity, and opening that make it thus—*partes extra partes*, body among bodies in a world of bodies.

7. Erich Auerbach, *Mimesis: The Representation of Reality in Western Literature* [1946], Willard Trask, trans. (Princeton: Princeton University Press, 2003). This theme is critically examined in a number of recent studies, for example: Alexandre Leupin, *Fiction and Incarnation: Rhetoric, Theology, and the Middle Ages*, David Laatsch, trans. (Minneapolis: University of Minnesota Press, 2003); Regina Schwartz, *Sacramental Poetics at the Dawn of Secularism: When God Left the World* (Stanford: Stanford University Press, 2008); and Johnson, *Made Flesh*. Jacques Rancière addresses Auerbach's underlying thesis and takes it seriously to task in *The Flesh of Words: The Politics of Writing*, Charlotte Mandell, trans. (Stanford: Stanford University Press, 2004), see especially, 71–93.

> Pursued and continually seized by the ancient Eucharistic formula, *hoc est corpus meum*, it seeks itself precisely in the figure that resolves and dissolves it in its own absolute interiority.[8]

Indeed, for Nancy, the ideal marriage of presence and its technical expression—a marriage underwritten by the metaphor of incarnation—turns a blind eye to the way each component limits the other.[9] If we are to take the Gospel at its word, the *logos* was already there, "in the beginning" (*en archē*), before it "became flesh" (*sarx egeneto*). In Nancy's reading, the antecedence of the *logos* necessarily relegates the body to a signifying function: a technical means for conveying the interiorized meaning that steers it; hence the contradiction that motivates Nancy's deconstruction: "The signifying body—the whole corpus of philosophical, theological, psychoanalytic, and semiological bodies—*incarnates* one thing only: the absolute contradiction of not being able to be a *body* without being the body *of a spirit*, which disembodies it."[10] In order to preserve the body *as* body, it would appear vitally important to divorce it from the knot tied by incarnational doctrine.

Yet behind the disembodying contradiction that Nancy discerns, there is another, perhaps more radical contradiction at work in the metaphor of Incarnation, namely the figure of two natures inhering in one person—a figure that no *logos* can possibly comprehend. Rather than functioning as the external body that signifies the internal spirit, the flesh could be construed as an external element that undoes the body from within. What results, then, is a carnism that radically escapes the logocentric orbit. Tellingly, across Christian Scriptures and commentaries, flesh is generally opposed to the spirit as the site of waywardness, lasciviousness, and sin. In brief, the flesh is mired in finitude. Any reading of the incarnational claim—"and the word became flesh and dwelt among us"—must consider the verse that directly precedes it, where the Gospel speaks of the

8. Roberto Esposito, "Flesh and Body in the Deconstruction of Christianity," Janell Watson, trans., *Minnesota Review* 75 (2010), 89–99, here 90. Esposito is referring to Jean-Luc Nancy, *Corpus*, Richard Rand, trans. (New York: Fordham University Press, 2008), 64–74.

9. For Nancy, the incarnate life of Christ does not illustrate "an invisible truth"—it is not merely a corporeal signifier—"rather,' this life *is* precisely the truth that appears [*se présente*] in being represented [*se représentant*]. [. . .] The *logos* is not distinct from the figure or the image, since its essential content consists precisely in the *logos*'s figuring, presenting, and representing itself." Nancy, *Noli me tangere: On the Raising of the Body*, Sarah Clift, Pascale-Anne Brault, and Michael Naas, trans. (New York: Fordham University Press, 2008), 4.

10. Nancy, *Corpus*, 69.

children of God, "who were born, not of blood, nor of the will of the flesh (*ek thelēmatos sarkos*), nor of the will of man, but of God" (John 1:13 [KJV]). Directly before announcing the divine Incarnation, the Gospel starkly contrasts the "will of the flesh" and the "will of man" from the "will of God." The Greek term for "flesh" (*sarx*), like the Hebrew term (*basar*), decidedly refers to a material condition that is vulnerable, impermanent, and destructible, which makes it extremely difficult to comprehend how the spiritual *logos* can become mortal flesh.

Paul is highly cognizant of this problem: "But we preach Christ crucified, to the Jews a stumbling block (*skandalon*) and to the Greeks foolishness (*mōrian*)" (1 Cor. 1:23 [NKJV]). The "scandal" of the Incarnation, the Incarnation as oxymoron, is precisely what drove the kind of Gnostic solutions that were attractive to more intelligent listeners insofar as they were far more comprehensible.[11] The fundamental Gnostic dualism, which rigorously separates the material body from the immaterial soul, resolves the uncomfortable if not impossible idea proclaimed by orthodox doctrine—that is, the idea of Christ as the intertwining of two distinct natures in a single, hypostatic union.

This feature of entwinement or intermingling has made the metaphor of incarnation attractive to a broad range of discourses beyond strictly theological ruminations. In general, it speaks to a desire to overcome the rigid dualisms that structure and organize knowledge by uniting opposing notions: the divine and the human, transcendence and immanence, the spirit and the flesh. In drawing together what cognition would keep separate, a distinct *carneology* may be discerned in a host of theoretical reflections on the visual arts, media and technology, and popular culture.[12] For example, figures of incarnation often motivate feminist and gender discourses, namely as a way of demonstrating how the embodied nature of an *écriture féminine* may resist masculine economies of

11. According to Daniel Boyarin, the Incarnation might indeed be incomprehensible to Hellenized Judaism but not to rabbinic Judaism. Whereas the former adopted a Pythagorean-Platonic conception of the soul as detachable from the base body, the latter insisted on the inseparability of the soul and body in animate life. In Boyarin's estimation, Christian theology would come to depend on an allegorical (Pythagorean) approach to reading, which purportedly supplants rabbinic physical practices and rituals with figurative meanings. Boyarin, *Carnal Israel: Reading Sex in Talmudic Culture* (Berkeley: University of California Press, 1993), 31–35. For a useful critique of Boyarin's contrastive interpretation of Paul, see John David Dawson, *Christian Figural Reading and the Fashioning of Identity* (Berkeley: University of California Press, 2002), 19–48.

12. For a critical overview of these various interventions, see Volker Demuth, *Fleisch: Versuch einer Carneologie* (Berlin: Matthes & Seitz, 2016).

abstraction and subjugation. For Hélène Cixous, "woman" speaks by "throwing her trembling body forward; she lets go of herself, she flies; all of her passes into her voice, and it's with her body that she vitally supports the 'logic' of her speech. Her flesh speaks true."[13] This gestural speech constitutes a *sarcologic* intervention—a conjugation of the word and the flesh—that contrasts with an exaggerated insistence on the *logos* alone; it protests the masculinist detachment of reason from embodied experience. In Cixous's view, those deemed repressed in psychoanalytic theory, those who have been marginalized by Freudian phallocentrism, are forcefully eloquent in their carnal fragility—

> a fragility, a vulnerability, equal to their incomparable intensity. Fortunately, they haven't sublimated; they've saved their skin, their energy. They haven't worked at liquidating the impasse of lives without futures. They have furiously inhabited these sumptuous bodies: admirable hysterics who made Freud succumb to many voluptuous moments impossible to confess, bombarding his Mosaic statue with their carnal and passionate body words, haunting him with their inaudible and thundering denunciations, dazzling, more than naked underneath the seven veils of modesty.[14]

The bodily revolt that Cixous and others have evoked confronts a broader dualism that has organized many theoretical reflections: namely, the dualism between subjective consciousness and the external world. This dualism has been persistently challenged by phenomenology and philosophical hermeneutics, two theoretical strands that have appropriated incarnational figures to illustrate their methods.[15] In terms of intellecutal history, phenomenology and hermeneutics share an orienting source in the work of Franz Brentano, whose lectures on empirical psychology at the University of Vienna from 1874 to 1895 attracted both Sigmund Freud and Edmund Husserl. Brentano, who studied

13. Hélène Cixous, "The Laugh of the Medusa," Keith and Paula Cohen, trans., *Signs* 4 (1976), 875–93; here, 881.

14. Cixous, "The Laugh of the Medusa," 886. Along similar lines, Luce Irigaray has frequently turned to incarnational metaphors in order to articulate an embodied feminine subjectivity. For a comprehensive overview, see Abigail Rine, *Irigaray, Incarnation, and Contemporary Women's Fiction* (New York: Bloomsbury, 2013).

15. Michael O'Sullivan provides a concise account of the centrality of incarnational metaphors in phenomenology and philosophical hermeneutics in *The Incarnation of Language: Joyce, Proust, and a Philosophy of the Flesh* (New York: Bloomsbury, 2008), 11–56.

scholastic theology and was ordained a Catholic priest, assisted a line of thinking that proliferates to varying degrees through the work of psychoanalysis and phenomenology, and onward through Martin Heidegger and Hans-Georg Gadamer, Maurice Merleau-Ponty and Jacques Derrida.[16] More recently, with the so-called theological turn in phenomenology, this tradition motivates a pronounced engagement with incarnational discourse.[17] In order to begin an assessment of the implications of philologies of the flesh, it would be worthwhile to review some of the more relevant aspects of this philosophical heritage.

For reasons that are more or less straightforward, Husserl persistently grappled with the role of the body in acts of consciousness. Insofar as my body is neither purely internal to my consciousness nor solely an external object in the environment, it appears to occupy the very threshold between subjectivity and objectivity that constitutes phenomenology's principal focus. As a threshold phenomenon, my body can never be an entirely concrete entity, since it is *my* body and thus also the seat of *my* individual consciousness. My embodied existence is therefore much more than an experience of having a body. Husserl designates this threshold existence as *Leib* ("lived body") in contrast to *Körper*, which denotes the material body that is found in the environment. The *Leib* is a psychophysical unity—the union of body and conscious soul—related to but distinct from the *Körper* that is encountered in the world. Precisely as a psychophysical unity, the *Leib* underscores our doubled nature as both *cognitive* and *sensory* beings—that is, as beings cognitively *detached from* but also sensorily *implicated in* the world we inhabit.[18] In sum, the *Leib* is a physical thing that is also a locus of internal feeling, situated on the border of consciousness and reality, touching and touched by the world.

16. See Otto Jachmann, *Denken wird Wahrnehmung: Die Philosophie von Brentano, Husserl, Heidegger, und Derrida und die Anthroposophie* (Borchen: Möllmann, 2009).

17. Dominique Janicaud was one of the first to identify a theological turn in European phenomenology. On the varied assessments and evaluations of this tendency, see *Phenomenology and the "Theological Turn": The French Debate*, Dominique Janicaud, ed. (New York: Fordham University Press, 2000). The most sustained consideration of the role of the incarnation in phenomenology is found in Michel Henry, *Incarnation: A Philosophy of the Flesh*, Karl Hefty, trans. (Evanston: Northwestern University Press, 2015).

18. Edmund Husserl, *Ideas Pertaining to a Pure Phenomenology and to a Phenomenological Philosophy*, vol. 2: *Studies in the Phenomenology of Constitution* [1913], Richard Rojcewicz and André Schuwer, trans. (Dordrecht: Kluwer, 1989), 151–58. For a comprehensive discussion on this theme in relation to metaphors of incarnation, see Natalie Depraz, *Transcendance et incarnation: Le statut de l'intersubjectivité comme altérité à soi chez Husserl* (Paris: Vrin, 1995).

The tactual constitution of the *Leib* is confirmed when we examine the sense of seeing. "An eye does not appear to one's own vision. [. . .] I do not see myself, my *Leib*, the way I touch myself."[19] Even though I may be able to see my physical eye in a mirror, it is not *my* eye in the strict sense, insofar as I cannot see my seeing; I cannot locate visual sensations in the eye. Nonetheless, I can feel myself feeling, which, for Husserl, validates "the privilege of the localization of the touch sensations" (158). Touch effects allow us to experience the body as a lived body, as a psychophysical unity, both conscious and real, and therefore not like some bodiless subject entirely detached from the world of experience. "A subject whose only sense was the sense of vision could not at all have an appearing *Leib*" (158). Thus, in perceiving the world of things, I come to experience my lived corporeality or *Leiblichkeit*.

For Maurice Merleau-Ponty, Husserl's description of the *Leib*, which clearly attempts to bridge the division between immanent consciousness and transcendent reality, is an important first step, but one that needs to be pursued further and revised. Although profoundly indebted to Husserl, Merleau-Ponty is critical of the distinctions that organize his phenomenological method overall. In particular, Merleau-Ponty is troubled by the binary series implicit in Husserl's investigations: most importantly, the dualism between consciousness and reality; and the dualism between immanent perception and transcendent sensation. In Merleau-Ponty's view, such divisions are symptomatic of an intellectualist tendency grounded in reflection, the very tendency that his own phenomenology attempts to defuse and one, moreover, that would go on to instigate projects of deconstruction. Whereas Derrida's careful work on Husserl yielded the key tool of *différance*, Merleau-Ponty comes to elaborate a complicated notion of the "flesh" (*chair*), which clearly stems from Husserl's meditations on the *Leib*. Indeed, some scholars—most notably, Didier Franck—would insist that Merleau-Ponty's *chair* is synonymous with Husserl's *Leib*; yet one should question the validity of this claim.[20] German would generally designate *chair* as *Fleisch* ("flesh" or "meat") and link *Leib* specifically to a sense of the *proper*, as in *one's own body*. In this regard, *Leib* tends to be far more personal and subjective than Merleau-

19. Husserl, *Ideas*, vol. 2, 155.

20. Didier Franck, *Flesh and Body: On the Phenomenology of Edmund Husserl* [1981], Joseph Rivera and Scott Davidson, trans. (New York: Bloomsbury, 2014). For an extensive critique of translating *Leib* as *chair*, see Jacques Derrida, *On Touching—Jean-Luc Nancy*, Christine Irizarry, trans. (Stanford: Stanford University Press, 2005), 233–38.

Ponty's rather neutral descriptions of the flesh—descriptions that decidedly deemphasize intentional acts of consciousness.

Merleau-Ponty's most sustained elucidations of the flesh are contained in his essay, "The Intertwining—The Chiasm," which appeared posthumously as the central chapter of *The Visible and the Invisible* (1964):

> The flesh is not matter, is not mind [*esprit*], is not substance. To designate it, we should need the old term "element," in the sense one employed it to speak of water, air, earth, and fire, that is, in the sense of a *general thing*, midway between the spatio-temporal individual and the idea, a sort of incarnate principle that brings a style of being wherever there is a parcel of being. The flesh is in this sense an "element" of Being. Not a fact or a sum of facts, and yet adherent to the *place* and to the *now*. Much more: the inauguration of the *where* and the *when*, the possibility and exigency for the fact: in a word: facticity.[21]

The flesh as "facticity," as an adhesion to the here and now, overturns all presuppositions of empirical positivism and subjective intellectualism. The metaphysical division between materiality and spirituality, which grounds the philosophy of reflection, breaks down with the notion of the flesh—a notion that is here explicitly connected to the Pre-Socratic conception of "element." Like Heidegger, Merleau-Ponty apparently wants to reach back before Plato, back to the world of Anaxagoras, whom Socrates cites in the *Phaedo* as claiming: ὁμοῦ πάντα χρήματα ἦν ("All things were the same"; *Phaedo* 72c). Socrates offers this statement to portray the chaotic state that flourished before the emergence of *mind* (*nous*): a turburlent realm that did not yet yield to the distinctions carved out by the intellect. According to Merleau-Ponty, in this primordial, homogeneous flux, we discern the "thickness of flesh" (1760/135), which offers an encounter with the carnal visibility that the seer shares with the seen—an encounter, therefore, that differs from any subjective, detached surveying of fixed objects. The flesh is somehow prior to the cognitive subject, prior to the transcendental ego, which observes the world from a removed position. For this reason, the flesh is also prior to objects stabilized as inert bodies. As Mauro Carbone explains concisely,

21. Maurice Merleau-Ponty, "L'entrelacs—le chiasme" [1964], in Merleau-Ponty, *Œuvres*, Claude Lefort, ed. (Paris: Quarto Gallimard, 2010), 1765 [Merleau-Ponty, *The Visible and the Invisible*, Alphonso Lingis, trans. (Evanston: Northwestern University Press, 1968), 139–40 (translation modified)].

the flesh is the elemental medium in which all beings participate, a "coarse, crude or wild" state in which "subject and object are not yet constituted."[22]

The monism implicit in the primordial nature of the flesh therefore precedes and overwhelms the dualism that is maintained in Husserl's account of intentionality, which rests on the *union* and hence the *distinction* between the *subjective-pole* and the *world-pole*. Tellingly, Merleau-Ponty backs away from any strict notion of union:

> If we can show that the flesh is an ultimate notion, that it is *not* the union or composite of two substances, but thinkable by itself, if there is a relation of the visible with itself that traverses me and constitutes me as a seer [*en voyant*], this circle which I do not form, which forms me, this coiling over [*enroulement*] of the visible upon the visible, can traverse, animate other bodies as well as my own. (1765/140; translation modified)

In Merleau-Ponty's view, this principle of animation is precisely what has eluded philosophical reflection, including Husserl's phenomenology. Intentionality is not dismissed outright, but rather shifted from the level of ego and consciousness to the level of incarnate investment. As Merleau-Ponty comments: "What we are calling flesh, this interiorly worked-over mass, has no name in any philosophy" (1772/147). Here, the flesh hardly marks the unification of spirit and body in glorious presence. Rather, it names the very element that opens the body up from within, giving it over to exteriority and escaping the guidance of a sovereign spirit, while still remaining bodily—*leibhaftig*. As Derrida points out: "The whole problem of 'flesh' itself is its corporeity before and beyond any incorporation [. . .], for 'flesh' is also a body."[23]

One returns, then, to the distinction between the organized, functional body and the almost anarchic flesh. Whereas the body can easily be integrated into a rational, theological system, the flesh remains somehow recalcitrant, persisting as something problematic or excessive, irritating and disturbing. The Hebrew institution of circumcision, the inscription of God's word upon the very site of

22. Mauro Carbone, *The Flesh of Images: Merleau-Ponty between Painting and Cinema*, Marta Nijhuis, trans. (Albany: SUNY Press, 2015), 7–20, here 9.

23. Derrida, *On Touching*, 237. With great care and nuance, Derrida reflects on phenomenology's pesistent preoccupation with the theme of "flesh" in the series of "Tangents" that constitute part 2 of *On Touching*, 135–262.

male sexual impulse, can thus be understood as a means of controlling the sinful extravagance of the flesh. Accordingly, as Eric Santner has recently shown, with reference to Merleau-Ponty and Esposito, the flesh has always constituted that "sublime substance" that "various rituals, legal and theological doctrines [. . .] attempted to manage," thereby providing the principal object of biopolitical endeavors as opposed to disciplinary actions.[24] Theory or the Law may strive to subordinate the flesh to the body, to domesticate the flesh's difficult or even anarchic impulses, yet the flesh continues to evade such systematization, which is perhaps why, in Merleau-Ponty's view, the flesh has no name in philosophy.[25]

Hans-Georg Gadamer likewise appeals to the metaphor of incarnation to develop a philosophical hermeneutics that would criticize the philosophy of reflection and the transcendent, detached subjectivity that it invariably posits and promulgates. Like Merleau-Ponty, Gadamer balks at distinguishing thinking from speaking—a distinction that he too ascribes to an exaggerated intellectualism. For Gadamer the severance of thought and expression has steered Western philosophy towards the instrumentalization of language, towards reducing all verbal expression to statements, logical propositions, and signifying codes. In order to remedy this limited view of language, Gadamer's hermeneutic theory proffers an "infinite conversation" among finite languages. To this end, in his magnum opus, *Truth and Method* (1960), Gadamer distinguishes "embodiment" from "incarnation." Whereas *embodiment* insists on the distinctiveness of verbal form and ideational content, *incarnation* illustrates their inseparability. "Incarnation is obviously not embodiment [*Einkörperung*]. Neither the idea of the soul nor of God that is connected with embodiment corresponds to the Christian idea of incarnation."[26]

24. Eric Santner, *The Royal Remains: The People's Two Bodies and the Endgames of Sovereignty* (Chicago: University of Chicago Press, 2011), ix–x. Santner's recent work on conceptions of the flesh in relation to political theology and political economy has played an important role in my own decidedly philological approach. See also Santner's *The Weight of All Flesh: On the Subject Matter of Political Economy* (Oxford: Oxford University Press, 2015); and Roberto Esposito, *Bios: Biopolitics and Philosophy*, Timothy Campbell, trans. (Minneapolis: University of Minnesota Press, 2008), 159–61.

25. George Lakoff and Mark Johnson clearly attempt to correct this namelessness on the basis of recent cognitive science in *Philosophy in the Flesh: The Embodied Mind and Its Challenge to Western Thought* (New York: Basic Books, 1999).

26. Hans-Georg Gadamer, *Wahrheit und Methode: Grundzüge einer philosophischen Hermeneutik* [1960] (Tübingen: Mohr, 1990), 422 [*Truth and Method*, Garrett Barden and John Cumming, eds. (New York: Crossroad, 1982), 378].

In Gadamer's view, the detachment modeled on the separateness of body and soul motivates misleading abstractions, which obfuscate the true relationship between words and things. To correct this approach, one must learn that the word is not a sign that one merely uses; rather, "the ideality of meaning lies in the word itself"; the word is not a discursive tool that one applies a posteriori; rather, "It is always already meaning" (421/377). Recognizing the true nature of language, and hence the true method for its interpretation, requires understanding how experience in the world entails a search for the right word that truly, mimetically belongs *to* the object. Gadamer writes:

> The experience [*Erfahrung*] is not wordless to begin with and then an object of reflection by being named [. . .]. Rather, it is part of experience itself that it seeks and finds words that express it. We seek for the right word, i.e., the word that really belongs to the object, so that in it the object comes into language [*zu Worte kommt*]. (422/377)

The Christian doctrine of Incarnation retains this mysterious mimetic bond of language, which is otherwise eradicated by philosophical reflection (422/379). Whereas the history of philosophy has tended to divorce language from thought, the Gospel of John joins them back together. As Gadamer concludes: "If the Word became flesh and the reality of the spirit was perfected only in this incarnation, then the logos is freed from its spirituality, which means, at the same time, from its cosmic potentiality" (423/379). An engagement with language that regards the *logos* as a word "freed from its spirituality" would be a philology of the flesh—an approach that loves the *logos ensarkos* and does not allow it to depart along a transcendent trajectory. It cares for a word that cannot dispose of its verbal medium, but rather one that deals with the immanent realm in which the word remains in the flesh among mankind.

Jacques Derrida explicitly engages with the Husserlian tradition that motivates both Merleau-Ponty's phenomenology and Gadamer's philosophical hermeneutics, particularly by way of Heidegger; yet he cautions against taking the theme of incarnation too far: "By making the flesh ubiquitous, one runs the risk of vitalizing, psychologizing, spiritualizing, interiorizing, or even reappropriating everything, in the very places where one might still speak of the nonproperness or alterity of the flesh."[27] It is precisely the unstable qualities of

27. Derrida, *On Touching*, 238.

"nonproperness" and "alterity" that point to the difficulty of reconciling the flesh with any theological system. Slavoj Žižek, following Hegel, refers precisely to this aspect of the flesh as "the monstrosity of Christ," which allows the Incarnation to allude not to the spiritualization of the flesh but rather to the death of transcendence. In brief, the flesh marks God's "eccentricity"—that God's *center of being* is outside himself, grounded in mankind. Žižek concisely explains Hegel's position: "God himself needs man in order to come to himself, to reach himself, to actualize himself. [. . .] man is the cause of God."[28] Here, the Incarnation implies "God's alienation from himself in Christ."[29]

Insofar as it affirms the conjunction of the divine and the human—the collocation of immanence and transcendence—the Incarnation has always been capable of affirming either the apotheosis of humankind or the humanization of the divine, either the *anabasis* of humanity to the status of a god or the *katabasis* of god to the status of human mortality. Regarding the latter alternative, Žižek further refers to Friedrich Schelling, who dismisses commonplace interpretations of human, temporal experience as a prison-house, as nothing but a long pilgrimage awaiting release into the glory of immortality; rather, for Schelling, "Eternity is the ultimate prison, a suffocating closure, and it is only the fall into time that introduces Opening into human experience. [. . .] The Event of 'incarnation' is thus not so much the time when ordinary temporal reality touches Eternity, but, rather, the time when Eternity reaches into time."[30] Whereas Nancy views the Incarnation as a spiritualization—as a disembodiment of the physical body—Schelling's sense of the flesh stresses humanization, a radical surrender to suffering and mortality. As Žižek concludes: "Once God became man, there was no longer a God one could return to or become [. . .] The point of Incarnation is that one cannot become God—not because God dwells in a transcendent Beyond, but because God is dead."[31]

Despite Nancy's claims to the contrary, then, it is not the *flesh* but rather the *body* that has traditionally functioned as a metaphor of totality, integrity, and subjective identity, as an appropriate vessel for the deathless spirit. The na-

28. Slavoj Žižek and John Milbank, *The Monstrosity of Christ: Paradox or Dialectic?* (Cambridge: MIT Press, 2011), 33.

29. Žižek and Milbank, *The Monstrosity of Christ*, 75.

30. Slavoj Žižek, *The Puppet and the Dwarf: The Perverse Core of Christianity* (Cambridge: MIT Press, 2003), 14.

31. Žižek and Milbank, *The Monstrosity of Christ*, 31.

ture of the *corpus* implies a transcendent, sovereign principle that is capable of organizing component parts into an organic, systematic unit. In other words, it is the integral body that works to *incorporate* its disparate elements, above all the diffusive, excessive, and disintegrating impulses of the flesh. The flesh can produce meaning only when it is incorporated into a representational system, when it is consumed and digested, when it is made to nourish bodies of sense.[32]

The philology of the flesh, then, would include a love for the word's material features that contribute to but are ultimately irreducible to information. It calls to mind that human subjects—speakers and listeners, readers and writers—exchange specific language, whose fleshly facticity, its adhesion to a specific time and place, exceeds subject-directed intentions and usages, without however neglecting meaning altogether. In this way, the philology of the flesh indulges in an oversaturation of meaning, which far outpaces the word's denotative functions. It demonstrates how we might disrupt the disruptions that bring language—our language—to a halt.[33]

Yet how valid is this appeal to philology? What would justify a turn to philology, one that, moreover, explicitly engages in incarnational doctrine? Certainly, both philology and theology have not fared well in a largely secular, rather cynical age, where it has become increasingly difficult to believe firmly in anything, either in a religiously dogmatic claim or in the irreducible uniqueness—that is, the nontranslatability—of words in the world's languages. The ideals of tolerance and translation have always better suited the enlightened mind. Most of us today rightfully denounce the blind obstinacy, the intransigent chauvinism, and, above all, the inhuman violence of fanaticism, just as we tend to celebrate multicultural exchange and pluralism, shared diversity, and world literature. For the sake of peace, and for the sake of commerce that flourishes with it, we may well

32. From a psychoanalytical standpoint, then, the flesh could be linked to whatever traumatically resists the symbolic production of meaning. Žižek illustrates this tension by referring to the roles of first and second readings: "It is usually said that the first reading is always deceptive, and that the meaning discloses itself only in a second reading—what, however, if the meaning which arises in the second reading is ultimately a defense mechanism against the shock of the first?" *For They Know Not What They Do: Enjoyment as a Political Factor* (2nd ed; New York: Verso, 2008), xiv–xv.

33. Accordingly, Charles Bernstein adduces "the flesh of the word" to spell out his own ars poetica: "The *intersection* / of absorption & impermeability is precisely / *flesh,* / as Merleau-Ponty uses this term / to designate the intersection of the visible / & the invisible." Bernstein, "Artifice of Absorption" in *A Poetics* (Cambridge: Harvard University Press, 1992), 86.

acknowledge difference, but only in the course of discovering common ground and mutual understanding. The basically exclusionary nature of monotheistic religions, which affirm that there is only one true, irreplaceable God, militates against this kind of appeasement. Such a claim implies that every other god is necessarily false and thereby undermines the very basis for accord. Analogously, the philological claim, that specific words in specific cultural-historical contexts are never equivalent with any other terms, disrupts attempts to arrive at perfectly adequate translations.

By not appealing to absolute singularity, by renouncing the distinction between true and false beliefs—or, for that matter, between true and false philologies—we presumably hold open the channels for intercultural and interhistorical communication. Cooperative *ecumenicalism* is *ecological,* setting up a welcoming "house" (*oikos*), where different views can be tolerated and exchanged. Ecumenicalism, concerning not only religious dogmas but also sociocultural positions, resolves the problem of mutual incomprehension by providing an all-encompassing ground for shared *inhabitance* (*oikoumenē*), a global *economy* or marketplace, wherein all ideas, opinions, and claims are exchangeable and understandable, consumable, and digestible. The enlightened age aims to find common denominators and thus grow more accepting of difference, which, in the end, is taken to be merely a matter of difference and nothing more. In contrast, exclusionary thinking, which is always implicit in any true-or-false distinction, insists, often quite violently, on nonexchangeability, which is precisely what today's ecumenicalism promises to defuse.

Understood as stubborn instances of nonecumenical resistance, it would appear that neither philology nor theological dogmatism has anything to contribute at the end of history. Extrapolating from Francis Fukuyama's infamous theory, Walter Benn Michaels diagnoses the present era as a moment where real disagreement is no longer viable. The end of history means that former ideological commitments, which used to drive arguments over what is and what is not true, have essentially disappeared, leaving us with mere differences of opinion. We no longer disagree over ideas or ideologies; we no longer affirm the truth of one position at the expense of another, because we now recognize that we simply see things differently. These differences are based on our different cultural identities—on who we are and where we come from—differences that readily allow for different things to be "true" for some people but not for others. Identity has trumped ideology. Michaels discerns this shift as a persistent feature of postmodern theory, which indulges in polysemy and undecidability, reception and perspectivism:

> Readers for whom the same text can have different meanings are not readers who have different beliefs about what the text means; they are readers who have different responses to the text, whatever it means. They do not, that is, have different interpretations of the text, they have different *experiences* of the text.[34]

Any philological argument that maintains the truthfulness of its claims, like any theology that insists on the veracity of its assertions, is thus consigned to a prior epoch, to a time when beliefs really mattered, when interpretations could indeed be verified or falsified, when variances in positions could ignite a crusade. If subjective experiences alone legitimize different readings, then philological expertise, like theological appeals to revealed truth, can no longer play a role in determining what a text does and does not say.

From a historical perspective, it is easy to understand how philology, like theology, came to be characterized in such a way that it would find itself incompatible with a pluralist worldview. Parallel to, but also at times intersecting with, the violent history of religion in the West, there is a history of linguistic and literary scholarship that is no less violent, no less embattled, one marked by importunity and unyielding conviction. Although the long struggle against clerical obscurantism and ecclesiastical power is more clearly recorded, the protest against institutional control over the transmission and interpretation of texts equally deserves a place in the story of present nihilism.

As in the case of Western anticlericalism, the critique of institutional knowledge has generally been a reaction to exaggerated pretensions to authority. From its emergence in the third century BCE, philology developed a polemical edge that fostered competitiveness, rivalry, and tenacity, attempting to exercise great disciplinary control over usage.[35] Subsequently, in the early modern period, the philologist's skills for testing authenticity and exposing forgeries—which in-

34. Walter Benn Michaels, *The Shape of the Signifier: 1967 to the End of History* (Princeton: Princeton University Press, 2006), 8.

35. See Robert Stockhammer, *Grammatik: Wissen und Macht in der Geschichte einer sprachlichen Institution* (Frankfurt a. M.: Suhrkamp, 2014), 9–29.

cludes, of course, the talent for producing forged documents—soon became a powerful political weapon.[36] The famous case of Lorenzo Valla and the *Donation of Constantine* would alone be sufficient to demonstrate how scholarship could wreak considerable institutional damage. Although philologists could just as well adopt a more humble position, playing the role of the quiet and unobtrusive servant, strong wills and adamant self-confidence continued to surface among professional readers and scholars. Philologists typically invited scorn whenever they acted insubordinately, persuaded that the value of their services surpassed the work of those they ostensibly aimed to serve. Repeatedly across history, institutions had to restrain philologists whenever they adopted an air of haughtiness, whenever they flaunted their hard-earned erudition and gloated over their superior knowledge and insight.

Motivated by imperturbable assurance, philologists as textual critics exercised great authority in establishing editions and fixing interpretations, often by means of the most intimidating tactics. From the pulpit of the academy, they employed formidable disciplinary power over language, dictating to all what was correct or incorrect usage. Scholars determined what should or should not belong to the *oikos,* deciding on what was native or foreign, legitimate or illegitimate, pure or corrupt. With intense training and Herculean memory, they could defeat any alternative judgment, silencing each opponent by adducing the definitive parallel passage or the conclusive textual citation. Otherwise, they might simply appeal to some quasi-mystical prowess, to their impeccable intuition, their connoisseur-like discernment, or their inborn competence in order to conquer anyone brave or foolish enough to disagree.

By its heyday in the German university culture of the mid-nineteenth century, backed by the compendious work of Friedrich August Wolf, August Boeckh, Wilhelm von Humboldt, and many others, philology—and above all, classical philology—established itself as the highest, most demanding, and therefore most elite science. Yet around the same time, roughly coincident with the *Gründerzeit,* these imposing pedagogues were being faulted for disdaining their humanistic mission, for supplanting the benefits of moral education with the hyper-professionalized pursuit of science, for ignoring the goals of *Bildung* in favor of *Wissenschaft.* It was precisely this kind of scientism that would

36. For highly illustrative examples, see Anthony Grafton, *Forgers and Critics: Creativity and Duplicity in Western Scholarship* (Princeton: Princeton University Press, 1990).

be targeted by the Third Humanism of the 1920s, which strived to remedy a guild that failed to convey the normative ideals that would be useful for society at large. The classicists who gathered around Werner Jaeger vilified the university bookworms, who were more concerned with the function of Greek particles or the employment of the Latin ablative than with imparting to young minds the courage of Achilles or the civic virtue of Cincinnatus.[37]

Yet when other philologists responded to the call of duty, applying their rigorous methods to endorse nationalist ambitions, their craft all too readily became complicit in the kind of racial science that fueled the most insidious chauvinism. As Geoffrey Harpham portrays this period: "Philologists adduced linguistic evidence in support of racialist theorizing, promulgated learned forms of anti-Semitism, represented as a fact of nature the domination of the weak by the strong, and claimed to deduce from the study of language the superiority of western European culture and its dominant religion, Christianity."[38] Here again, but now at the most repulsive level, we find the exclusionary beliefs that would aggravate the pluralist, egalitarian mind. Indeed, the perfidious collaboration of philology and racial pseudoscience, whereby the radical heterogeneity or non-exchangeability of one's language raised it to a sovereign position above every other (*über alles!*), would ultimately lead, after the Second World War, to the broad condemnation of philology in favor of a more politically neutral, less determinative approach to cultural artifacts.[39]

It is in this spirit that we should understand New Critical and poststructuralist theories. Both New Criticism and poststructuralism perform a decisive shift in focus from authorial-centered meaning (*intentio auctoris*) to reader-centered responses (*intentio lectoris*). Accordingly, Roland Barthes famously called for replacing a conception of the authorial and authorized "work" (*œuvre*), which is ascertained or fixed by philological labor, with a conception of the "text," which

37. For a comprehensive account, see Barbara Stiewe, *Der "Dritte Humanismus": Aspekte deutscher Griechenrezeption vom George-Kreis bis zum Nationalsozialismus* (Berlin: de Gruyter, 2011).

38. Geoffrey Galt Harpham, "Roots, Races, and the Return to Philology," *Representations* 106 (2009), 34–62, here 50. See also Maurice Olender, *The Languages of Paradise: Race, Religion, and Philology in the Nineteenth Century*, Arthur Goldhammer, trans. (Cambridge: Harvard University Press, 1992), 88–92.

39. See Sheldon Pollock, "Future Philology: The Fate of a Soft Science in a Hard World," *Critical Inquiry* 35 (2009), 931–61, here 936–37.

unworks the work by way of semiological investigation.[40] By renouncing philological control, the reader would be liberated from imperialistic designs and allowed to roam freely in the empire of signs. The material conditions of the text, its rhetoricity and its traces, are what eludes authorial control and thus invites readerly exploration. Whereas traditional philology reinforced the ontotheological system of authorized guidance and principled meaning, the new reading practices emancipated the reader from any such dogmatic management.

For this reason, Sheldon Pollock—who here echoes Walter Benn Michaels's judgment—attributes philology's fall from academic status to "the hypertrophy of theory," which is regarded as symptomatic of our age, one marked by "the devaluation of the strictly textual in favor of the oral and the visual; the growing indifference to and incapacity in foreign languages, especially in the historical languages, worldwide; and the shallow presentism of scholarship and even antipathy to the past as such."[41] It would not be an exaggeration to say that these developments, which have for decades recalibrated the study of literature and culture, are directly linked to a deep-seated suspicion over philology and what the term is believed to represent. In the words of Werner Hamacher, this and analogous suspicions constitute altogether "an antiphilological affect":

> More and more among the human sciences, philology is seen as a petty, narrow, elitist, and in extreme cases hostile enterprise of specialists who presume to practice as a profession what any literate person does naturally. This affect—hostility toward concentrated attention to language, words, pauses—turns into defensiveness and often to disdain across a wide public, and the affect is also shared by many philologists, fueled as it is by energies closely related to philology.[42]

Indeed, as an academic practice, philology persists as an embarrassment, a source of shame, blameworthy for its flagrant fetishization of language. As one scholar confesses:

40. Roland Barthes, *De l'œuvre au texte* (1971), in *Œuvres complètes*, vol. 2, E. Marty, ed. (Paris: Seuil, 1994), 1211–17, here 1213 ["From Work to Text," in *The Rustle of Language*, R. Howard, trans. (Berkeley: University of California Press, 1989), 56–64, here 58]. See Ika Willis, "Philology, or the Art of Befriending the Text," *Postmedieval* 5 (2014), 486–501.

41. Pollock, "Future Philology," 934–35.

42. Werner Hamacher, *Minima Philologica*, Catherine Diehl and Jason Groves, trans. (New York: Fordham University Press, 2015), 109.

> In the company of many humanists or social scientists—to say nothing of colleagues in more quantitative disciplines, who might not even recognize the word—to claim to be a philologist could excite at best condescension, at worst denunciation. Like a covert drug habit or a particularly bizarre romantic predilection, even if you did philology, it was better not to admit it.[43]

Yet is it fair to reduce the entirety of philological labor to tyrannical and hostile pursuits, to the determination of unambiguous truth? Should philology be dismissed outright simply because of its tarnished past—its former presumptuousness, its ideologies, its racism? Can we not envision a philology that exhibits gestures of reception and response, which would not be incongruous with the New Critical, poststructuralist turn? Is it not at least possible that the contemporary antiphilological temperament—one that opts for openness as opposed to foreclosure, for freedom as opposed to constraint—targets in fact what one could arguably identify as false philology, as philology of the dead letter?

Certainly, even in the era of postmodern theory, philology has found no lack of endorsements in tune with a pluralist position and its emphasis on subjective responses and experiences of texts. Hamacher's bid to promulgate philology as the careful attentiveness to form, to *how* meaning is produced and not merely *what* meaning is, reaches back to Paul de Man and his efforts to encourage a "return to philology" as a method of tirelessly close reading.[44] The general project of revisiting the "philological question" is well represented by many German and American scholars in literary theory, language criticism, and media studies: Friedrich Kittler, Hans Ulrich Gumbrecht, Thomas Steinfeld, Karl-Heinz Bohrer, and Thomas Schestag.[45] Prior to this recent efflorescence, now in the area of medieval studies, Stephen Nichols drafted a "New Philology" that impels a return to the material vagaries of manuscript culture.[46] In a kindred spirit, Edward Said aspired to rehabilitate philology as an openly democratic and hu-

43. Whitney Cox, review of James Turner, *Philology: The Forgotten Origins of the Modern Humanities*, *Bryn Mawr Classical Review* (2015), 02.18.

44. Paul de Man, "Return to Philology," in *The Resistance to Theory* (Minneapolis: University of Minnesota Press, 1986), 3–26; and Hamacher, *Minima Philologica*.

45. See, e.g., the contributions by Kittler, Gumbrecht, Steinfeld, Bohrer, and others in Jürgen Paul Schwindt, ed., *Was ist eine philologische Frage?* (Frankfurt a. M.: Suhrkamp, 2009); and Thomas Schestag, "Philology, Knowledge," *Telos* 140 (2007), 28–44.

46. Stephen G. Nichols, "Introduction: Philology in a Manuscript Culture," *Speculum* 65 (1990), 1–10.

manistic practice that would free itself from perverse orientalist prejudices.[47] In addition, we have seen of late calls for "metaphilology," "feminist philology," "radical philology," and other varieties.[48] An all-out dismissal of philology would appear to be based on the belief that there is but one kind of philology, a belief that can readily be discounted, if only on the basis of these and many other recent interventions.

Understood within a political-theoretical context, a philology of the flesh—one that explicitly turns on metaphors of incarnation—could in fact be seen as a force that counteracts homogenizing pressures. For example, Michael Hardt and Antonio Negri contrast the synthetic, identifiable sameness of the *people* with the lateral *multitude*, which they define as a "set of singularities," as a "social subject whose difference cannot be reduced to sameness, a difference that remains different."[49] Hardt and Negri thus question the validity of homogenization, the guiding metaphor of which has always been the *organic body*. They criticize the *incorporation* of the multitude into a hierarchical system of parts that are organized into a working whole, into the traditional *body politic*, which functions by means of a clear division of labor and a clear chain of command. Given that the persistent metaphor of the body politic historically derives from the medieval theory of the "King's Two Bodies," which, as Ernst Kantorowicz has definitively shown, rests on the Christian doctrine of Incarnation, it comes as no surprise that Hardt and Negri revert to the metaphor of the flesh in order to specify the political force of the multitude. In their view, the multitude is "a kind of social flesh, a flesh that is not a body, a flesh that is common, living substance."[50] Reminiscent of Merleau-Ponty's musings on the elemental "flesh" and Gilles Deleuze's adoption of Antonin Artaud's figure of the "body without organs," Hardt and Negri refer to the living, singular, *nonincorporable* flesh of the

47. Edward Said, *Humanism and Democratic Criticism* (New York: Columbia University Press, 2004).

48. Mieke Bal, "Virginity: Toward a Feminist Philology," *Disposito: Revista hispánica de semiótica literaria* 12 (1987), 30–82; Sean Alexander Gurd, *Iphigenias at Aulis: Textual Multiplicity, Radical Philology* (Ithaca: Cornell University Press, 2005), x; and Jan Ziolkowski, "Metaphilology," *Journal of English and Germanic Philology* 104 (2005), 239–72.

49. Michael Hardt and Antonio Negri, *Multitude: War and Democracy in the Age of Empire* (New York: Penguin, 2004), 99.

50. Hardt and Negri, *Multitude*, 192. Further reference is made to Ernst Kantorowicz, *The King's Two Bodies: A Study in Mediaeval Political Theology* [1957] (Princeton: Princeton University Press, 1997).

multitude as always exceeding "the measure of any traditional social bodies."[51] The postmodern political climate may be, as Walter Benn Michaels proposed above, one that no longer supports disagreements over truth and falsehood, yet that is not to say that politics itself has come to an end. What may have come to an end is a politics founded on committed beliefs, while Hardt and Negri envision a political network wherein "the old standards of measure no longer hold," where "old social bodies decompose and their remains fertilize the new production of social flesh."[52]

The distinction between the integral body and the disintegrating flesh should enable a reassessment of the role of religious sentiment within a pluralist or even nihilist framework. To be sure, although religion, and particularly organized monotheism, can effortlessly be charged with despotic feats of oppression, coercion, and ideological pretension, claiming for itself a monopoly on the "truth" and thereby promoting the vilest acts of fanaticism, there are across history countless examples of religiously coded principles and dispositions that contravene the assured security of dogmatic beliefs and instead display the kind of freedom and openness that is otherwise associated with enlightened viewpoints, a freedom and openness that does not shy away from experiences, responses, and even responsibility. The critique of religion, like the critique of philology, may well stand as long as one limits the meaning of these terms to practices that have historically worked against radical freedom. Yet these lines of critique would be invalidated as soon as their targets are shown to be grossly facile generalizations. At the very least, these critiques should themselves be subject to critique—to a metacritique—as soon as one recognizes that the limitation of meaning is itself the primary gesture of the objects under suspicion: The wholesale dismissal of philology and theology would then be but an ironic demonstration of the kind of philological-theological thinking that is being denounced.

Philology rightfully instigates condescension whenever it resolutely sides itself with death. Insofar as it traffics in dead languages and promotes a life-

51. Hardt and Negri, *Multitude*, 196.

52. Hardt and Negri, *Multitude*, 196. More recently, Eric Santner pursues a similar trajectory to describe how the two-body political theory breaks down after the French Revolution, allowing the mysterious, glorious flesh of the monarch to relocate to the people in the postrevolutionary period. Santner, *The Royal Remains*.

less pedagogy, which fixes meaning, thwarts innovation, and suffocates young minds, philology comes across as mortifying. Its perversely loving devotion to a changeless past causes it to be cast as necrophilia, which cultivates a passion for the deceased, a desire to possess what no longer moves or breathes, turning the seminar room into a graveyard. Those who wish to restore the legitimacy of philological methods must invariably underscore the discipline's connection to life; they are obliged to reveal the manner by which philology opens onto rather than obstructs the way of life. Even in an ecumenical age, philology can become defensible, but only when the historical curatorship of written texts aims to revivify the past and thereby revivify the present.

It is precisely in this sense that George Steiner values philology as a performative critique—a critique in action, which hinges on *presence* or the *present* as opposed to *absence* or the *preterite*: "Such acts of criticism and self-criticism within the critical motion perform the pre-eminent function of all worthwhile reading. They make the past text a present presence [. . .] a vitalizing assessment of past presentness."[53] Especially when motivated by an interpretive drive, by the ideals of hermeneutic inquiry, philology can be a source of reanimation: "Hermeneutics reads the living text which Hermes, the messenger, has brought from the undying dead" (14). Here, philology cannot be charged with decadent necrophilia, but rather praised for its powers of necromancy.[54]

Steiner's allusion to the Catholic doctrine of "Real Presence," which insists on the substantial presence of Christ in the Eucharist, turns the words of all past discourse into the Word Incarnate. His philology turns reading into the sacramental union that combines signs and things. And certainly, the power of this kind of fleshly presence can be frightening. It exacerbates a perhaps instinctively human fear of ghosts or the walking dead. For this reason, Steiner claims that we "crave remission from direct encounter with the 'real presence' or the 'real absence of that presence' [. . .]. We seek the immunities of indirection. In the agency of the critic, reviewer or mandarin commentator, we welcome those who can domesticate, who can secularize the mysteries and summons of creation" (39). In this regard, the condescending attitude towards philology is a defense mechanism disguising a deep-seated anxiety that the dead are not truly dead, that the weight of the tombstone has not held the past in its grave. Snick-

53. George Steiner, *Real Presences* (Chicago: University of Chicago Press, 1989), 13.

54. Steiner's point here corresponds closely to Gadamer's conception of literature; see, e.g., Gadamer, *Wahrheit und Methode*, 395–96 [*Truth and Method*, 352–53].

ering at philologists, we childishly laugh at what frightens us. We protest the real presence of the incarnate word with iconoclastic fury. On a quotidian level, we flee the haunting, uncanny presence of what should have remained repressed by taking refuge in the homey comfort of the secular. "Like sleepwalkers, we are guarded by the numbing drone of the journalistic, of the theoretical, from the harsh, imperious radiance of sheer presence" (49). Yet even on a more sophisticated level, Steiner discerns cowardice, for example in the success of a poetics and a theory of language best represented by Stéphane Mallarmé and Ferdinand de Saussure, respectively. For Steiner, Mallarmé's poetics consistently promote "real absence," which severs the vital link between word and world. "Mallarmé's repudiation of the covenant of reference, and his insistence that nonreference constitutes the true genius and purity of language, entail a central supposition of 'real absence'. [. . .] The truth of the word is the absence of the world" (96). Similarly, Saussure's systematic, differential theory of language, which hinges on a repudiation of referentiality, may be understood as "antinomian to philology" (105), insofar as it entails the selfsame divorce of the signifier and the signified, the *signum* and the *res*. Steiner thus suggests that, by detaching language from the world, the antiphilological attitude is in fact the one more closely allied with moral blindness and death.

In order to overcome the theoretical consequences that have characterized modernity, Steiner insists that we turn once again to philology as a mode of receptivity, as an approach that touches the world that touches us. "The informing agency is that of *tact*, of the ways in which we allow ourselves to touch or not to touch, to be touched or not to be touched by the presence of the other" (148). In this sense, philology is likened to a tactful "courtesy" or *cortesia*, one that welcomes the other into the *court* of one's private space, inviting real presence to haunt our homes, uncannily. Thus, philology comes to be defined as an ethical obligation, one that is based on a religious or quasi-religious credence, as the term *real presence* immediately implies. "The numinous intimations, which relate hospitality to religious feeling [. . .], the intuition that the true reception of a guest, of a known stranger in our place of being touches on transcendent obligations and opportunities, helps us to understand the experiencing of created form" (155). It is this conception of philology as gracious host that aims to correct modernity's secularized devotion to absence and its complacent negligence of the world.

For Steiner, the philological attention to the forms and functions of particular languages ensures the referential trajectory, which leads from the word to the world. Here, the way of reading does not obstruct the way of life, but rather coincides with it. Philology is thereby not deadly but altogether vital, insofar as it maintains the referential connection to the living. That said, Steiner's conception of philological vitalism does not escape charges of lethality, perhaps not on the part of philology but rather on the part of the *logos* that the philologist ostensibly loves. For *reference* depends on the ultimate transparency or effacement of the word itself. By courteously inviting the dead into our homes, by transforming the words of the past into the living flesh of real presence, we treat the material form of discourse as a means to an end, as a vanishing mediator, which defines the word as "the executive passage of means into meaning" (162). The word dies, so that reference may live. Philology may indeed remain vital when it perpetuates referentiality, yet this operation still requires the sacrifice of the word—the word that must surrender its own life for the sake of the nonverbal reality it denotes. As a *sign*, the *verbum* must pass into the *res* and thus must be left behind. Explicitly in the Christian sense, crucifixion is the prerequisite of redemption.

Alternatively, one may repudiate this sacrificial economy by adopting a model of *potentiality*, which still aims for real presence, not on the level of the signified but rather on the level of the signifier. To do so, one must disavow precisely the hermeneutic drive that motivates Steiner's charitable courtesy. Interpretative domestication, preparing a welcoming home for the language of the past, renders the word transparent and therefore makes the word dispensable as a thing (*res*) in its own right. In a purely communicative model, the formal conditions of the message are no longer required once the message has been received as an idea. In contrast, a rejection of hermeneutic processes that operate without remainder would seem to hold on to the material thingness of language, to preserve the life of the word itself. By renouncing interpretation, one respects the *verbum* as tangible *res*. The real presence of meaning is abandoned for the real presence of the means.

For Hans Ulrich Gumbrecht, this encounter with the life of the word constitutes a certain "power" or "potentiality": "the potential of occupying or blocking spaces with bodies."[55] This potential is therefore a "physical" power, one that is opposed to any "intellectual" or "cognitive" capability (6). On this basis, Gumbrecht characterizes this power as nonviolent, insofar as he defines "violence"

55. Hans Ulrich Gumbrecht, *The Powers of Philology: Dynamics of Textual Scholarship* (Urbana: University of Illinois Press, 2003), 5.

as the transformation of "potential into performance" (6)—that is, precisely the kind of sacrificial violence implicit in Steiner's notion of "performative critique." Accordingly, Gumbrecht's potential speaks to a desire for presence that is much different from the presence endorsed by Steiner, which is based on the ultimate transparency of the verbal medium. For Gumbrecht, potential consists in the enduring presence of the word itself as a physical thing, as an ineradicable body—in a presence that exceeds "the explicit goals of philological practice" by producing "effects of tangibility" (6). Whereas Steiner's courteous tact aims to touch meaning, Gumbrecht's tangible power longs to touch the means.

Gumbrecht's potentiality, which tries to evade a sacrificial economy, must therefore refrain from hermeneutic violence, turning instead to "noninterpretive ways of dealing with cultural objects that would escape the long shadow of the humanities as *Geisteswissenschaften* [. . .] which dematerialize the objects to which they refer" (8). While Steiner's courteous philology, like Gadamer's hermeneutics, works to achieve a temporal proximity—the communication of past and present—Gumbrecht insists upon a kind of "spatial proximity" that exceeds ideational exchange. Gumbrecht, too, refers to "real presence," yet with a more emphatically physical sense of reception. This insistence on the word's physicality militates against the predominant tendency of the *Geisteswissenschaften*, which, at least since Wilhelm Dilthey, have relied on hermeneutic procedures that privilege the *spirit* (*Geist*) over the *letter*. The "powers of philology" that Gumbrecht's project adumbrates speak against this privilege of the spirit. It may therefore be aligned with Friedrich Kittler's critical turn to "media studies" (*Medienwissenschaft*), which explicitly and boldly intend to carry out "the expulsion of the spirit from the humanities"—*Die Austreibung des Geistes aus den Geisteswissenschaften.*[56]

Yet what remains after the spirit has been expelled? Where do we find ourselves after this exorcism? Is the focus on mediation as opposed to the mediated content simply a reiteration of our hyper-technologized, hyper-virtual, hyper-medialized lives? Or would it not, rather, confront issues and counter trends specific to our age? What can the philology of the flesh promise? What do we stand to benefit from attending to this particular love for the *logos*? What would be its relevance today—particularly for cultures that supply and demand constant flows of information while appearing to drift ever further away from the

56. Cf. Friedrich Kittler, ed., *Austreibung des Geistes aus den Geisteswissenschaften: Programme des Poststrukturalismus* (Paderborn: Schönigh, 1980).

sustained difficulties of textual engagement? In pursuing these and related lines of questioning, the following chapters offer scattered episodes across past history, which may or may not speak to the present—episodes that may in fact speak by not speaking at all: varied instances of boisterously silent verbal flesh, words that solicit and frustrate every attempt at complete incorporation. At the very least, the case studies below call into question the needs and desires that, today, all too hastily cause us to view problems, including problems of language, as annoying hindrances rather than productive thresholds. The following readings should serve to check the obsession with convenience and accessibility, with transparency and functionality—an obsession that compels us to leap for solutions, grab hold of straightforward, consumable information, and therefore overlook any *ellipitical* remnants, what every solution leaves out or behind.

2

Before the Word

From all appearances, it was a profound love for language that drove Lorenzo Valla to subject ancient texts to the most severe philological scrutiny. Regardless of the consequences, he consistently applied his profound erudition and critical skills to improve the accuracy and authenticity of what tradition had bequeathed. With a keen awareness of historical usage, semantic nuance, and register, he proposed countless emendations, collating variants, correcting scribal errors, removing anachronisms, and—most notoriously, in the case of the *Donation of Constantine*—exposing forgeries. That his polemical flair would excite the envy and animosity of many of his peers comes as no surprise. Yet causing offense by interrogating personal or institutional claims to legitimacy was of minor importance: Valla's loyalties were firmly on the side of language. His love for the word—his *philia* for the *logos*—set him on his noble quest: to purify our textual inheritance of corruption, even if it meant questioning powerful authorities who boasted an unimpeachable control on the form, meaning, and interpretation of these texts. Although extraordinarily knowledgeable, Valla took his philology at its word. Unlike those who contended that they *possessed* the truth, he characterized himself as one who *desired* the truth, fondly rehearsing, in the preface to his *Repastinatio* (1439), the story of Pythagoras, who specified "modestly" that he was not "wise" (*sophos*), but rather a "lover of wisdom" (*philosophos*).[1]

However disingenuous self-assertions of modesty may be, a desire for the truth of what language transmits led Valla, without ecclesiastical approval, to examine Jerome's canonical translation of the New Testament by measuring it carefully against the Greek text. An initial redaction of his annotations was prepared around 1443 during his time in Naples and subsequently revised and expanded a decade later after his return to Rome.[2] As expected, the work sparked controversy when Poggio Bracciolini, papal secretary to Nicholas V and Valla's long-time nemesis, charged the scholar with having the audacity to correct Holy Scripture. In an *apologia* published around 1450, Valla attempted to clarify his objectives.

> Accordingly, in order that I may not be excessive (*ne multus sim*), if I am correcting anything (*siquid emendo*), I am not correcting Sacred Scripture, but rather its translation (*interpretationem*), nor am I being insolent toward scripture but rather pious, nor am I doing anything other than translating better (*melius . . . transfero*) than the earlier translator (*prior interpres*), so that my translation (*tralatio*)—should it be true (*vera*)—must be called (*appellanda*) Sacred Scripture, not his.[3]

1. Lorenzo Valla, *Repastinatio totius dialectice et philosophie*, 2 vols., G. Zippel, ed. (Padua: Antenore, 1982), 1, praef. 1–2. The anecdote is recorded in Diogenes Laertius, *Lives*, 8.1.1. For its usage in Renaissance Humanist culture, see Christopher Celenza, "Lorenzo Valla and the Traditions and Transmissions of Philosophy," *Journal of the History of Ideas* 66 (2005), 483–506.

2. On the history of the two redactions, see the editor's introduction in Lorenzo Valla, *Collatio Novi Testamenti*, Alessandro Perosa, ed. (Florence: Sansoni, 1970), xxiii–l; and Jerry H. Bentley, *Humanists and Holy Writ: New Testament Scholarship in the Renaissance* (Princeton: Princeton University Press, 1983), 32–69. For a general introduction to Valla's approach in the *Annotationes*, see Christopher Celenza, "Renaissance Humanism and the New Testament," *Journal of Medieval and Renaissance Studies* 24 (1994), 33–52.

3. Lorenzo Valla, *Antidotum Primum: La prima apologia contro Poggio Bracciolini* [ca. 1450], Ari Wesseling, ed. (Assen, Germany: Van Gorcum, 1978), 112: "Itaque, ne multus sim, siquid emendo non Sacram Scripturam emendo, sed illius potius interpretationem, neque in eam contumeliosus sum, sed pius potius, nec aliud facio nisi quod melius quam prior interpres transfero, ut mea tralatio, si vera fuerit, sit appellanda Sancta Scriptura, non illius." Cited in Christopher Celenza, "Lorenzo Valla's Radical Philology: The Preface to the *Annotations to the New Testament*

Valla exhibits his usual prideful humility by declaring his intention not to overspeak (*ne multus sim*), claiming that he is "not doing anything other" (*nec aliud facio*) than translating better than Jerome, while neglecting to acknowledge that Jerome was traditionally thought to have been guided by divine inspiration. All arrogance aside, the parenthetical purpose clause—*ne multus sim*—does point to Valla's aim to let the Greek text communicate clearly in Latin, unencumbered by the translator's interference. He believes that his interventions work to reduce the effects of intervention. This gesture should be proof of his piety. The terms that Valla employs to contrast his work from Jerome's is telling: whereas the Vulgate is designated as an *interpretatio*, Valla refers to his accomplishment as a *tralatio*.

Although in the fifteenth century *interpretatio* and *tralatio* (or *translatio*) were more or less synonymous, Valla seems to be making a nuanced distinction. In classical usage, *interpretatio* primarily denotes an explanation, which invariably employs one expression to clarify another. This specification is discernible in Quintilian, one of Valla's most important authorities.[4] The *interpres*, who provides this explanation, is a "middle-man," someone who negotiates the terms between (*inter-*) two parties. In contrast, *translatio* and its verbal form *transferre* connote a physical transport from one place to another (*trans-*, as opposed to *inter-*). The implication here is that Valla wants to carry the Greek into Latin without "excessive" explanation (*ne multus sim*). If he is successful, then his *translatio* will be "true" (*vera*), for he will have borne the contents of Holy Scripture from one textual site to the other. And if his translation is indeed true, then it "must be called Sacred Scripture" (*appellanda Sancta Scriptura*). All will be compelled to agree, insofar as it is the Word of God, not the Word of Valla; for the philologist is "not doing anything" more than finding the most suitable words to deliver the divine message.

The ideal here is one of transparency, which corresponds to the majority of Valla's work: to implement historical scholarship and critical insight so that the original intention of the author shines through.[5] Collation requires an unam-

in Context," *Journal of Medieval and Early Modern Studies* 42 (2012), 365–94; here 390n1. I have modified Celenza's English translation on p. 365.

4. On the use of *interpretatio*, see, e.g., Quintilian, *Institutio oratoria* 2.14.1–2, L. Radermacher and V. Buchheit, eds. (Leipzig: Teubner, 1971), 103.

5. Cf. Celenza, "Lorenzo Valla's Radical Philology," 366.

biguous source, divine or human, which acts as the transcendent guarantor of sense and thereby steers the philologist's emendations, which aim to clear the path back to this authorial mind: the greater the distance from the origin, the greater the difficulty in returning there. In the first preface to his *Annotationes,* Valla elaborates on all the obstacles that have come between modern readers of Scripture and the source. In addition to infelicities that occur in Jerome's Latin version of the Greek, there is the historical fact of written transmission. Even Jerome complained how, already in the fourth century, the New Testament "had as many exemplars as there were codices."[6]

> If it is true that, after only four hundred years, that stream was flowing so wildly from its source, is it any wonder that after another thousand years—for it is indeed so many years from Jerome to now—this stream, which was never cleansed, has in part taken on some mud and filth? The unlearned copyist pollutes it, the negligent scribe pollutes it, the bold emendation of those who comprehend badly pollutes it, and the corruption (*corruptio*) that is more frequent than rebuke (*correptio*).[7]

Located far along the stream of history, Valla laments the "mud and filth" that have polluted the purity of the original text. That said, Valla nowhere questions the uncorrupted validity of the Greek New Testament, even though the Byzantine text type was itself the result of a lengthy and complicated transmission history.[8] Nonetheless, in perfect humanist fashion, Valla goes back to the Greek sources—*ad fontes.* Time has compromised the timelessness of the truth, because human and therefore fallible agents have interfered. Valla vividly demon-

6. Cited by Lorenzo Valla. The Latin text of both prefaces, with English translation, is provided in Celenza, "Lorenzo Valla's Radical Philology," 383–89. Subsequent citations are from this article. Translation modified.

7. "Verum si post quadringentos solum annos ita turbidus a fonte fluebat rivus, quod mirum si rursus post mille annos — tot enim ab Hieronymo ad hoc evum sunt — hic rivus nunquam repurgatus aliqua in parte limum sordesque contraxit? Inquinat aliquid indoctus librarius, inquinat negligens scriptor, inquinat audax male accipientium emendatio et corruptio frequentior quam correptio."

8. On the Greek sources for Valla's *Annotationes,* see Salvatore Camporeale, *Lorenzo Valla: Umanesimo e teologia* (Florence: Instituto nazionale di studi sul Rinascimento, 1972), 285–88; and John Monfasani, "Pseudo-Dionysius the Areopagite in Mid-Quattrocento Rome," in James Hankins et al., eds., *Supplementum Festivum: Studies in Honor of Paul Oskar Kristeller* (Binghamton: Medieval and Renaissance Texts and Studies, 1987), 189–219.

strates how easy it is for an "unlearned copyist" or "negligent scribe" to mistake a *correptio* ("rebuke") for a *corruptio*. Such failings cause the textual baggage to be transported (*transferri*) poorly: goods are damaged; parcels are lost.

Yet apart from these defects, fault must also fall on the translator:

> Add to this that many things are translated (*transferri*) obscurely, not by the fault of the translator but rather by the law and requirement of translation (*interpretationis*), at least of that kind of translation that is not sense for sense but word for word, such as this translation, which those unlearned in the Greek language are incapable of understanding, in their expositions they pour out many things that are false and unsuitable and shrinking far from the truth, and they often argue stubbornly among themselves over worthless matters (*de caprina lana*), as they say.[9]

Valla is alluding to the "law" (*lege*) or "rules" that Jerome imposed upon himself in preparing the Vulgate. As Jerome explained in his letter to Pammachius, although he agreed generally with Cicero, preferring to translate sense for sense, he explicitly adopted a more literal method for Holy Scripture, "where even the order of words is a mystery."[10] Valla does not consider the possible appropriateness of Jerome's literalism—a method that is arguably more aligned with the metaphor of verbal transport—because, on a practical level, the consequence of such literalism is a language that is often unidiomatic and obscure, particularly for those who have no knowledge of the source text.[11] And it is obscurity above all that Valla wishes to dispel. Again, his ultimate goal is to provide a sound, comprehensible Latin text—a clear channel, which bears the divine author's original intention.

In order to achieve this goal, Valla must arrange his priorities. Above all, he must make sure that the Latin text is articulated clearly and forcefully, even if

9. "Adde huc multa transferri obscure, non intepretis vitio, sed interpretationis lege atque necessitate, utique illius que non ad sensum sit sed ad verbum, qualis hec ipsa est, que indocti grece lingue cum intelligere non possunt, in exponendo falsa multa et impropria ac longe a vero abhorrentia effundunt, et de caprina, ut dicitur, lana inter se pertinaciter sepe contendunt."

10. Jerome, *Liber de optimo genere interpretandi*, Ep. 57, G. J. M. Bartelink, ed. (Leiden: Brill, 1980), 13.

11. Valla's explicit critique of literalism also conflicts with his own insistence on lexical consistency, translating the same Greek word by the same Latin word in every case. See Celenza's comments on Valla's method in "Renaissance Humanism," 41–43.

it means breaking occasionally with fidelity to the Greek. As Valla confesses in the later preface:

> The fact [is] that I am not always examining the Greek words, but rather laying bare any ambiguities occurring in the Latin and illuminating any instances when the law of translating literally may have made things more obscure.[12]

Despite adopting a humble position, claiming to minimize the extent of his interventions, it is ultimately Valla's love for the *Latin* language that guides his efforts throughout. Eloquence trumps accuracy. Thus, although his philology anticipates on many points the textual criticism of subsequent centuries, his primary aim is to improve the textual corpus, allowing it to communicate unhampered.[13]

To this end, attention must be paid to the smallest detail. In the earlier preface, Valla indulges in a corporeal metaphor: "For something, howsoever small, that is a member of the precious body [*pretiosi corporis*], cannot be considered anything but precious."[14] The figure of the body (*corpus*) introduces a number of implicit, interrelated concepts that determine Valla's approach, not only to translation but also to language overall. To begin, the body is here understood as an organized whole, a systematic structure, wherein even the smallest member contributes to its integral operation. For this reason, debility in one place threatens to enfeeble the entire organism. In addition to this idea of the collaboration of every part in relation to the whole, the body is further taken to be a vessel that contains a precious message, which deserves untroubled transport—a message that should be able to reach its audience without difficulties or distractions. When the verbal body is corrupted in any of its parts, "however small"—when it becomes weak, sickly, or overburdened—it suffers in its capacity to perform this vehicular function. A body impaired calls attention to itself—it calls attention to its material conditions and limitations—and thereby risks obstructing the content it should be transporting. By refining the body, by training it into good, healthy form, the philologist helps it perform its task of transmission. Finally, in carrying out this mission, the text affirms its corporate identity. It

12. "quod non semper excutio greca, sed in latinis siquid ambiguum contingit aperio, siquid lex ad verbum transferendi obscurius facit illustro."

13. Cf. Celenza, "Lorenzo Valla's Radical Philology," 373.

14. "Neque enim nisi pretiosum censeri potest, quod pretiosi corporis quantuluncunque membrum est."

should, therefore, not be questioned but rather received as an embodied entity that communicates authoritatively. Refining the Latin corpus in accordance with these desiderata is precisely what Valla wants to achieve. His philology, which loves the mediating function of words, is a *philology of the body*.

Valla stands before the Word as a corpus: as something organized, vehicular, and identifiable. This kind of integrity confirms the text's authenticity, even in cases like the *Donation of Constantine*, the *Letter to Agbar*, and the *Corpus Dionysiacum*, which prove the identity of the forger, however anonymous, by providing clues to the text's historical and cultural origin. Valla's frequent tropes of humility, apart from attempting to disarm likely opponents, underscore above all his self-assigned role as an assistant, as someone who attends to the textual corpus, addressing its needs, accommodating it, improving it, and thereby preparing it for reception in the world. Supplying this body of true knowledge is, again, a sign of his piousness. He recognizes that the careful attentiveness to words—to vocabulary, morphology, and syntax—is essentially menial work, analogous to the labor of a domestic servant, who facilitates the more valuable endeavors of his master. In this way, the philologist of the body poses as a *minister*. Whereas the *master* (*magister*) engages in matters that are *greater* (*magis*), the *minister* deals with issues that are *lesser* (*minus*)—slighter, yet equally important, since higher things are supported by the basis below. Thus, in *ministering* to the word, the philologist sets theology on a sound footing, which includes the philologist's own theology. In editing and clarifying the textual corpus, in devoting oneself to the *literal* shape of Scripture, philological scrutiny prepares the way for the *spiritual* sense, which must ultimately supersede the former—"For the letter kills, but the spirit gives life" (2 Cor. 3:6 [NKJV]). The *way*, although necessary, should in no way block or obfuscate the *destination*. Valla's critique of Jerome's literalism goes hand in hand with the ideal of authorial transparency, which consigns the letter to a subordinate status.

Valla's numerous opponents would doubtless have agreed, at least in principle, with the indispensable usefulness of philology, but they would have also insisted that it maintain its subservient role. It should limit its tasks to this ancillary office, assisting and facilitating the superior work of theological reflection and the teaching of the Church, and therefore refrain from too much needless complaining or nitpicking. For the sake of salvation, understood as the redemption from death in eternal life, theology must at some point restrict philology from posing tiresome questions. The ecclesiastical institution that confronted Valla might appreciate the philologist's efforts, yet when too much time is spent judging correctness and testing variants, when too much time is expended on considering errors or corruptions, on spotting anachronisms and lacunae, there is less time for taking the divine message to heart. Again, Valla would concur; yet he would indicate that God's authorial intention does not always correspond to the intention of His interpreters. However difficult, philology—forever in love with the word—must raise whatever issues emerge, even if, or precisely because, it hinders complacent, undisturbed reading. Whereas theologians might protest that the philologist gets stuck on minutiae and lost in details, threatening to obscure the larger picture, the philologist responds that it is at times necessary to halt the reader's intention for the sake of the author's. Valla was well aware that philological scrutiny might imperil the order of things, thwarting efforts to *incorporate* a text into a domineering idea or ideology. He realized that his work discomforted those authorities bent on promulgating what they believed to be the true message and thus preserve their power over doctrinal interpretation. Yet, piously loyal to the word, he would not hesitate to break in and overturn dogma, even if it sparked controversies and made everything troublesome and less simple.

That said, when focused on the *true* spiritual sense—on the original intention of God—Valla's theology too must put an end to the philological inclination to detain the passage of reading. Ultimately, philology must arrive at a *body of truth*, characterized by cohesiveness and integrity. As one can see in his work on the New Testament, each annotation raises a problem in order to solve it definitively.[15] Valla is confident that his emendations are correct, insofar as they allow what he understands to be the authorial intention to find unhindered expression. The corporeal metaphor—the text-as-body—presents the text as a material form that contains an immaterial sense within. The operative premise is that the idea or concept is entirely separable from its corporeal form, that meaning is distinct from its verbal manifestation. Meaning may be housed within the confines of a book, it may subsist within the limits of the physical corpus, but it is always capable of release or even redemption, precisely because it is detachable from its material vehicle. On the analogy of the soul's independence of the

15. Cf. Christopher Celenza, "Lorenzo Valla's Radical Philology," 378. "As one moves on to read the individual annotations to the New Testament, one is struck initially not by open-ended interpretation but by an initial opacity that belies the philological virtuosity behind them. Far from opening conversations, Valla seems to believe that, with each individual annotation, he is settling a specific problem of meaning within the text. Episodes of overt, lengthy acts of interpretation are rare; and Valla always seems certain that he is right."

body, the text's meaning can readily be discharged from its physical container, liberated from its finite or contingent conditions, including the history of fallible transmission, and then imported into the reader's consciousness.

The philology of the body works devotedly on behalf of this immaterial and immortal idea; it insists on the text's transparency and transitivity, so as to free meaning from its mediation, even though the medium remains indispensable. The philologist of the body labors on the written corpus in order to render the text more readable through emendation and clarification. In brief, the philology of the body refines language, turning it into an efficient instrument or transportation system and thereby facilitating the passage from page to mind. Having arrived at the idea, having reached the destination, the role of language—a role that dutifully serves meaning—has been accomplished. Should the role of language be understood differently, it would entail a different approach, a different way of standing before the Word, a different philology.

Nearly half a millennium after Valla helped to inaugurate the basic principles for textual criticism, after centuries of biblical research and historical scholarship worked to establish ever more definitive editions of the New Testament, the true aspiration of philology would remain in question.

> The interpretation of the Johannine *Logos* however may be the final goal of a "philology," which, taking itself at its word, perceives in the word the secret of the spirit and its revelation as the true philology; mere readers of the dead letter, incapable of making themselves "receivers of the word," naturally know nothing about this. For the philologist, because of his profession, the most living language—when the concepts of his knowing grasp its words—becomes a dead language. For the true philologist, every word of a dead language can once again become alive.[16]

16. "Die Interpretation des Johanneischen Logos aber mag das letzte Ziel einer 'Philologie' sein, die, sich selbst beim Worte nehmend, als die wahre Philologie im Wort das Geheimnis des Geistes und seine Offenbarung wahrnimmt, wovon die bloßen Leser des toten Buchstabens, unfähig, sich zum 'Hörer des Wortes' zu machen, natürlich nichts wissen. Für den Philologen von Berufs wegen wird die lebendigste Sprache, nach deren Worten die Begriffe seines Wissens greifen, zur toten Sprache. Für den wahren Philologen kann jedes Wort einer toten Sprache wieder lebendig werden." Ferdinand Ebner, "Nachwort zur Mitarbeit am 'Brenner,'" in *Schriften*, vol. 1, Franz Seyr, ed. (Munich: Kösel, 1963–65), 581.

Ferdinand Ebner, an autodidact philosopher, who taught elementary school in the industrial city of Wiener Neustadt, could hardly be counted as being of the same philological caliber as Lorenzo Valla. Instead, he is today recognized, together with Franz Rosenzweig and Martin Buber, as a main representative of the "new thinking" or "dialogic thinking" that emerged in the first decades of the twentieth century.[17] What these thinkers share is a decided emphasis on interrelationships and reciprocal dialogue, which overcome any rigorous distinction between subjectivity and objectivity. As an entity that, in addressing another, is also being addressed, the dialogic subject is fundamentally implicated and therefore constituted by other mutually implicated and constituted subjects. The subject's transcendence—its detachment from the world—is therefore rejected as a philosophical illusion, a species of solipsism. To a certain extent, Valla's emphasis on rhetoric and the fact that the majority of his work developed as a direct response to current debates also reflect this dialogic mode of thinking. Yet Valla's acutely polemical nature, reaffirming his position at every turn, caused him to enter exchanges in a way that is far removed from the sense of dialogue that Ebner and others represent. In Ebner's view, dialogue should not be *polemical* but rather profoundly interactive, to the point where the positions between both interlocutors begin to merge. For Ebner, the capacity for an open-ended interrelation forms the basis of human spirituality—a spirituality that bespeaks the authentic reality of the self, which is always in relation to other selves, and therefore explicitly distinguished from physical or psychological definitions of humankind, which rely on strict individuation.[18] The Prologue to the Gospel of John is a central text for Ebner, insofar as language or *logos* is the basis for the sharing and receiving of spiritual being.[19] For human being *qua* spiritual being is the entity that is addressed and the entity that expresses itself in language.[20] It is with this dialogic principle in mind that Ebner stands before

17. For a comprehensive discussion, see Bernhard Casper, *Das dialogische Denken: Franz Rosenzweig, Ferdinand Ebner und Martin Buber* (Freiburg: Alber, 2002).

18. See Nunzio Bombaci, "Der Prolog des Johannesevangelium als Epiphanie," in *Pneumatologie als Grammatik der Subjektivität: Ferdinand Ebner*, Ermenegildo Bidese, Richard Hörmann, and Silvano Zucal, eds. (Vienna: Lit Verlag, 2012), 173–86; here, 175.

19. Cf. Samuel H. Bergman, *Dialogical Philosophy from Kierkegaard to Buber* (Albany: State University of New York Press, 1991), 155–61.

20. Cf. Jitianu Liviu, "Dialogisch Denken: Prämissen für eine Theologie der Gegenseitigkeit," *Studia Universitatis Babes-Bolyai: Theologica Catholica Latina* 1 (2003), 47–61; here, 57–58.

the Word, proposing that the interpretation of the word-as-flesh "may be the final goal of a 'philology.'"

At least for those who listen or read in a particular way, the Christian doctrine of Incarnation appears to invite *philological* reflection while submitting its *theological* claims, promising not only to provide some religious sense concerning the Creator and His engagement in the world, but also to offer some insight into how any message may be verbally formulated, communicated, and received. With extraordinary concision, the doctrine affirms that God is the one who relates to humankind and the world by means of the Word that created the world and humanity. *What* God may be directly corresponds to *how* God is perceived—that is, through *language* (*logos*). The *narrative* (*logos*) of God's intervention in human history is therefore itself the *Word* (*logos*) that intervenes. And it is precisely this conflation of message and medium—the conflation of *logos* and *logos*—that would seem to warrant Ebner's general claim.

Although similar in appearance, the composite terms, *theology* and *philology*, feature the word *logos* in two very different, though not necessarily opposing, ways. At first sight, *philology* may be presumed to name a scholarly field or a scientific discipline, given the fact that the *–logy* morpheme is generally taken to be a suffix denoting *the study of* the object indicated by the root, as in *anthropology*, *biology*, *cosmology*, and *theology*—terms that unambiguously signify the study of *humankind*, *life*, the *cosmos* and the *divine*. Yet *philology* patently does not deal with the study of *love* or *friendship* (*philia*). The term *philology* is not constructed like the names of the various sciences but rather like the term *philosophy*. As Pythagoras underscored, the *philosopher* is not *wise* (*sophos*) but rather displays the *love* (*philia*) for *wisdom* (*sophia*). Analogously, *philologia* denotes the *love* of *discourse*, *argument*, or the *word*—*logos*. Thus, whereas the suffix in *theology* denotes a studious *account* (*logos*) of its object (*theos*), the *logos* in *philology* designates the very object of *love* (*philia*). It attends to the studiousness that motivates every study. To take *theology* and *philology* at their word entails recognizing that the *-logy* in *theology* represents a methodical attentiveness to God and therefore differs significantly from the *-logy* in *philology*, which names the object of loving attention. With *theology*, the *logos* refers to the scientific procedures, concepts, and criteria for approaching the nature of God; it uses its words (*logoi*) as instruments for acquiring, producing, and disseminating knowledge, even though this knowledge is ultimately insufficient. In contrast, *philology*, in the strictest sense, affectionately attends to the *logos* itself, not for the sake of the knowledge it may bear, but rather for its own sake. In loving the Word, in inclining toward words, philology resists definitive knowledge, including knowledge about God. Philology interrupts or suspends the scientific drive of theology—it enacts an *epochē*—because it turns the *means* for knowledge, the *logos*, into the *end* of its affection.[21]

All the same, at least from the perspective of Christian doctrine, theology and philology seem to work in concert, insofar as the *logos* that aims to transmit the nature of God is in fact God, the *logos* in the flesh. With the Incarnation, the *logical* means for approaching God becomes the *logical* end of the search. As the Word Incarnate (*logos ensarkos*), Christ is the means and the end, the medium and the message: "the way, the truth and the life" (John 14:6 [NKJV]). On the one hand, the *truth* of Christ constitutes the *way*, the mediating *via*, which marks out the path to salvation: no one arrives to the Father except by passing through Christ. On the other hand, however, Christ is not simply the way to the Father, but also the *life* itself, the *vita*, the very destination to which the path leads. Thus, in proposing that coming to terms with the Prologue to the Gospel of John may be the "final goal" (*das letzte Ziel*) of philology, Ebner suggests that the true purpose of studying words in human history and culture is to engage with this life, with the word as flesh, wherein "the secret of the spirit and its revelation" may be encountered.

On this basis, Ebner distinguishes between a philology that is "true" from one that is not. In his estimation, in order to become true, philology must "take itself at its word," which implies that it must learn to trust itself, to believe itself, to give itself credit or credibility, without any need for further verification. And insofar as it denotes the *philia* of the *logos*, the word *philology* decidedly proclaims a *love* for the *word* in itself. That is to say, when philology takes itself at its word, it takes every word at its word; it loves every word for what it is. True love is arguably not attracted to someone or something for the sake of something or someone else. Accordingly, true love for the word does not traffic with discourse merely for the sake of some other thing, some other *logos*, or some other knowledge. As in Immanuel Kant's "judgment of taste," philology's love for the word must be "disinterested"—that is, not motivated by any desire that would lead to something extrinsic, to something beyond the word.[22] This

21. Cf. Schestag, "Philology, Knowledge," 30–31.

22. Immanuel Kant, *Kritik der Urteilskraft* [1790], §5, in *Gesammelte Schriften* (Akademie-Ausgabe), 23 vols. (Berlin: Reimer/de Gruyter, 1900–2004), 5: 181–86.

aesthetic disinterestedness and the concomitant "purposive purposelessness" (*zweckmäßige Zwecklosigkeit*) of the artwork corresponds to the "Humanity" formulation of Kant's categorical imperative, which presents the moral precept of treating humanity, both others and ourselves, never as a means but always as an "end" (*Zweck*) in itself.[23] Accordingly, for Ebner, "true philology" involves perceiving the "secret of the spirit and its revelation" *in the word itself* and not in any other transcendent cause.

With Augustine, one could say that Ebner's true philologist must not turn the word into a transitive object "to be used" (*uti*)—that is, it should not "refer it to obtain what one loves" (*ad id quod amas obtinendum referre*)—but rather approach the word as an intransitive object "to be enjoyed" (*frui*), "to rest in love for something for its own sake" (*amore inhaerere alicui rei propter seipsam*).[24] It is important to underscore the contrast that Augustine posits between *referre* in matters of use and *inhaerere* in matters of enjoyment. In loving the word, Ebner's true philologist should not exploit the word by *carrying it back* (*referre*) to a nonverbal entity, but instead tarry with the word in an *act of inherence*, holding on to the word, adhering to it and to it alone—*inhaerere*. When philology takes itself at its own word, it acknowledges that all thinking, and therefore all knowing, takes place *in* language and not merely *through* language.

When it neglects to make such acknowledgment—when it declines to take itself at its own word—philology is reduced to dealing with the "dead letter," which turns every reception of the word into a failed reception. In Ebner's view, this failure is particularly discernible among professional philologists, whom he charges with turning "the most living language" into a "dead language." Professional philology is mortifying because it attempts to "grasp" or "comprehend" (*greifen* or *begreifen*) words through "concepts" (*Begriffe*)—concepts that persuade readers to turn their backs on the words in which those concepts are invariably formulated. Philologists of this ilk achieve no true knowledge, because they treat words as mere signs referring beyond themselves, because, in their will to science, they fail to see that knowledge inheres in the word. These philologists of the body construe the word (*logos*) as the corporeal bearer of meaning, as a kind of vehicle of sense, without realizing that the *logos*—the divine Word—is the meaning, that the *way* is the *life*. For this reason, according

23. Kant, *Grundlegung zur Metaphysik der Sitten* [1785], in *Gesammelte Schriften,* 4: 29.

24. Augustine, *De doctrina christiana,* R. P. H. Green, trans. (Oxford: Clarendon Press, 1995), 1.8, 14.

to Ebner's evaluation, these philologists practice false philology, misleadingly seeking out theological truths that they presume to be transcendent to the word, rather than discovering truth as immanent to language. They supplant the word for an allegedly nonverbal Idea, turning linguistic expression into a vanishing mediator, killing the word off for what the word denotes. In the wake of their work, they are left with a language that is empty and dead. In this regard, sign usage is fatal.

Ebner claims that true philology alone can resuscitate the dead language of false philology. Again, philology is true when it loves the word wherein the "secret of the spirit and its revelation" is perceived. This *logos* is the *logos ensarkos*—the Word Incarnate—and therefore a word that breathes and lives. For Ebner this living breath is the spirit (*spiritus*)—a principle of life, which recalls that the transcendent Word of Creation became flesh in order to dwell immanently among mankind—that is, "in order to express itself, in order to speak to man."[25] It is, of course, precisely because this language lives and breathes that it is able to die. Death is the prerequisite for resuscitation or even resurrection, a resuscitation that is enacted when true philologists, as true "receivers [*Hörer*] of the word," take the Word at its word rather than grasping at it by means of concepts and abstractions. To encounter the life of the Word means that we breathe, live, and think in the Word and thus in words. True philology, therefore—at least in Ebner's assessment—is *philology of the flesh*, an approach to language that responds to the word's carnal uniqueness, which evades definition and thereby resists any *ontotheological* determination, the kind of determination that presumably occurs whenever the word becomes but an object of knowledge.

In contrast to a philology of the body, Ebner's philology of the flesh unremittingly adheres to the verbal medium, in which meaning and form are indissolubly entwined. As Paul Virno puts it, the word-as-flesh marks "the full coincidence between expression and content."[26] A philologist of the flesh remains en route, forestalling the utter detachment of ideational content from its concrete expression. For dialogic thinkers like Ebner—as well as for phenomenologists like Merleau-Ponty—the flesh and the spirit remain perfectly

25. Ebner, "Nachwort," in *Schriften*, 1.630.

26. Paolo Virno, *When the Word Becomes Flesh: Language and Human Nature*, Giuseppina Mecchia, trans. (South Pasadena: Semiotext(e), 2015), 150.

intertwined.[27] Any rigorous distinction between the two is simply a result of analytical intellectualism or a mere habit of thinking. As Ebner writes at the head of his notes on the Johannine Prologue: "The opposition Nature-Spirit, over which philosophy has always stumbled, is perhaps nothing other than a matter of perspective. Should one just once remove the perspective, which it imposes on us, it would then no longer exist."[28]

The philology of the flesh, therefore, may have theological import, no less than the philology of the body, yet without promulgating a spiritual sense at the expense of the literal. Indeed, the tension between metaphorical accounts of the word-as-body and of the word-as-flesh has motivated numerous difficult debates throughout the history of the Christian Church. In the early Christological writings of Tertullian and Irenaeus, it is precisely the "scandal of the Incarnation" that misleadingly compels thinkers to adopt the more comforting and more feasible solution provided by Gnostic dualism.[29] Since the earliest centuries of Church history, Gnostic heresies consistently solved the many theoretical problems pertaining to the Incarnation by insisting on a strict division between the body and the soul, between the letter that kills and the spirit that gives life. For this reason, Docetism in its various configurations treated the doctrine of the Word becoming mortal flesh with arrogant condescension. Even though the Pauline distinction between the fatal letter and the vitalizing spirit is directly prefaced by the assertion that the "spirit of the living God" writes not "on tablets of stone but on tablets of the fleshly heart" (2 Cor. 3:3 [NKJV]), the Gnostics were repelled by all fleshliness and combatted it, ostensibly because they were incapable of recognizing what orthodoxy repeatedly affirmed, namely that the mortal and immortal aspects of Christ are fully intertwined in a single hypostatic union. In the Docetist view, the flesh of the Word Incarnate was no ordinary flesh, but merely appeared to be so—a kind of phantom or illusion (a *dokēsis*) that, having no material reality, would not threaten to impede the redemptive elevation

27. On the spirit in relation to the flesh in Merleau-Ponty, see Christopher B. Simpson, *Merleau-Ponty and Theology* (London: Bloomsbury, 2014), 131–32.

28. Ferdinand Ebner, *Glossen zum Introitus des Johannesevangeliums*, in Schriften, I.563. "Der Gegensatz Natur-Geist, über den die Philosophie seit jeher stolperte, ist vielleicht doch nichts anderes als eine perspektivische Tatsache. Schaffe man nur einmal die Perspektive, in der er sich uns aufdrängt, weg, so besteht auch er nicht mehr."

29. See Mayra Rivera's provocative discussion of Tertullian in *Poetics of the Flesh* (Durham: Duke University Press, 2015), 43–54.

of the immaterial soul. In contrast, for those who targeted the heresiarchs, the flesh of Christ must be taken as real flesh. Indeed, for Tertullian, flesh is pivotal (*caro cardo est*), the very hinge without which the portal to salvation falls apart.[30]

Ebner's philology of the flesh takes the Incarnation of the Word as the very basis for revealing the ontological truth of human being—a revelation that consoles us by putting us, as carnal beings, into relation with each other through the spirit we share. To illustrate, he cites from the *Notebooks* of Fyodor Dostoevsky, who writes that faith in the "Incarnation of the Word" (*Fleischwerdung des Wortes*) or in the "humanization [*Menschwerdung*] of God in the life of Christ" is "the source of life, the reassurance of man and the redemption of all mankind from despair and the condition *sine qua non* for the being of the entire world."[31] Ebner endorses this notion of redemption, which, in linguistic terms, depends wholly on the union of materiality and referentiality. His philology of the flesh differs, therefore, from Valla's philology of the body, which ultimately serves the vehicular word by reducing the verbal material to a means that must vanish before the communicated idea.

One could therefore imagine a direct confrontation between the word-as-body and the word-as-flesh. Again, Dostoevsky comes to mind. For such a dramatic encounter seems to unfold in his famous parable, "The Grand Inquisitor." In addition to its explicit themes, this enigmatic story could also be read as an *allegory of philology*, broaching issues pertinent to the formulation, communication, and reception of verbal language by personifying the two basic inclinations we have been tracing. Concurrent with the many points that touch on existential, moral, and ethical questions—points that clearly engage a broad range of interests in literature, history, social theory, political science, religious studies, and philosophy—Dostoevsky's text offers fundamental insights into differences in our approaches to discourse, writing, and reading; and does so by portraying these positions in the starkest of contrasts. The fact that Dostoevsky's depiction caricaturizes his antagonists simply underscores the story's allegorical intention.[32]

30. Tertullian, *De resurrectione*, 8.2.

31. Ebner, *Glossen zum Introitus des Johannesevangelium, Schriften* I.574. "Im Glauben an die Fleischwerdung des Wortes, an die Menschwerdung Gottes im Leben Christi ist 'die Lebensquelle, die Beruhigung des Menschen und die Rettung aller Menschen vor der Verzweiflung und die Bedingung sine qua non für das Sein der ganzen Welt,' wie es einmal in den Notizbüchern Dostojewskys heißt."

32. On "The Grand Inquisitor" episode and its departures from historical veracity, see the important and insightful reading by Romano Guardini, "The Legend of the Grand Inquisitor," Sally Cunneen, trans., *Cross Currents* 3 (1952), 58–86.

Although "The Grand Inquisitor" has prompted an inordinate amount of critical reflection, it is typically not regarded as addressing the structural conditions and functions of language in general. Nonetheless, even without entering into a detailed discussion about the formal elements of Dostoevsky's nineteenth-century Russian, a specially attuned reading would demonstrate that verbal form and function should be counted as one of the text's major, albeit implicit, themes. That is to say, the main personages of the drama, including their speech and behavior and the manner in which they interact with each other, personify conceptions of language that consequently delineate how one understands the roles of the word in the world, in history, and in culture—conceptions that clearly fall under the rubric of philology.

The story, from the fifth book of the author's last novel, *The Brothers Karamazov* (1879–80), is well known. It is presented as an idea for a poem envisioned by Ivan Karamazov, a highly rational and enlightened atheist with strong sympathies for socialist reform. While admitting that he is incapable of writing verse, Ivan relates and explicates the plot of his poetic idea to his younger brother Alyosha, a devout Christian novice of mystical bent. Set in sixteenth-century Seville at the height of the Jesuit inquisition, the work would describe how Christ quietly reappeared in flesh and blood among the people: not in some glorious eschatological moment at the end of time but rather firmly within historical time: "He simply wanted to appear, if only for a moment, to visit his children at the very place where the heretics' fires crackled."[33] Specifically, Christ shows up the morning after nearly a hundred condemned apostates perished in a "magnificent *auto-da-fé*" ordained by the Grand Inquisitor and showcased before the aristocracy, the clergy, and "the thronging populace" (312). Whereas this second coming of the Messiah is explicitly not eschatological, the Jesuitical fervor to execute *ad majorem gloriam Dei* amply compensates with a *Dies Irae* of its own design. In the dawn's light, as the embers of the mass pyre continue to smolder, Christ walks again among the people; and He is immediately recognized for who He is. Once again, He embraces the crowd, blessing them and healing them. He causes "their hearts to throb with a reciprocal love" (312). And when, on the cathedral steps, a bereaved mother implores Him to resurrect her young daughter, His lips gently pronounce the Aramaic command recorded in the Gospels, "Talitha cumi" (Mark 5:41), and thereby summons the girl to rise from her coffin.

33. Fyodor Dostoevsky, *The Brothers Karamazov*, Ignat Avsey, trans. (Oxford: Oxford University Press, 1994), 311.

The Grand Inquisitor, who happens to be passing by, witnesses the spectacular miracle. Without hesitation, the cardinal orders that the stranger be imprisoned in the Holy Office. After nightfall, the Inquisitor himself enters the dark cell to interrogate his captive. The remainder of the tale discloses how Christ was received and handled, how He was indicted and sentenced to the stake.

The private meeting between Christ and the Church official is therefore depicted as the confrontation between two incompatible, mutually exclusive positions: the catechism of the Roman Catholic institution and the Word as living flesh. It is altogether clear that the high priest finds Christ's physical presence threatening. In his view, the efficacy of the Church relies on the inaccessible transcendence of God's unique Son. With Christ's reappaearance, Dostoevsky stages an encounter of two instantiations of language: between the Word Incarnate and the priestly interpretation of scripture. Ecclesiastical authority, which is presumably founded on and legitimized by the words of Christ, is made to grapple with the difficulties posed by the fleshly presence of the Word. Thus, over the course of the interaction, two philological positions come into focus, two competing understandings of what language does and how it operates. The way the Logos-in-the-flesh acts suggests how words may function; and how this divine figure is received—how He is treated and processed—can by extension signal how one may treat and process words in general. Moreover, by being confrontational, the scene provides the opportunity to assess the scope of the two positions, the philology espoused by the Inquisitor and the philology illustrated by Christ's all too real presence.

Although both sides are portrayed as discontinuous, they appear to share a capacity to love: the cardinal's professed *love of mankind* and Christ's instigation of *reciprocal love,* including the enigmatic kiss at the story's conclusion. In the tale, the one kind of love is made to clash with the other. The Word Incarnate, who according to the Christian Gospels instructed the "scribes" (*grammateis*) to practice "affectionate love" (*agapē*) as the greatest commandment (Mark 12:28–31 [KJV]), arguably aims to turn every grammarian into a "loving friend" of the "Word"—a *philos* of the *Logos.* Yet here, in Dostoevsky's text, the Inquisitor boldly questions the viability of that love by positing an affection that he believes to be wholly different.

An appropriate place to begin a closer reading is the start of the interrogation session. In a way that anticipates Kafka's enigmatic "Judgment" (*Das Urteil*), Dostoevsky's old priest collapses accusation and sentence into a single powerful moment:

> "Is it you? You?" There being no answer, he adds quickly: "Don't answer, remain silent. After all, what could You say? I know only too well what You would say. And You have no right to add anything to what You have already said. So why have You come to disturb us? For You really have come to disturb us, and You know it. But do You know what is going to happen tomorrow? I don't know who You are and I don't want to know—whether You are He or whether You are just a semblance of Him—but tomorrow I shall judge You and burn you on the pyre, like the vilest of the heretics, and that same crowd which today kissed Your feet, tomorrow, at a sign from me, will rush to stoke up the fire, do You know that?" (313–14)[34]

The interrogator's initial question, demanding self-identification, is retracted nearly as soon as it is uttered. In the first of many ironic gestures, Dostoevsky has the Inquisitor rehearse the question posed by John the Baptist from the dark depths of his dungeon cell: "And when John had heard in prison about the works of Christ, he sent two of his disciples and said to Him, 'Are You the Coming One, or do we look for another?'" (Matt. 11:2–3 [NKJV]). Like the Baptist, Dostoevsky's cardinal resides in a prison, not as a prisoner but rather as the warden; unless, of course, we interpret the old priest as being imprisoned in his own viewpoints—an interpretation that a full reading of the tale would certainly bear. And like Christ in the Gospel account, the Christ in Ivan's portrayal performs miraculous works and is, indeed, the "Coming One," not as the cornerstone of the Church but rather as the Church's gravest enemy. The Inquisitor recognizes this enmity, he acknowledges a fatal contradiction between the verbal precepts of the Church and the living Word itself, and therefore must exert sovereign control over the one who comes unexpectedly and uninvited. The cleric's *philology*, his love for the words of the ecclesiastic institution, is therefore also a *misology*, a hatred for the Word Incarnate.

34. Dostoevsky, *Brat'ja Karamazovy* in *Collected Works,* 30 vols. (Leningrad: Academy of Sciences, 1972–90). "Это ты? ты? –Но, не получая ответа, быстро прибавляет: –Не отвечай, молчи. Да и что бы ты мог сказать? Я слишком знаю, что ты скажешь. Да ты и права не имеешь ничего прибавлять к тому, что уже сказано тобой прежде. Зачем же ты пришел нам мечшать? Ибо ты пришел нам мешать и сам это значешь. Но знаешь ли, что будет завтра? Я не знаю, кто ты, и знать не хочу: ты ли это, или только подобие его, но завтра же я осужу и сожгу тебя на костре, как злейшего из еретиков, и тот самый народ, который сегодня целовал твои ноги, завтра же по одному моему мановению бросится подгребать к твоему костру угли, знаешь ты это?" (14: 228).

The Inquisitor expresses this misological philology by pronouncing the conflicting message or the impossible command that binds the prisoner in a double bind: *Speak! Don't speak!—speak*, because I love words, and *don't speak*, because I hate the Word. And in Ivan's legend, Christ readily acquiesces to the priest's impossible demand. The Word-in-the-flesh says not a word and will not utter a single syllable for the remainder of the parable. In decisive contrast, the custodian speaks incessantly in a monologue that strives to domineer the conversation by presuming to know the answers that are, in fact, never articulated ("I know only too well what You would say"). His reception of the captive is but an antireception. When the Word falls silent, there are always many words to fill the gap. The Inquisitor's strategy may appear to be a winning move, yet it is doomed to fail before the muteness of his detainee. One cannot be victorious over silence, if only because one cannot fight against nothing. The astute cardinal is aware of this problem, which is why he presumes so much, finding it necessary to supply his opponent's responses in order to set up something to oppose.

To this end, the old priest appeals to logic and justice: "You have no right to add anything to what You have already said." If in the first Incarnation Christ established his Church by words and deeds, then any subsequent speech or action would undermine what had been founded; any additional *logos* would disrupt and potentially dismantle what the Logos had erected. After this inaugural installation, any extra word could function as a dangerous supplement, threatening to replace what has already taken place. The full presence or *parousia* of the Savior would risk overturning the very institution of salvation, namely the Church: *extra ecclesiam nulla salus*. Certainly, since the early centuries of theological speculation, writers have sought to reconcile any potential contradiction by underscoring the Pauline claim that Christ "is the head of the body, the Church" (Col. 1:18 [NKJV]); that salvation comes from Christ as it is transmitted through the Church. Ivan's poem, however, not only exposes the fragility of this reconciliation but also forces both positions—Christ and the Church—into an irresolvable battle. From the Inquisitor's perspective, the incarnate presence of the Messiah and the organizational structure of Church necessarily operate at cross-purposes—"You really have come to disturb us, and You know it." The present potency of the institution's words depends upon the impotent absence of the Word.

In staging a collision between Christ and the Church, Dostoevsky essentially pits one body against another—two bodies that came to be distinguished over the course of ecclesiastical history, albeit with great difficulty and much debate: the *corpus mysticum*, which denotes the mystical body of the Church, and the *corpus verum*, the true flesh of Christ, which once dwelled among mankind, was crucified, and is now presumed to be physically present in the consecrated host of the Eucharist—a miraculous consecration performed by ecclesiastic power, which thereby held control over the sacrament.[35] Yet the *real presence* of the Eucharist is decidedly not *full presence*. Whereas the sacrament of the Eucharist can readily be *incorporated* into the institutional structure of the Church, the fleshly presence of the Savior would arguably disintegrate this edifice of power. And it is precisely this disintegration that the Inquisitor wants to avoid. In the old man's pessimistic view, humankind is too "weak and base" for the freedom that Christ offers (321). *Mundus vult decipi*. With Hobbesian insight, the Inquisitor argues that free choice only serves to increase human suffering. As he later claims, freedom is wholly destructive. The Church is therefore the Antichrist, providing a system of beliefs based on "miracle, mystery, and authority" (322)—the very powers that Christ renounced in the desert as satanic temptations. As the Antichrist, the Church gives the weak what they truly want: to surrender their terrible freedom and be led as a gentle flock, comforted by a set of established doctrines and rituals that offer security and peace of mind. The Inquisitor therefore feels compelled to execute Christ immediately. The disruptive power of the flesh must be annihilated for the sake of the ecclesiastical corpus.

The philological bearing of this imperative would appear to be the following: The fate of the Word-as-flesh is to become the word-as-body or a body of words. With the annihilation of the living Word, the Inquisitor aspires to determine and maintain a verbal corpus that will convey definitive meanings. He wants to confine sense in order to ensure the kind of unambiguous understanding that the enervated people presumably crave. He must limit the freedom of the Word Incarnate by means of corporate comprehensibility, controlled and therefore controlling. Here again, the metaphor of the body connotes integrity and stability, something that presents itself as a fixed system of beliefs to which mankind, in its misery, gladly will bow. This body—the *corpus mysticum* that is the Church—will be integral as long as it integrates the disintegrating nature of the flesh; it will be stable as long as it stabilizes the destabilizing freedom of

35. For a comprehensive overview of this historical distinction, see Henri de Lubac, *Corpus Mysticum: The Eucharist and the Church in the Middle Ages* [1944], Gemma Simonds, trans. (Notre Dame: University of Notre Dame Press, 2007), esp. 128–68.

the signifier. Should the Word return in the flesh—as the *corpus verum* that is Christ's living body—the liturgical establishment of doctrinal coherence would be undercut.

The legend of the Grand Inquisitor thus forces two types of philology to confront and thereby limit each other: one that works to authorize verbal definition and legitimate interpretations; and another that unworks any such inscription of fixed sense. Whereas the Inquisitor seeks to transform the flesh into a body of beliefs, the fleshly presence of Christ presents an excessive surplus beyond any authorial or authorizing economy. The cardinal is certainly a philologist, but one who loves the words that constitute a corporate system of doctrines, rituals, and power. For the love of mankind, he loves the language that grants his congregation security and therefore renounces any love for the flesh that would override his claims and plunge the people into the pits of anxiety. Accordingly, he rejects the Christ, who "thirsted for love freely given" (321), and replaces fleshly love with a love that has a much different goal:

> Have we not really loved man when we have so humbly recognized his weakness, have lightened his burden out of love, and out of consideration for his feeble nature have even allowed him to sin, so long as it is with our permission? So why then have You come to interfere now? And why do You look at me so silently with your humble, piercing eyes? Why are You not angry? I do not want Your love, because I do not love You. (322)[36]

The affection that the Inquisitor displays for his flock is in fact a disincarnate love, the only kind of love that Ivan himself is capable of practicing. In the previous chapter, "The Rebellion," Ivan refers to the story of Saint John the Merciful, who invited a decrepit beggar into his bed and resuscitated him by breathing "into his mouth, which was purulent and stinking from some dreadful disease" (296). According to Ivan, this revolting gesture was not performed out of any love for one's neighbor, but rather out of self-hatred, as an act of "hypocrisy, in response to a dutiful love, as a self-imposed penance" (296–97). Ivan's interpre-

36. Dostoevsky, *Brat'ja Karamazovy*: "Неужели мы не любили человечества, столь смиренно сознав его бессилие, с любовию облегчив его ношу и разрешив слабосильной природе его хотя бы и грех, но с нашего позволения? К чему же теперь пришел наме мешать? И что ты молча и проникновенно глядишь на меня кроткими глазами своими? Рассердись, я не хочу любви твоей, потому что сам не люблю тебя" (14: 234).

tation is clear: "One can love a man only when he's out of sight; as soon as he shows his face, that's the end of love" (297). Fleshly presence is too intrusive, too messy, too uncontrollable, and therefore altogether abhorrent. Ivan thus concludes: "One can love one's neighbor in the abstract and sometimes even at a distance, but close up almost never" (297).[37]

An abstract love is one that derives a general idea that is presumably detachable from the particular instance. It requires the dispensability of the instance. The particular must be dispensable lest it obfuscate the abstraction. This kind of love correlates to a philology of the body that rigorously distinguishes form from content, as if particular words are mere corpuscular vessels that transport a meaning that is unencumbered by the means of transmission. Yet as we have seen, the fact of incarnation disturbs clear conveyance and hence abstraction, if only because it confounds form and content. The distinction between these two conceptions of language is pivotal for how the word is processed. It is, indeed, a hermeneutic issue, as Hans-Georg Gadamer explicitly demonstrates:

> Incarnation is clearly not embodiment [*Inkarnation ist offenbar nicht Einkörperung*]. Neither the conception of the soul nor the conception of God, which are linked with such embodiment, correspond to the Christian concept of Incarnation. The relationship of soul and living body [*Leib*], how it is thought in these theories, as in the Platonic-Pythagorean philosophy, and how it corresponds to the religious conception of the soul's migration, posits rather the complete otherness of the soul to the body [*Leib*]. It [the soul] retains its being-for-itself [*Fürsichsein*] in all embodiments, and the dissolution of the living body counts as purification, i.e., as restoration of its true and actual being. Even the appearance of the divine in human form [*Gestalt*], which makes the Greek religion so human, has nothing to do with incarnation. Here, God does not become man, but rather shows himself to men in human form, while at the same time entirely retaining his superhuman form. By contrast, that God became man [*Gottes Menschenwerdung*], as the Christian religion teaches, involves the sacrifice that the crucified as the son of man takes upon himself, i.e. [it involves] however a mysteriously different relationship, whose theological interpretation occurs in the doctrine of the Trinity.[38]

37. For further discussion of this theme in relation to the flesh, see Dennis Patrick Slattery, *The Wounded Body: Remembering the Markings of the Flesh* (Albany: SUNY Press, 1999), 115–30.

38. Gadamer, *Wahrheit und Methode*, 422 [*Truth and Method*, 378–79].

The "Platonic-Pythagorean" theory of embodiment describes the body as a prisonhouse, locking an incorporeal soul within. Throughout its sojourn in life, the soul subsists on its own (*für sich*) and longs for emancipation from the body that encloses it. For Gadamer, the Pythagorean conception of the body-soul relationship is analogous to a Platnonic theory of language, whereby words are believed to contain an Idea, which transcends particular expressions and is in fact, strictly speaking, nonverbal. Here, the Idea is regarded as *absolute*: τράπεζα, *mensa*, and *Tisch* all refer to the idea of "table"—an idea that is not compromised by the formal specificities of the Greek, Latin, or German terms used to express it. According to Gadamer's analogy, in construing words to be hollow corporeal containers, one postulates that some immaterial, ideational content can be detached or abstracted from them, like a soul from a body. The Jesuit handling of heretics in Dostoevsky's parable is legitimized by this theory: the *auto-da-fé* is thought to liberate the immortal soul from its mortal, sinful encasement. Here, the pyre is purifying.

In contrast, Gadamer's metaphor of "incarnation" describes the inadequacy of abstraction—inadequate, because the Idea is not detachable from the concrete words that formulate it. Gadamer's theological illustration is crucial: the ancient Greek doctrine of the soul's migration correlates to an understanding of the gods that regards them as incorporeal and therefore immortal. To cite a well-known example, in the first book of Homer's *Odyssey*, when Athena disguises herself as the old sea-captain Mentes to visit Telemachus, the goddess is not compromised by the mortal form. She freely enters the body and can freely escape it without injury. With the Christian Incarnation, however, Christ becomes man—he lives and breathes in mortal form, is tortured and crucified. In Gadamer's view, it is the doctrine of Incarnation that better reveals the true "Being of Language"; for the fact of condescension, the nondistinction of Christ's divinity and humanity, underscores the nondistinction of the soul and the body, and ultimately the nondistinction of form and content, or rather, their complete intertwinement: a flesh endowed with spirit or breath. Here especially, one detects the teaching of Heidegger, who bases his hermeneutical phenomenology on a key lesson from Nietzsche: "We do not 'have' a body; rather, we 'are' bodily."[39] Analogously, the incarnate word is no mere medium or vessel; it

39. Martin Heidegger, *The Will to Power as Art, Nietzsche*, vol. 1, David Farrell Krell, trans. (New York: Harper & Row, 1979), 99.

is not a body that contains some detachable, incorporeal message; rather, the word-as-flesh communicates itself.

The flesh that communicates itself is still a word, a living word, which calls for a philology of the flesh that lovingly abides with the word as living presence. That this living presence remains completely silent throughout Dostoevsky's depiction of the inquisition is telling. One could say it is the mark of the Word's *responsibility*. The ability to respond rests on a capacity to remain open, to keep things in question, to maintain freedom, and not to retreat into an ontotheological dogmatism wherein all things have already been decided, wherein all answers have already been determined. Christ's failure to respond—the incapacity of the flesh to say anything definitive—is paradoxically the greatest sign of His responsibility. By refusing to speak *definitively*, the Word-as-flesh renders speech *infinite*; it hinders any detachment of some timeless and therefore lifeless Idea. Hence, the Inquisitor complains: "Why have You come to disturb us?"

From a slightly different angle, one can see how Christ's silence instigates the Inquisitor's ceaseless monologue, as if Christ's responsible, palpable muteness were itself inquisitive, calling upon the cardinal to respond without pause. Yet whereas the priest's body of words aims to foreclose freedom, the incarnate Word—a word that is not articulated into any discernible statement—persists in disclosing the excess of the flesh. Both discursive acts, the cardinal's monologue and Christ's silence, are performative, yet they perform to different ends. Even when we consider Christ's words in the Gospels, particularly as recorded in the Gospel of John, it becomes evident that the majority of what Jesus says exhibits a concrete efficacy—healing the blind and the crippled, curing the leper, and raising the dead. These words lead to powerful outcomes, rather than serving as vehicles for ideas or information—that is, these words have a performative effect that lacks ideational objectivity and thereby evades the division into signifier and signified.[40] When we return to Dostoevsky's legend, we recall the single phrase that Christ actually utters in the tale—"Talitha cumi"—is an act of speaking that grants renewed life. In contrast, the Inquisitor's barrage of words amounts to little more than a death sentence.

The philology of the flesh would seem therefore to concern itself more with

40. Cf. Werner H. Kelber, "Die Fleischwerdung des Wortes in der Körperlichkeit des Textes," in Hans Ulrich Gumbrecht and K. Ludwig Pfeiffer, eds., *Materialität der Kommunikation* (Frankfurt a. M.: Suhrkamp, 1995), 31–42; here 34–35.

the open clearing of potentiality, a potentiality (and a power, *potentia*) that relates to the verbal the field of living possibility, as opposed to any determinate figure or identifiable position. The Word Incarnate works counter to the rigor mortis of finality; it nourishes open-ended, nonterminal potential. This capacity to sense this potentiality comes very close to what Merleau-Ponty refers to as the recognition of the "flesh":

> My flesh and that of the world [. . .] involve clear zones, daytimes, about which pivot their opaque zones, and the primary visibility, that of the *quale* and of the things, does not come without a second visibility, that of the lines of force and dimensions, the massive flesh without a rarefied flesh [*chair subtile*], the momentary body without a glorified body [*corps glorieux*].[41]

Just as Gadamer alludes to the Incarnation in order to demonstrate the inseparability of verbal form and content, Merleau-Ponty invokes the flesh in order to motivate an authentic response to experience, one that resists falling into the intellectualist and naturalist dualisms that disengage the perceiving subject from the perceived object. With the metaphor of the flesh, Merleau-Ponty encourages seers not only to see the "clearing" that grounds the subsequent qualities of things—the *how* that is prior to the *what*—but also to see that they, too, in their carnal experience belong to the realm of the seen. Merleau-Ponty's difficult musings on the flesh offer an encounter with the flesh of the visible, an encounter that is rigorously distinguished from any subjective, detached surveying of fixed objects. The flesh precedes the cognitive subject, who observes the world from a removed position, and therefore also precedes the object stabilized into an inert body. Before these facts of intellectual or objective fixation, the flesh instigates a free response. And precisely as openness to the field that is prior to any defined figuration, the response to the flesh prompts an excess of responses.

Almost intuitively, Dostoevsky seems to anticipate both Gadamer and Merleau-Ponty in their appeals to a principle of incarnation. In *The Brothers Karamazov*, even when the flesh is no longer alive, it still mobilizes responsible, open faith. With the death of Father Zosima, Alyosha's beloved elder, we observe how the flesh, even in its decomposition, may serve as an antidote to disincarnate abstraction. In the opening chapter of the seventh book, "Odor of

41. Merleau-Ponty, "L'entrelacs—le chiasme," 1773 [*The Visible and the Invisible*, 148].

Putrefaction," Zosima's fresh corpse attracts multitudes of visitors, who expect the body's integrity to be preserved as a miraculous confirmation of the starets's sanctity. Yet already by the first day, the putrescent stench cannot be denied, causing confusion and scandal among the faithful. The uneducated masses begin to question Zosima's legacy: "His teaching was false [. . .]; he practiced his faith the modern way, he wouldn't accept there was real fire in hell. [. . .] He was not strict in his fasting [. . .]" (419). Even Father Païsy, who administered the last rites, clothing the monk's cadaver in all the accoutrements of the Eastern Orthodox Church, is shaken by the fact of decay. The corruption of the monk's flesh is disturbing and disorienting; it cannot be circumscribed; it exceeds the comprehension of the people, who must struggle to find reasons for this shocking event. As the Inquisitor would note: there is no miracle, no mystery, no authority that would reinforce and secure their system of belief.[42] Alyosha alone realizes how to respond authentically and freely to the difficulty of the rotting flesh. He recognizes how the evidence of mortal disintegration constitutes a challenge to every complacent belief. At the episode's conclusion, the young novice decides to leave the hermitage and enter into the world. The monk's decomposition, like Christ's condescension, marks the fleshly excess that occasions a renewed engagement with the human world. Needless to say, it is this very excessiveness that bespeaks freedom, which frightens the Inquisitor to the core. It is what drives him to consolidate doctrinal positions that do not ask for a free response but rather for docile submission. He scurries to turn the disorienting word-as-flesh into the orienting flesh-as-word. Therein lies his power—not *potentia*, but rather *dominatio*.

All the same, as Dostoevsky's text finally reveals, the conflict presented by this allegory—between the *dominatio* of the integral, foreclosing body and the *potentia* of the disintegrating, disclosing flesh—does not construct an opposition. Rather, it hinges on the gap within the initial *Speak! Don't Speak!* Certainly, the Inquisitor does not hesitate to dismiss the interference of the flesh. He plans to exterminate at once the interminable freedom offered by the Messiah's return to earth. In his view, the durability of the Church, its efficacy in saving the people from themselves, requires the continued absence of the Savior. As long as Christ remains inaccessible, hidden away in heavenly transcendence, the word of the

42. Cf. Slattery, *The Wounded Body*, 120. My reading here follows Slattery's insightful discussion.

Church can function unhindered. All the same, the final execution never in fact arrives. Christ is released. The fleshly presence of this unique prisoner may be dismissed, but it cannot be entirely eliminated.

Ivan's concluding scene is particularly striking: Christ "suddenly approaches the old man in silence and calmly kisses him on his bloodless ninety-year-old lips":

> That is His only response. The old man shudders. His lips quiver; he goes to the door of his cell, opens it, and says, "Go and don't come back any more . . . never . . . never!" And he releases Him into the dark backstreets of the city. The prisoner walks away. (329)[43]

The Inquisitor who skirted responsibility by taking control of all the questions, the ecclesiastical sovereign who sought to close the living presence of the Word within the confines of secure, unchangeable doctrine, ends up opening the door of the cell. The fermata reveals itself to be an overture. "The kiss sears his heart, but he doesn't let go of his Idea" (329). Although he insists on the disappearance of the flesh, although the strength of the "idea" reduces the fleshiness of the word to the level of a vanishing mediator, the flesh nonetheless persists and thereby affects the body's integrity, including the corporeal integrity of the priest himself. Tellingly, Merleau-Ponty notes how the experience of the flesh produces "a sort of dehiscence [that] opens my body in two."[44] Suffering from the accessibility opened by Christ's searing kiss, the "bloodless" lips of the Inquisitor still stir and the Word Incarnate is granted release, however reluctantly. What burns within the tired heart is the recognition that a body without flesh is but an abstraction. The determination of sense requires the interminability of the flesh, even when it commands its evanescence.

The philology of the flesh and the philology of the body confront each other and limit each other—a confrontation and limitation that consign philology in general to a dynamic oscillation between determination and indetermination, closing and opening sense. The morphemic similarity between *philology*

43. Dostoevsky, *Brat'ja Karamazovy*: "Вот и весь ответ. Старик вздрагивает. Что-то шевельнулось в концах губ его; он идет к двери, отворяет ее и говорит ему: 'Ступай и не приходи более . . . не приходи вовсе . . . никогда, никогда!' И выпускает его на 'темные стогна града'. Пленник уходит" (14: 239).

44. Merleau-Ponty, "Interrogation et Intuition." "[. . .] une sorte de déhiscence ouvre en deux mon corps" (1750) ["Interrogation and Intuition," *The Visible and the Invisible*, 123].

and *philosophy* is again revealing. Although Pythagoras is cited with defining the philosopher as someone who desires wisdom and is therefore not wise, in Plato's *Symposium,* Diotima teaches the youthful Socrates that the nonwisdom of the philosopher is in fact more complicated. She asserts that Eros is a philosopher, "situated between the wise man and the ignorant man" (*Symp.* 204a–b), which means that the philosopher is caught between the same resourcefulness and penury that constitutes Eros, precariously poised between ignorance and wisdom, lacking understanding but at least wise to the lack. Although the philosopher never fully possesses the *sophia* he desires, he still recognizes, rather wisely, the fact of his poverty. Socrates, who elsewhere describes himself as a "philologist" (*Phaed.* 236e), doubtlessly held on to Diotima's every word, knowing, however ironically, that he knew nothing. For just as philosophers know that their knowledge hosts nonknowledge at its core, so philologists attend to words that they can never fully possess. Determination is always provisional.

For this reason, in Plato's *Theaetetus, philologia* simply refers to affection for conversation, discussion, or debate, without presuming cognitive proprietorship of the topics broached, yet all the while aware of what is or is not topical (*Theat.* 146a). If a discipline entails a body of knowledge to be learned, understood, and mastered, if it marks out some intellectual territory that has been acquired, some space that has been delineated by a particular horizon, then philology and, by extension, philosophy are perhaps better regarded as predisciplines, as modes of free but rational questioning that, analogous to the university's "lower faculty" described by Kant, comprise the groundwork for authorized, regulated, disciplinary work.[45] For Kant, the pre-disciplinary quality of philosophy—and implicitly of philology—underscores not only a traditionally ancillary role in relation to the sciences but also a moral freedom from every determined horizon of sense.

Yet despite their close relationship, philology is not philosophy, as it has been persistently stressed throughout antiquity.[46] Although both are grounded

45. See Immanuel Kant's last published essay, *Der Streit der Fakultäten* (1798), in *Gesammelte Schriften,* 7: 17–21. The question of philology and philosophy's relation to other scholarly fields—that is, the relationship between "Erkenntnis" and "Wissenschaft," is explored by Peter Szondi, "Über philologische Erkenntnis," in *Schriften,* 2 vols., J. Bollack et al., eds. (Frankfurt a. M.: Suhrkamp, 1978), 1: 263.

46. For a general overview of usage, see Axel Horstmann's article on "Philologie" in the *Historisches Wörterbuch der Philosophie,* 13 vols., J. Ritter, ed. (Basel: Schwabe, 1971–2007), 7: 552–72.

in the loving motivation of *philia*, philosophy clearly differs from philology, insofar as the former reaches out toward wisdom, while the latter inclines toward speeches and the written word. Whereas philosophy finds its end in knowledge, philology finds its end in the mediating *logos*. In addressing the employment of multiple languages, in pursuing their grammatical, morphological, and lexical components, in tracing how these verbal and syntactic elements developed historically and cross-culturally, philology ceaselessly poses questions concerning human words, including of course the word *philology* itself. Indeed, philological research inevitably arrives at self-questioning, raising and formulating questions about its own functions and operations, about its relation to other disciplines as well as its own status as a discipline. As Werner Hamacher points out, philology is always also a *philo-philology*—a desire for the desire for the word:

> Consequently, considering its questionability, philology is neither a science nor is it a theoretical discipline with well-defined procedures that lead to the acquisition of knowledge [*Wissen*]. The question concerning itself can thus at best make use of the right [*Recht*] of a propaedeutic and therefore proto-philological enquiry. It is not a question of philology as science, but rather—*sit venia verbo*—of philo-philology, which stays at the edge, in the forecourt or at the gate of philology, but whose interior it does not enter and whose law [*Gesetz*] it does not know.[47]

Because philology approaches every aspect of language or *logos* as a loving question, it comes to question itself, to such an extent, according to Hamacher, that it undermines its own disciplinary stability. Philo-philology, provided we allow Hamacher the use of this term (*sit venia verbo*), underscores the nondisciplinarity of every philological enterprise. Indulgence (*venia*) is called for and readily granted, insofar as every word emerges as something provisional or ephemeral. Philology has the right (*das Recht*), but is unfamiliar with the instituted law (*das Gesetz*). Philology, so to speak, stands "before the law"—*vor dem Gesetz*—perhaps like Dostoevsky's Christ before the legalistic Inquisitor. In any case, Hamacher's light allusion to Kafka is not unimportant: Philology falls outside of every disciplinary *Gesetz*, but does so by standing by, before the law closes

47. Werner Hamacher, "Für—die Philologie," in *Was ist eine philologische Frage?* J. P. Schwindt, ed. (Frankfurt a. M.: Suhrkamp, 2009), 21–60, here 28; Hamacher, *Minima Philologica*, Catherine Diehl and Jason Groves, trans. (New York: Fordham University Press, 2015), 120.

the gates, before meaning is locked within its institutional limits. In reaching toward words, toward language itself, philology remains at the margins of every discipline, before every meaningful horizon. Its fundamental priority subsists in this reaching out—in this *orexis*—which can be either negatively or positively charged. On the one hand, it consigns philology to the outside, removed from disciplinary authority; while on the other hand, it diagnoses every discipline with terminal anorexia. As a bodily affect, the *philia* of the *logos* takes place through the body, with a sound, a stroke, a kiss. Through this confrontation of the body and the flesh, philology is made to remain before the word.

3

This Loved Philology

It has already been suggested that the relation of philology to incarnational doctrine underscores a long-standing problem that pertains to the figuration of Jesus Christ, whose nature is said to consist in the hypostatic union of the distinctly divine and the distinctly human. In linguistic terms, precisely as the Word made flesh, Christ serves both as *reference* and as *referent*, both as the *word* and as the *object* denoted by that word. Both philologically and theologically, this twofold nature proves to be particularly scandalous and problematic, if only because it confuses the verbal signifier and the signified. As the Word Incarnate, Christ's *truth* consists in being both mediating *via* and mediated *vita*. Thus, according to the doctrine proclaimed in the Chalcedonian Creed of 451, Christ concurs "in one person and subsistence" (ἓν πρόσωπον καὶ μίαν ὑπόστασιν, *in unam personam atque subsistentiam*) but "in two natures" (ἐν δύο φύσεσιν, *in duabus naturis*).[1] Without entering into the

1. For a critical discussion, see Sarah Coakley, "What Does Chalcedon Solve and What Does It Not? Some Reflections on the Status and Meaning of the Chalcedonian 'Definition,'" in *The Incarnation: An Interdisciplinary Symposium on the Incarnation of*

possible meanings and historical interpretations of the key terms—*prosōpon/persona, hypostasis/subsistentia*—the notion of a single entity with two natures sufficiently spells out the fundamental duplicity of any Christology. As Jesus affirms consistently throughout the Gospel accounts, he is servant and master, representation and revelation, reference and referent, medium and message—a powerful sign of life but also the life itself.

It is no doubt his specific function as a referential sign that consigns Jesus to suffering and death. Sign usage can, indeed, be fatal, especially given the operative premise of direct reference, which insists that verbal signs denote ontologically independent realities and entities, that language points to what is extrinsic to it. Again, *reference* consists in language's capacity to *carry* the word's content *back* to its object. This notion of carrying back—*referre* or *reportare* in Latin, *anapherein* in Greek—is premised on the idea of truth as the adequation of word and object, that the verbal sign matches what it indicates without remainder. This signifying movement further characterizes the utilitarian function defined by Augustine above: "use" means "to *refer* something to obtain what one loves" (*ad id quod amas obtinendum referre*). At least here, reference, as opposed to inherence, entails employing a word to grasp something else, using language as a means and therefore using it up. In having the word refer or relate or report to what it names, one acts in confidence that the signifying term will float assuredly to its final resting place and never again stir. It is therefore perfectly apt that the Greek word for "sign" (*sēma*) also names the "tomb" that divulges the identity of the deceased. Semantics seals the grave. And readers who approach words with the expectation of discovering this ultimate sense do little else than pay their respects to a language lying in state.

Even when theories of reference are qualified—when it is acknowledged that words are more than mere nomenclature assignable to a ready-made world, when it is conceded that phenomena are produced by the very concepts that designate them, that language makes or discloses the world it represents—even here, the sign still suffers a curtailed lifespan, if only because, after performing its function, the word quietly exits the scene of meaning and passes out of view. The efficient use of signs strives to dissolve the material-formal conditions of communication in order to yield to its ideational content. Signs work best when they work as vanishing mediators. The classical but by no means incontestable

---

the Son of God, Stephen T. Davis, Daniel Kendall, and Gerald O'Collins, eds. (Oxford: Oxford University Press, 2002), 143–63.

definition of the sign as "something that stands for something else" (*aliquid stat pro aliquo*) always implies the eventual dispensability of the sign; *dispensable*, because the sign, by pointing beyond itself, indicates a meaning elsewhere, which exhausts the function of the indication itself. In arriving at the signification, the act of signifying comes to an end. In a figurative sense, therefore, including the figure of figuration itself, the sign, which carries meaning back, dies, so that its message can live, even if this "life," understood as some stabilized, immobile sense, is but a euphemism for death.

Here again, but now in semiotic terms, philology and theology corroborate each other. For the idea that death should serve as the condition for life not only demonstrates a fundamental principle for students or lovers of language, but also elicits the love of God. The theological import is present, for example, in another well-known verse from the Gospel of John: "Unless a corn of wheat falls into the ground and dies, it remains alone; but if it dies, it produces much fruit" (John 12:24 [NKJV]). In the agricultural sense reminiscent of mystery cults across the ancient world, death is understood as the prerequisite for flourishing. In the Gospel of John, the verse alludes above all to the Crucifixion, where the flesh is sacrificed in the figure of the Lamb of God. Just as wheat bursts from the buried corn, just as meaning emerges from the vanishing verbal medium, so everlasting life sprouts from Christ's death. For those who believe, the life of Christ *signifies* because it mediates the way to the Father. Within systems of reference and communication, the *power of the sign* is the *sign's power to die*. More specifically and more provocatively, the life of Christ signifies because the omnipotence of God who became flesh does not preclude God's power to die. That is to say, the power of the Word Incarnate must also involve the power to be powerless before death. For only in this way, only by consigning God as well as the faithful to death, can the Incarnation deliver all to an eternal, meaningful postmortem life.

In addition to the existential problem of understanding what a *postmortem life* may be, there are other issues that emerge as soon as we recall that Christ is not only the way to the Father, but also the endpoint or terminus in himself, *via* and *vita*. The Messiah's status as an end in himself—and not merely a means to an end—is best revealed through the figure of John the Baptist, who also plays an explicitly mediating role in the Gospel story and thereby reiterates the requirement of death and its relation to the function of signs. As the iconographical tradition bears out, the Baptist is to be regarded as someone who points to Jesus Christ and therefore as someone who himself is already marked out to die.

As the Baptist explains: "You yourselves bear me witness, that I said, 'I am not the Christ,' but, 'I have been sent before Him. [. . .] He must increase, but I must decrease" (John 3:28–30 [NKJV]). In his gloss on this passage from one of his sermons, Augustine allows the statement to address a philological theorem by reminding his readers that the Baptist as *voice*—as the *vox clamans in deserto*—ultimately expires in Christ as the Word made flesh. Augustine writes:

> The voice precedes the Word and it makes possible its understanding. [. . .] This voice which merely resonates and gives no sense, this sound which comes from the mouth of someone screaming [*clamans*], not speaking, we call it the voice, not the word. [. . .] "He must increase, but I must decrease"? Why? Because the voices are being effaced as the Word grows. The voice gradually loses its function as the soul progresses to Christ. So Christ has to increase and John the Baptist has to be obliterated.[2]

For Augustine, the voice is but the bearer of verbal meaning and therefore meaningless in itself, merely "resonating" and "giving no sense." As pure sound—"screaming, not speaking"—the voice is the enunciating act, an act that Augustine sharply distinguishes from what is being said. If the voice says anything at all, it simply announces its presence; it claims, "I am here"—that is, it functions as a gesture of self-referentiality. Yet this present claim to presence is already fated to absence. For the voice, in its mediating function, must ultimately vanish into the word, so as not to obstruct the arrival of sense. The enunciation yields its place to what is enunciated. Verbalized meaning amounts to *devocalization*. The voice is "effaced as the Word grows." The Word, of course, is Christ Himself—the word toward which the voice points before it is obliterated. Still, the nature of this word remains ambiguous. On the one hand, understood as the *referent* of the Baptist's screaming, Christ is the living flesh that reveals Him to be a man among mankind, to be revered as the immanent presence of the Word in the world; yet on the other hand, understood as a *reference*—as the word that itself points to the transcendent Father—he is the body that will be given up for the salvation of mankind.

Philology tends to situate itself on the threshold between reference and referent. It upsets smooth reading even though it may aim to provide a smooth

2. Augustine, Sermon 288; cited by Mladen Dolar, *A Voice and Nothing More* (Cambridge: MIT Press, 2006), 16.

text. This is because each word potentially addresses the philologist as a discrete utterance, as a request or even a plea, like a voice that cries out before being sacrificed to the logic of the sentence. And while a philological interrogation necessarily proceeds by taking the entire passage into consideration, by the sheer act of pausing to question each word, the philologist appears to attend to this intrusive voice before it is silenced, that is to say, before it is perfectly worked into the discourse at hand. If one insists on an opposition between voice and signifier, then reading to track the sense of a text indeed requires efforts of devocalization, of compelling the voice to evanesce into signification, of transforming the mere fact of phonation into a sign.[3] In contrast, philological care tarries with the word that has been charged to dissolve into meaning, listening to it in its solitary cell, administering the last rites, striving to stay the execution of the *vox moritura*, however provisionally. And when the time arrives to move on, to let the words assume their discursive purpose, the philologists stand to the side, willingly or begrudgingly, and accept their traditionally ancillary role, a mute witness to the sacrifice of the beloved voice.

The Christological ambivalence—Christ serving as both human indicator and divine terminus—turns entirely on the ambivalence of the *flesh*. In Christian dogma, the material body that is vulnerable, sinful, and slated for putrefaction is also the flesh in which God's Word appears to humankind and thus offers salvation from death. How, one should ask, does the willful flesh, which is generally denigrated, relate to the glorious flesh in which God was incarnated? How should one evaluate the flesh, which clearly functions as both the site of waywardness and a promise of salvation? The entire history of the heresies that plagued the early Church ensues from the difficulty in evaluating the flesh.[4]

The striking ambivalence of the flesh comes to the fore in the sixth chapter of the Gospel of John, which first recounts the story of feeding the multitude in Galilee at the time of Passover, followed by a sermon at Capernaum. Here, Jesus informs His disciples, "I am the living bread which came down from heaven. If anyone eats of this bread, he will live forever; and the bread that I shall give is My flesh, which I shall give for the life of the world" (John 6:51 [NKJV]). The core

3. On this procedure of semanticization as devocalization, see Adriana Cavarero, *For More than One Voice: Toward a Philosophy of Vocal Expression*, Paul Kottman, trans. (Stanford: Stanford University Press, 2005), 33–41.

4. For a comprehensive overview of the ambivalence of the flesh in Christian doctrine, see Adam G. Cooper, *Life in the Flesh: An Anti-Gnostic Spiritual Philosophy* (Oxford: Oxford University Press, 2008), 34–58.

idea is reiterated throughout the passage: "Whoever eats my flesh and drinks my blood abides in me and I in him" (John 6:56 [NKJV]). These lines clearly foreshadow the Eucharistic meal, which depends on the ultimate sacrifice of Christ's flesh upon the Cross. Yet further along and quite resolutely, Jesus insists that the flesh itself is of no benefit, no use: "It is the Spirit who gives life; *the flesh profits nothing.* The words that I speak to you are spirit, and *they* are life" (John 6:63 [NKJV]). "The flesh profits nothing"; "the flesh is of no help"—ἡ σὰρξ οὐκ ὠφελεῖ οὐδέν; *caro non prodest.* The Greek term *ōphelein* denotes being of use, succor, or assistance, giving some advantage, and hence is nearly synonymous with the Latin *prodesse,* which implies "being" (*esse*) "for" (*pro*) the use of something else. In this passage, then, the flesh appears to mark simultaneously both distance from and proximity to God, both extreme worthiness and extreme worthlessness: The flesh that is given "for the life of the world" itself lacks benefit or use-value; unless, of course, its use is grounded in its very uselessness.

The ambiguity may be clarified from a theological perspective, which would ascribe the ambivalence of the flesh to the realm of the *sacred,* identifying Christ's carnal nature as a nature dedicated to the divine by way of its utter destructibility. The sacral accursedness of the flesh—its complete uselessness—consigns it, by means of the Eucharist, to an economy that founds the body of the Church. The proclamation of the *incarnation* ("the word became flesh"—*verbum caro factum est*) ultimately yields to the ritual of *incorporation* ("this is my body"—*hoc est corpus meum*). As Saint Paul underscores, what is necessary for salvation is "the crucifixion of the flesh with its passions and desires" (Gal. 5:24 [KJV]). By means of sacrifice, by means of fatal expiration, the Word made flesh—flesh that is all too mortal—is to become flesh made eternal Sign. All the same, the complete uselessness of the flesh (*caro non prodest*) would appear to signal some crucial excess, something extravagant or nonrecuperable, something that resists final incorporation. If the flesh were to be subject to perfect integration, it would forfeit the very extravagance that founds integration itself. In the Vulgate's terms, the curious distinction between the flesh (*caro*) of the incarnational decree and the body (*corpus*) of the Eucharistic consecration persists, alerting us to the difficult tensions that subtend Christian theology, and thus philology as well: between *verbum caro factum est* and *hoc est enim corpus meum,* between the present perfect of accomplishment (*factum est*) and the deictic present (*hoc est*), between the passive voice and the active, between telling and showing, narrative and action, statement and event.

As we observed with the efforts of Dostoevsky's Inquisitor, in order to consolidate the Church into a "mystical body" (*corpus mysticum*), theology must reclaim and incorporate the flesh. Roberto Esposito therefore stresses how, beginning with the Patristic writings, "the words *sōma* and *corpus* begin to displace those of *sarx* and *caro* with ever greater frequency [. . .]. More than an expulsion of the flesh, this concerns its incorporation into an organism that is capable of domesticating flesh's centrifugal and anarchic impulses."[5] Although the flesh provides the material energy for animating the body, it must not overwhelm the latter's integrity. Henri de Lubac focuses explicitly on the persistent tension between flesh and body across medieval theory, where the *corpus* generally denotes "an idea of totality"—an integral organism, wherein different members work together for the sake of the whole. In contrast, the flesh was reserved for the Eucharist, which emphatically referred to Christ as a sacrificial victim. Flesh is food and thus a means for spiritual salvation. The sacramental connotations of flesh include the flesh as nourishment and the flesh as sacrificial meat. Thus, for Jerome, the flesh is the true, historical body of Christ (a *corpus verum*), which consequently formed the mystical body (the *corpus mysticum*) of the Church.[6] With Augustine, the flesh is even further neutralized, redefined as the "spiritual flesh"—that is, "a body that is now heavenly and spiritual, an angelic body in the society of angels."[7] Augustine therefore cautions his readers against indulging in the "habit of the flesh" (*consuetudo carnis*), which lures us into *enjoying* what should instead be *used*. Only with the death of our flesh-bound will are we capable of assuming the "habit of the spirit" (*consuetudo spiritus*).[8] As Augustine outlines elsewhere in *De Trinitate*, true peace or *tranquillitas* will only occur when the spirit is victorious over the flesh.[9] The spiritual flesh therefore is the flesh that is entirely obedient to the spirit, a flesh that no longer disturbs the soul—a "transfigured flesh."[10] At least from a theological perspective, in order to produce meaning, the flesh must be *incorporated* into a representational system, into a signifying body, by means of the spirit.

Compared with the theological perspective, philology is less equipped to establish definitive significations. In the history of academic study, beginning

5. Esposito, *Bios*, 164.

6. Henri de Lubac, *Corpus Mysticum*, 128.

7. Augustine, *In psalmum 145*, n. 3; cited in Lubac, *Corpus Mysticum*, 131.

8. Augustine, *De doctrina christiana*, 1.19, 34.

9. See Augustine, *De Trinitate*, chap. 15 [*On the Trinity*, Gareth B. Matthews, ed. (Cambridge: Cambridge University Press, 2002)].

10. Lubac, *Corpus Mysticum*, 132.

in the Christian Middle Ages, this incapacity tended to relegate philology to an ancillary role. The early university displayed a feudal structure wherein all the faculties worked together in a very clear distribution of labor premised on hierarchies of power: Philosophy served jurisprudence and medicine, which in turn served theology, which was the highest faculty insofar as it involved the eternal salvation of souls. This distribution of labor is clearly discernible in the opening monologue of Goethe's *Faust*:

> Habe nun, ach! Philosophie,
> Juristerei und Medizin,
> Und leider auch Theologie
> durchaus studiert, mit heißem Bemühn.
> Da steh' ich nun, ich armer Tor,
> Und bin so klug als wie zuvor!
>
> Have now studied, ah! Philosophy
> Jurisprudence and Medicine,
> And unfortunately also Theology
> Thoroughly, with fervent zeal.
> Here I stand now, I poor fool,
> And no wiser than before
>
> 354–59[11]

Faust does not mention *Philologie*, because philology is not a faculty in any proper sense. A *faculty* names a specific "capability" or "power to achieve knowledge." Derived from *facilitas*, a faculty denotes the "ease" that well-defined methods and correct training should provide. In contrast, philology tends to make everything *difficult*, not facile. Rather than accomplishing stable knowledge, it undermines the methods of the various faculties by posing questions about the language, by pointing out difficulties in the text. Only once those difficulties have been resolved can language *facilitate* the transmission of knowledge. Yet it is Faust's frustration with his acquired facilities that eventually leads him back to the difficulties of philology. In a subsequent scene, Faust turns to translating

11. Johann Wolfgang von Goethe, *Faust: Der Tragödie erster und zweiter Teil*, Erich Trunz, ed. (Munich: Beck, 1987), 20 [*Faust: A Tragedy*, Walter Arndt, trans. (New York: Norton, 1976), 10 (translation modified)].

the Prologue to the Gospel of John, bothered by rendering *logos* too readily or too easily as *Wort* ("word"). That is to say that here Faust no longer approaches language as a facile transmitter of univocal meaning, but instead struggles with the word *word* itself (1224–37).

Viewed as a troublesome source of difficulty, Philology was consistently treated with condescension. Rather than being given too much power, she was generally reduced to serving as the "handmaiden of the faculties"—the *ancilla facultatum*. Like a handmaiden, Philology should rest content in her subservient role, facilitating the more valuable work of interpretation and reflection. When left to her own devices, she slows reading down by pointing out some difficult crux, by calling attention to endless obstacles and stumbling blocks—*problēmata* and *skandala*—problems and scandals that philology should expeditiously remove, so as to clear the way for meaning. Philology loves language—she is the intimate friend of the *logos*—but she should not allow this friendship to be restrictive or oppressive. All too often, she gets lost in endless detours and complications, indulging in the sheer pleasure of the text, forestalling the arrival of good sense by never allowing the way to be forsaken. When Philology blocks the conveyance of meaning, when she calls attention to the textual corpus in itself, she stops readers in their tracks, reminding them of the flesh that constitutes the body. Here, the interpreter of language should be on guard. He should not fall in love with Philology but rather treat her with the condescension appropriate to her humble station. Otherwise, a loved Philology threatens to hold on to her lover, smothering him with affection and thereby preventing him from achieving the real work of reading. It is always a serious problem and an embarrassing scandal, when the master becomes infatuated with the servant.

The philology of the flesh thus constitutes a poetic challenge, one that may result in the failure of the word to be carried up or back—a failed *anapherein* or *referre*. It would entail the failure to be *reported,* which is explicitly announced in Emily Dickinson's resonant poem:

> A word made flesh is seldom
> And tremblingly partook
> Nor then perhaps reported
> But have I not mistook
> Each one of us has tasted
> With ecstasies of stealth

The very food debated
To our specific strength —

A word that breathes distinctly
Has not the power to die
Cohesive as the Spirit
It may expire if He—

"Made Flesh and dwelt among us"
Could condescension be
Like this consent of Language
This loved Philology[12]

With a literal citation from the Johannine Prologue ("And the Word was made flesh, and dwelt among us"), Dickinson's poem explicitly engages the Christian doctrine of the Incarnation, which passes directly into an evocation of the Eucharist: the "word made Flesh" is that which is "tremblingly partook." Read from a biographical perspective, the "very food debated" may refer to Dickinson's rejection of the exclusivism preached in her family's Congregational faith, which called for a formal conversion before granting participation in the Holy Communion. Although Dickinson fully accepted the Trinitarian beliefs endorsed by Amherst College, which explicitly distinguished itself from the staunch Unitarianism of Harvard College, she insisted on a more liberal interpretation of communion, where all should be welcomed to the altar. As she once divulged to a friend: "I do not respect 'doctrines.'"[13] Thus, in protest, Dickinson refused to be converted, and eventually ceased attending Sunday services altogether. As she famously writes: "Some keep the Sabbath going to Church— / I keep it, staying at Home."[14] A moral objection drove her to stand apart in a kind of *ekstasis*, which resulted in "seldom" participation in the Eucharist. When received, the

12. Emily Dickinson, *The Poems, Variorum Edition*, 3 vols., Ralph William Franklin, ed. (Cambridge: Harvard University Press, 1998), no. 1715A (undated), 3: 1489–90.

13. Dickinson to Mrs. Joseph Haven (no. 200), in *Letters of Emily Dickinson*, Thomas Johnson and Theodora Ward, eds. (Cambridge: Harvard University Press, 1997), 149. On Dickinson's problematic relationship to conversion in relation to this poem, see Siobhan Phillips, "'Loved Philology': Emily Dickinson's Trinitarian Word," *ESQ: A Journal of the American Renaissance* 51 (2005), 250–75.

14. Dickinson, *The Poems*, no. 236 (1861), 1: 259.

Host was taken—or in light of her congregation's doctrine, *mistaken*—"with ecstasies of stealth." Her communion, therefore, rests on a private sanctification, whereby "each one of us" can find his or her "specific strength."

This biographical explanation does not prevent reading the poem otherwise. By concluding with allusions to "Language" and "Philology," it also clearly points to a metapoetic motive, suggesting that the poem is a reflection on poetry itself. Of course, Dickinson is not the first or only poet who has taken the opportunity of turning to the Johannine Word as an *ars poetica,* which can concisely describe how the Word comes to be incarnated in the poet or how the poem is an incarnation of the poet's lived experience—in Dickinson's terms, how the Word constitutes "our specific strength."[15] Particularly in the wake of secularism, Eucharistic motifs were often adduced to offer poetic compensation for a perceived evacuation of meaning. In her study of post-Reformation English poetry, Regina Schwartz regards this turn to sacramental figures as a powerful remedy for the "feeling of profound loss [that] reverberates through the work of the early modern writers, a keen sense that something is missing, a real hunger for the real presence of God."[16] Yet, whereas a "Eucharistic poetics" generally strives for a sacredness that transcends the verbal sign, Dickinson's poetic word persists in revealing transcendence in the immanence of the human word.

Such a poetic word breathes and communicates itself; it lives as a sentient person who "dwells among us," as a Word that has descended from a transcendental realm to find expression in the poet. This departure from transcendence into immanence is precisely what theologians define as Christ's *condescension,* used in the sense as it is found in Paul's Epistle to the Romans: "Be of the same mind one toward another. Mind not high things, but *condescend* to men of low estate. Be not wise in your own conceits" (Romans 12:16 [KJV]). The English imperative *condescend* translates the Greek participle *sunapagomenoi* ("leading away with"), which features an analogous pair of prefixes (*sun-* "with" and *apo-* "away from"). In the Vulgate, the Greek participle is translated into Latin as *consentientes,* which employs only the *con-* prefix and thereby expresses the *shared feelings* that produce agreement.[17] Dickinson's poem retains both the notion of

15. For instructive examples in the early-modern poetic tradition, with particular emphasis on English poets, see Schwartz, *Sacramental Poetics,* and Johnson, *Made Flesh.*

16. Schwartz, *Sacramental Poetics,* 15.

17. The SBL Greek New Testament reads: τὸ αὐτὸ εἰς ἀλλήλους φρονοῦντες, μὴ τὰ ὑψηλὰ φρονοῦντες ἀλλὰ τοῖς ταπεινοῖς συναπαγόμενοι. μὴ γίνεσθε φρόνιμοι παρ' ἑαυτοῖς; the Vulgate:

consent and the doctrine of *condescension,* linking the two closely together: "A word that breathes distinctly / Has not the power to die . . . if He . . . Could *condescension* be / Like this *consent* of Language / This loved Philology." The condescension of Christ—God's readiness to become man, His *consent* to leave the heavens and dwell among mankind as a man—functions therefore as a figure for the "consent of language" to participate in this poem, to inspire the poet or poetry in general.[18]

A metapoetic interpretation of Dickinson's poem, then, would understand it as a portrayal of inspiration, which also relates to metaphors of eating and digestion. "A word made flesh" becomes "a word-made flesh," that is a flesh made of words: both Incarnation and Eucharist, both living person and food. Christ is to be venerated as God, but also received and consumed as a meal. These two senses of the word—as sacrificial meat and as living flesh—are reflected in the two equal halves of the poem. Whereas the first eight lines describe the event of reception—a word, in which the poet *partakes,* a word that she *tastes*—the last eight lines present the process of creativity: "a word that breathes distinctly." The repetition or *anaphora* ("A word made flesh" [1], "A word that breathes distinctly" [9]) underscores the continuum between the word of reception in the first octave and the word of poetic expression in the second. The poem's first word—"A word made flesh"—is therefore a word that will be *carried back,* an object of *anapherein* or *reportare.* Strikingly though, the poem explicitly undermines the very concept of anaphora: it disrupts the poetic act of carrying back by placing it under negation: "nor then perhaps *reported*" (line 3, emphasis added). The poem's anaphora thus carries back a word that *perhaps* cannot be carried back. The anaphoric "word that breathes distinctly" in line 9 can and cannot *refer* back to the initial "word made flesh" in line 1. It is precisely the reporting of this word, which "perhaps" is not "reported," that engenders the ambiguous energy of this poem.

"This loved Philology" is both a philology of the body, which refers words back to produce meaning, and a philology of the flesh, which finds it difficult to carry words back. Love for the word makes all reference difficult because it hesitates to let language go. The philology of the flesh perceives a meaning that

---

id ipsum invicem sentientes non alta sapientes sed humilibus consentientes nolite esse prudentes apud vosmet ipsos.

18. See Helen Vendler, *Dickinson: Selected Poems and Commentaries* (Cambridge: Harvard University Press, 2010), 506.

inheres in the word itself and therefore never wants the verbal way to pass away into a secure referent. This philology focuses on the verbal medium to such an extent that it conflates the way toward life with life itself. It fuses the *via* to the *vita*. For this reason the *word* of the poem's latter half—the "word that breathes distinctly"—explicitly "has not the power to die." It lacks the power to die not because it is immortal, but rather because it does not have the strength to be carried back—reported or transported—to a transcendent realm. What the anaphora of the line 9 shows, however, is that the word does refer back to the first line; yet this reference decidedly never departs from language: the "word" of the second octave refers to nothing more and nothing less than the "word" of the first octave, to a "word made flesh." Here, at least, the philology of the body, which rests on *reference*, underwrites the philology of the flesh, which insists on *inherence*.

The capacity of the poetic word to breathe distinctly was a persistent concern for Dickinson. Already in her first letter to Thomas Wentworth Higginson, she asks:

> Are you too deeply occupied to say if my Verse is alive?
> The Mind is so near itself—it cannot see distinctly—and I have none to ask—
> Should you think it breathed—and had you the leisure to tell me, I should feel quick gratitude—[19]

The implicit feeling of isolation—a mind so near to itself that there is no one near to ask—colors the poetic desire with a sense of urgency. The solitariness of the mind, which renders it incapable of seeing "distinctly," may be well on the path to extinction, because it reinforces a delusion of disembodiment; and without a body, there can be no breath. An unread poem, like a bodiless mind, may or may not be alive; it may or may not breathe. In this regard, the missive itself could be read as a lonely mind seeking a breathing body. As Dickinson writes in a subsequent letter: "A Letter always feels to me like immortality because it is the mind alone without corporeal friend."[20] Here, one should take *immortality* as a euphemism for death, insofar as it negates the mortality that defines our humanness. Dickinson suggests that immortality is "the mind alone without corporeal

19. Dickinson to Higginson, April 16, 1862 (no. 260), in Dickinson, *Letters*, 403.
20. Dickinson to Higginson, June 1869 (no. 330), in Dickinson, *Letters*, 460.

friend"—at best, a mere ghost consigned to eternal lifelessness. As Ferdinand Ebner would insist, life obtains only in the spirit or breath (*spiritus*)—in the spirit that constitutes the interrelationship and dialogic interaction between two subjects, in the shared spirit that liberates the mind from isolation and solipsism. It is the spirit or breath that gives life, while the *letter*, like immortality, kills. The mind alone cannot know whether the verse breathes or not; for that, it needs to enter the spiritual space that unites the poet and her correspondent. Incapable of *distinguishing* itself from the outside, the solitary mind is unable to enter into this vitally necessary relation with another. If Higginson should be "too deeply occupied," he would suffer from the same isolation, the same incapacity to relate. Yet should he not be so occupied, he would be in the position to resuscitate the poetic word. And should the verse be alive, it would be a word that does not have the power to die. The *inspired* word, therefore, both can and cannot *expire*. The poem can expire or breathe out the spirit that inspired it without expiring, without being carried back to a purely discarnate sense—expiring without expiring, "cohesive as the Spirit," *co-herent* in the common breath.[21]

The stipulation formulated in the conditional sentence at the poem's end ("[The word] may expire if He [. . .] Could condescension be") not only evokes this expiration without expiration, but also marks the point in the poem where the play of the poem's prefixes coalesce. Most relevant is the oscillation of composite forms with the prefixes *dis-* and *con-*. As a prefix, *dis-*, like its cognate *de-*, denotes a sense of withdrawal, negation, or descent, as opposed to the prefix *con-*, which denotes a joining, a bringing together or a being-with. *Distinct* describes something that is separate or set apart, generally opposed to *cohesive*, which implies a hanging together. Following the logic of Dickinson's poem, two alternatives emerge. On the one hand, a word made flesh, or partaking in it, is "seldom"—a rare occurrence: isolated, sporadic, or unusual: it is "a word that breathes *distinctly*"—a quality that could be "*cohesive* as the Spirit," but only if it would expire. In this case, as the prefixes would suggest, the word's *distinctness* prevents its *cohesiveness*. On the other hand, the poem also envisions an idea of cohesiveness that includes distinctness—an accomplishment that is achieved by the word *condescension*, which combines both the prefix of cohesion (*con-*) and the prefix of distinction (*de-*).

21. On the significance of breath in the poem, see Matthias Bauer, "A Word Made Flesh: Anmerkungen zum lebendigen Wort bei Emily Dickinson," in "Bibeldichtung," Volker Kapp and Dorothea Scholl, eds., special issue, *Schriften zur Literaturwissenschaft* 26 (2006), 373–92; here, 384.

As noted, *con-de-scension* aptly demonstrates the claim of the Christian Incarnation, insofar as it expresses the cohesion of two distinct natures: transcendent and immanent, immortal and mortal, divine and human. The separating power of *de-* theologically states how God detaches Himself from the purely transcendent realm, while the binding force of *con-* underscores His connection to human life. Both gestures are clearly heard in Dickinson's biblical citation: "[The Word was] made flesh [*de-*] and dwelt among us [*con-*]." Poetically, the separating force is found in the word that "breathes *dis*tinctly"—yet, it is a word that could also be "*co*hesive as the spirit," at least when the word could be *con-descension*. The mutual limitation of the philology of the flesh and the philology of the body results in the possibility of breathing both *distinctly* and *coherently*. "This loved Philology"—this loved love for language—holds off transforming the word-made-flesh into a body, into a form that would surrender, yielding itself to some discarnate content; yet it is also a philology that does not neglect reference, even if the word ultimately refers to the Word. Dickinson's philology of the body aims at a destination, which is breathing *life*, yet this objective needs the philology of the flesh to provide the *way*. Should the way perpetually hinder the arrival to life, it would be insubordinate, if not altogether scandalous; but should the destination ignore the way, it would pass away into the transcendent signified. As *condescension*, however, the poet's "loved philology" offers a word that expires or "breathes distinctly" without breathing out its last. As an earlier poem asserts:

> A word is dead
> When it is said,
> Some say.
> I say it just
> Begins to live
> That day
>
> *The Poems*, no. 278
> (1862), 1: 297

The flesh is mortal but it does not have the power to die, for as soon as it dies, it is no longer breathing flesh but rather a dead body, a corpse. The flesh feels and senses and thereby gives us the capacity to feel and to sense; it gives us the power to react to the world, to touch the world and to be touched by the world. The flesh enables us to know that we live in a distinct, living body. In contrast, a discarnate body destines us to become alienated, reified, exposed to incorporation, assigned to hierarchies of meaning. Unchecked by the philology of the flesh, the philology of the body fatally determines the word, causing the inspired body to expire. The philology of the body dutifully works with the conviction that the verbal medium will exhaust itself in its function. Like a deferential handmaiden, it performs its tasks quietly and unobtrusively, ensuring that words accomplish their mediating function. Yet for this very reason, it fails to recognize that the way is also the life. In this regard, the philology of the flesh is transgressive, if not altogether revolutionary: mistaking the way by never abandoning the way. "With ecstasies of stealth," it insists, as Hegel's famous dialectic shows, that the servant is the master. Insofar as it attends to what is both *distinct* and *coherent*, Dickinson's loved philology casts doubt on the validity of a meaning that uses up and dispenses with the means of meaning. Thus, the incarnation of the divine word serves as the paradigm for the incarnation of a poet's word.[22] *The* word made flesh underwrites Dickinson's word made flesh. In both cases, the descent interrupts and thereby qualifies the consent. The antithetical forces of *de-* and *con-*, of being apart and being with, which inform the word *condescension*—and which perhaps could also be heard in the proper name *Dickinson*—postpones the final exhalation.

Dickinson's poetry recognizes the contradictory nature of immortal life. It bears witness to the idea that immortality is nothing more than eternal lifelessness. In a later letter to Higginson, she explains: "To be human is more than to be divine, for when Christ was divine he was uncontented 'til he had been human."[23] What is "uncontented" seeks to be contained—to be limited, to discover boundaries that would test a being's powers. Dickinson's insight corroborates Hans Blumenberg's probing reflections on the significance of the Incarnation. For Blumenberg, the timelessness of eternity is where nothing happens. Eternity is vacuous, unending, *uncontained*, and therefore "boring" (*langweilig*); and "those who are powerful, the nearer they approach the superlative, are seized with an inclination toward adventure."[24] In Blumenberg's view, therefore, it was God's desire for limitation that led to the Word of Creation: both the Word that was "at the beginning" and, subsequently, the Word that was made flesh, which marks

22. Cf. Bauer, "A Word Made Flesh," 380.
23. Dickinson to Higginson, 1877 (no. 519), in Dickinson, *Letters*, 592.
24. Hans Blumenberg, *Matthäuspassion* (Frankfurt a. M.: Suhrkamp, 1988), 11.

the presence of the creative Word in the World. Because nothing is impossible for God as an omnipotent "absolute power" (*potentia absoluta*), it was possible for Him to employ an "ordained power" (*potentia ordinata*) to create an ordered world composed of horizons, which limit possibility. In God's infinite capacity He produced the incapacity that contains or restricts His infinite power; for the *potentia ordinata* means that not every possibility remains possible. Accordingly, in the Genesis account, the Creation is followed by a judgment or distinction: "And God saw every thing that he had made, and, behold, it was very good" (Gen. 1:31 [KJV]). To judge something to be good implies distinguishing it from everything else, from everything possible that was not created. To create something means to withhold something, which—for Blumenberg, and perhaps also for Dickinson—motivates the Incarnation. Blumenberg elaborates:

> What was withheld came as that Word itself, through which the World was commanded into being, and it came as a "piece of the World": it became flesh. It lived as a man among men, for whom the burden of the world-adventure of the godhead had been imposed.[25]

The Incarnation is therefore compensation for the dispensation of the Creation. With the Incarnation, God gives what He had initially withheld. If the Creation makes God guilty (*schuldig*)—guilty of holding something back in His effort to contain infinite possibility—then the Incarnation pays off this debt (*Schuld*).[26] As Dickinson observes, "to be human is more than to be divine," because the noncontainment of divine power is ultimately empty—*empty*, because it lacks the containment that spells contentment. To be human is to face finitude, to be measured in time, and thus to evade the infinite "boredom" or *Langweiligkeit* that characterizes God's *discontent*—a discontent that motivates His *condescension*.

Dickinson's dynamic philology is further evident in her relationship to the printed word. The physical form of the codex alone—as text enclosed by covers, traditionally composed of animal skin: parchment, vellum, and leather—already suggests an embodied or incarnate quality. That Dickinson would be attracted to these quasi-sacred objects, to the subcutaneous, fleshly nature of the words of past authors, corroborates her engagement in a loved philology.

25. Blumenberg, *Matthäuspassion*, 12.
26. Blumenberg, *Matthäuspassion*, 65.

Handling a bound volume has always been a complexly sensuous affair: visual, tactile, and olfactory, in addition to being intellectual and imaginative. For those who are particularly sensitive, the printed word offers a fairly convincing experience of real presence, with the absent author miraculously accompanying the sacramental act of reading. Certainly for Dickinson, how she related to books and how books related to her held out the promise to create that spiritual, dialogic space, for which she longed.

In the spring of 1864, Dickinson became so debilitated by an eye affliction that she was driven to seek treatment from Dr. Henry Willard Williams, one of Boston's leading ophthalmologists. The prescribed therapy required her to reside with her cousins in Cambridge for eight months, far away from her quiet, seldom-abandoned home in Amherst. More than simply disturbing her accustomed solitude, the cure imposed a horrifying injunction, which she later reported to her friend Joseph Lyman:

> Some years ago I had a woe, the only one that ever made me tremble. It was a shutting out of all the dearest ones of time, the strongest friends of the soul—BOOKS[.] The medical man said avaunt ye ~~books~~ tormentors, he also said 'down, thoughts, & plunge into her soul'. He might as well have said, 'Eyes be blind', 'heart be still'. So I had eight ~~weary~~ months in Siberia.[27]

The fact that Dickinson describes time spent in an urban setting with family as imprisonment and exile is striking, but rhymes perfectly well with what we know of her disposition, ensconced in the provinces of Western Massachusetts. While gratefully acknowledging the care and attention that her recently orphaned cousins have shown her, Dickinson's letters consistently characterize the Cambridge boardinghouse as "jail," "prison," and "wilderness."[28] Yet for this enigmatic claustrophile, seclusion had always been wonderfully profitable, composing and sending out poems for spiritual intercourse. And in no time, as she confesses elsewhere, throughout her sojourn to the east she was able to write poems with pencil, albeit stealthily, against the doctor's orders: "I work in my

27. Joseph Lyman wrote out seven "snatches" of his correspondence with Emily Dickinson, first published in Richard Sewall, *The Lyman Letters: New Light on Emily Dickinson and Her Family* (Amherst: University of Massachusetts Press, 1965), 76.

28. For an account of Dickinson's ordeal, see Elizabeth Phillips, *Emily Dickinson: Personae and Performance* (University Park: Pennsylvania State University Press, 1988), 61–67.

Prison, and make Guests for myself. [. . .] The Physician has taken away my Pen."[29] Solitude, then, was not the problem: she could people her room with verse in Cambridge as readily as she had done in her private chamber in Amherst. Rather, as we see in this note to Lyman, what transformed her into a detainee, specifically into a desolate sybirak starving and shivering in the middle of summer, was the oculist's strict order that she refrain from all reading. This was the restriction that she identified, the one that made her truly "tremble," apparently for the first time in her life, for it was a prohibition that deprived her of "the strongest friends of the soul." To be without books meant to be utterly alone, regardless of the company that daily busied itself about her, regardless of the "Guests" that she concealed in her desk.

Acquiescence to so severe a restriction was no doubt motivated by the fear of permanent blindness, of being forever cut off from her kindred spirits. Temporary abstinence is often the price to pay for subsequent indulgence. Yet this cure appears to have been especially vicious. The banning of books, which was intended to prevent a complete loss of eyesight, was itself taken to be a form of blinding. "The medical man said avaunt ye ~~books~~ tormentors, he also said 'down,' thoughts, & plunge into her soul'. He might as well have said, 'Eyes be blind', 'heart be still'." The ophthalmologist's dual conjuration, as Dickinson presents it, is not without some complexity. According to the bereaved patient, the doctor assumed a manner reminiscent of an exorcist, seeking to drive out the demonic volumes—the deletion of the very word "~~books~~" is a telling gesture. The archaic *avaunt*, synonymous with the imperative *begone* (as in Macbeth's cry to the Ghost of Banquo: "Avaunt, and quit my sight! Let the earth hide thee!"),[30] calls more specifically, in light of the common French cognate, for a departure in the sense of moving *avant*: the books are dispatched by advancing them to the front, by compelling them to proceed along their course and move forward before everything else.

Dickinson's characterization of the medicine man's witchery could therefore imply the conviction that books are merely dispensable instruments of mediation: once a book's contents are sufficiently processed, decoded, and interpreted—once the information has found entrance into the mind of the reader, digested and incorporated—the physical medium itself should no longer be necessary. In addition to aiming to reduce eye strain, then, the physician's

29. Dickinson to Higginson, June 1864 (no. 290), in Dickinson, *Letters*, 431.

30. William Shakespeare, *Macbeth* III.4.

dismissal of books may at least partially be motivated by an adherence to the principle of the vanishing mediator, just as the poet's torment is caused by a refusal to let the mediator go. The doctor is thus also portrayed as a mesmerist or animal trainer, who strives to domesticate the drive that would otherwise pull her towards harm's way, commanding his patient's "thoughts" to lie "down" and "plunge into [the] soul," hoping to train the woman's dogged will and thereby prevent misbehavior and forgetfulness. Psychic therapy entails mental discipline. But Dickinson will know nothing of asceticism. She longs for traffic with the "strongest friends of [her] soul," which must persist apart from the information they convey to the mind. Her bibliophilia refuses to send the books off, because it has always dissuaded her from having them move along. Instead, she relishes in their loved, comforting presence. If she is condemned to suffer a life without books, she might as well be blind.

For Dickinson, the frightening ban, a quasi-biblical *Bücherverbot*, has all the weight of a terrible fate. The absence of books banishes her to the unwelcoming climes of Russia's notorious penal colony as decisively as their presence would have conveyed her to more inspiring shores.

> There is no Frigate like a Book
> To take us Lands away
> Nor any Coursers like a Page
> Of prancing Poetry —
> This Traverse may the poorest take
> Without oppress of Toll —
> How frugal is the Chariot
> That bears the Human Soul
>
> Dickinson, *The Poems*, no. 1286
> (1873), 1:1116–17

It is arguably the physical format of the codex—unbounded pleasure bound by two covers—that provided the model for the poet's productive confinement, the "finite infinity" that she consistently cultivated.[31] Within the limits of a book,

31. "There is a solitude of space / A solitude of sea / A solitude of death, but these / Society shall be / Compared with that profounder site / That polar privacy / A soul admitted to itself — / Finite infinity." Dickinson, *Poems*, 3 vols., Thomas H. Johnson, ed. (Cambridge: Harvard University Press, 1955), no. 1695 (undated), 3: 1149.

as well as within the sacred precincts of her room, she could travel swiftly and thriftily, frugally and fruitfully, without oppression. She moves forward by taking up the rear; she advances by never leaving the vessel. On this basis, the limitlessness that unfolds within the binding's specific limits modifies the general distinction between form and content, one that rests on a particular conception of the book, which is the signal achievement of the poem cited here. While a book may be understood as a container, that is, as a mediating *form* that transmits content, here, the *content* itself serves as a container or vessel: a "Chariot that bears the Human Soul." By engaging with the meaning borne by the page, the soul is carried along as freight or passenger. The opportunity for this kind of sublime transport is precisely what is lost when the poet is bereft of her books. Condemned to the doctor's prohibition, Dickinson is robbed of the chance to be transported to pleasurable lands. Instead, she finds herself deported to a weary wilderness, a woeful experience that exacts a heavy, oppressive toll.

Although one might conjecture that Dickinson's symptoms, which included photophobia, blurred vision, and recurrent headaches, point to inflammatory ailments like iritis or uveitis, Dr. Williams, who would soon be appointed as the first chair of ophthalmology at Harvard Medical School, would not have ruled out a more psychological etiology, for example the "hysterical hyperaesthesia" that he would come to describe in the 1867 edition of his *Practical Guide to the Study of Diseases of the Eye*.[32] With no medical records of the case extant, it is impossible to know for certain the outlines of the cure. What is known, however, is that throughout her life Dickinson reported being assailed by "phantoms" and other frightening hallucinations, which led neighbors to designate her as "the myth of Amherst"; and if we take Dickinson at her word, the doctor's verbal commands confirm a diagnosis focused more on nerves or hysteria than on physiological debility.

As Dickinson describes it, in keeping her away from books, the doctor might just as well have said, "Eyes be blind, heart be still." Dickinson thus interprets

32. Henry Willard Williams, *Practical Guide to the Study of Diseases of the Eye: Their Medical and Surgical Treatment*, 2nd ed. (Boston: Ticknor and Fields, 1867), 262–63, cited in Martin Wand and Richard Sewall, "'Eyes Be Blind, Heart Be Still': A New Perspective on Emily Dickinson's Eye Problem," *New England Quarterly* 52 (1979), 400–6; Norbert Hirschhorn and Polly Longsworth, "'Medicine Posthumous': A New Look at Emily Dickinson's Medical Conditions," *New England Quarterly* 69:2 (1996), 299–316; and Donald Blanchard, "Emily Dickinson's Ophthalmic Consultation with Henry Willard Williams, MD," *Archives of Ophthalmology* 130:12 (2012), 1591–95, which includes extensive bibliography on the topic.

her cure as a punishment. There is, of course, nothing unusual in viewing a project of restoration as a form of chastisement. Rehabilitation often entails harsh measures. Yet the expression that Dickinson employs here seems to allude to a more devastating outcome. In the Book of Isaiah, God calls for a scourge upon the wayward Israelites in order to clear a future path for the righteous:

> Make the heart of this people fat, and make their ears heavy, and shut their eyes, lest they see with their eyes, and hear with their ears, and understand with their heart, and convert and be healed. (Isaiah 6:10 [KJV])

A heart made "fat" is one made lethargic: the English Standard Version renders the Hebrew term *hashmen* ("make fat, stouten") as "dull," which underscores how God punishes those who have grown negligent or complacent in regard to his word.[33] The initial command therefore corresponds to the subsequent ones in the series, making the ears "heavy" and closing the eyes. The Vulgate demonstrates this correspondence by translating the opening imperative as *excaeca,* "make blind"—*excaeca cor populi huius,* "Blind the heart of this people." The plague therefore realizes or literalizes what is already metaphorically the case: in God's view, the Israelites are already blind in their hearts, their ears are listless, they look but do not see; and so the punitive command—*excaeca!*—seals their emotional, moral, and cognitive blindness by means of a physical debility, which will prevent any future conversion.

Construed as a warning, the passage finds its place across the Christian Gospels, for example John 12:40: "He hath blinded their eyes and hardened their heart, that they should not see with their eyes, nor understand with their heart, and be converted, and I should heal them" (KJV).[34] As mentioned above, the problem of conversion as expressed here played an essential role in the development of Calvinist theology, especially among the Puritans, who insisted on giving public testimony to one's faith as a prerequisite for membership into the

33. The Masoretic pointing of the Hebrew forms the imperative, yet the Septuagint employs the indicative mood: ἐπαχύνθη γὰρ ἡ καρδία τοῦ λαοῦ τούτου, "For the heart of this people was fat." In the latter reading, the people's heart is already hardened, whereas in both the Masoretic text and the Targum the prophet is instructed to dull the heart. See Craig Evans, "Isaiah 6:9–10 in Rabbinic and Patristic Writings," *Vigiliae Christianae* 36 (1982), 275–81, 280n5.

34. See also Mark 4:12: "That seeing they may see, and not perceive; and hearing they may hear, and not understand; lest at any time they should be converted, and their sins should be forgiven them" (KJV).

community of the blessed. Such conversion narratives vitally informed the religious life of the American Colonies and motivated the revivalist spirit of the First Great Awakening that flourished across New England in the 1730s. The revivals staged by Jonathan Edwards, beginning in 1733 in Northampton, Massachusetts, centered on the extent and obstinacy of human blindness and the pressing need to convert willfully. As he expresses it in a sermon from 1739:

> The blindness that is in the heart of man [. . .] is neither for want of *faculties*, nor *opportunity* to know, but from some positive cause. There is a principle in his heart, of such a blinding and besotting nature, that it hinders the exercises of his *faculties* about the things of religion; exercises for which God has made him well capable, and for which he gives him abundant opportunity.[35]

Edwards goes on to identify "those who are judicially given up of God, to the blindness of their own minds" and cites Isaiah 6:10—the command to "make the heart of this people fat, and their ears heavy, and shut their eyes"—explaining, "This judgment, when inflicted, is commonly for the contempt and abuse of the light which has been offered, for the commission of presumptuous sins, and for being obstinate in sin, and resisting the Holy Ghost, and many gracious calls and counsels, warnings and reproofs."[36]

Edwardsian theology had a lasting impact in framing the debates regarding individual piety and salvation that defined the religious experience of the Congregational movements in the following century; and it was explicitly in order to sustain this heritage that Amherst College was founded in 1821 with generous support from Samuel Fowler Dickinson, the poet's paternal grandfather.[37] This tradition was dutifully maintained by Mary Lyon, the founder of the Mount Holyoke Female Seminary, which Emily Dickinson began attending in 1847. Here, in accordance with revivalist enthusiasm, a public profession of faith and display of conversion would demonstrate to the community that you were not blind to the truth, and consequently that you would not incur divine wrath.[38]

35. Jonathan Edwards, "Man's Natural Blindness in the Things of Religion," in Edward Hickman, ed., *The Works of Jonathan Edwards*, 2 vols. (London: William Ball, 1839), 2: 247.

36. Edwards, "Man's Natural Blindness," 254.

37. Barton Levi St. Armand, *Emily Dickinson and Her Culture: The Soul's Society* (Cambridge: Cambridge University Press, 1984), 20–21.

38. See Roger Lundin, *Emily Dickinson and the Art of Belief*, 2nd ed. (Grand Rapids: Eerdmans, 2004), 36–43.

Dickinson, however, could not bring herself to participate, as one of her classmates, Clara Newman Turner, recounts:

> To illustrate the independence and honesty of [Emily's] convictions, — Miss Lyon, during a time of religious interest in the school, asked all those who wanted to be Christians to rise. The wording of the request was not such as Emily could honestly accede to and she remained seated—the only one who did not rise. In relating the incident to me, she said, "They thought it queer I didn't rise"—adding with a twinkle in her eye, "I thought a lie would be queerer."[39]

The young woman would suffer the same doubts and hesitation a few years later during the great revival at her home in Amherst, deeply concerned about conversion yet unable to commit.[40] Although it is unclear whether she was undergoing a profound spiritual crisis or was instead scrupulously reacting to a superficial and hence meaningless show of piety, around this time, in a letter to her friend Abiah Root, Dickinson's tone elevates to the point of dark rebellion:

> Where do you think I've strayed, and from what new errand returned? I have come from "*to* and *fro*, and walking up and down" the same place that Satan hailed from, when God asked him where he'd been, but not to illustrate further I tell you I have been dreaming, dreaming a *golden* dream, with eyes all the while wide open.[41]

With stunning audacity, Dickinson not only refuses to submit to religious coercion, but does so by citing Scripture: "And the LORD said to Satan, Whence comest thou? Then Satan answered the LORD, and said, From going to and fro in the earth, and from walking up and down in it" (Job 1:7 [KJV]). Moreover, hardly admitting that her rejection is a mark of spiritual blindness, she emphasizes the clarity of her vision—"with eyes all the while wide open." It is the same boldness that motivates her interpretation of Dr. Williams's ban on reading—

39. Cited in Jay Leyda, *The Years and Hours of Emily Dickinson* (New Haven: Yale University Press, 1960), 136.

40. For an extensive account, see Cynthia Griffin Wolff, *Emily Dickinson* (Reading, Mass.: Addison-Wesley, 1988), 99–104.

41. Dickinson to Abiah Root, May 17, 1850 (no. 36) in Dickinson, *Letters*, 1: 99.

"He might as well have said, 'Eyes be blind', 'heart be still'"—which, if heard as an allusion to Isaiah's harsh mission, would constitute a scriptural quotation to affirm an unorthodox matter: blindness would rob her of salvation, not the salvation of Christian faith, but rather the salvation of books, presumably the cruelest punishment she could imagine.

This interpretive gesture is not only heterodox but also unconventional. In brief, Dickinson's plight stems from a relationship with books—a technology of mediation—that resolutely departs from any desire for nonmediation. An earlier generation of Romantics might have regarded blindness either as a threat that would divorce them from the glories of nature, leaving them incapable of observing and adoring the inexhaustible richness of divine Creation, or as a gift of true inner vision, no longer distracted by quotidian falsehood and deception. Both the threat and the promise of blindness speak to the hindrances of bookish mediation, insofar as books written by mankind commonly constituted an obstacle to God's great Book of Nature. To observe and drink in life meant to look away from the mediation of the page. Instead, Dickinson's despair derives from the possibility of losing mediation itself. To be sure, at one point during her treatment, she complains to her sister Lavinia that she is unable to enjoy the season—"the calls at the Doctor's are painful, and dear Vinnie, I have not looked at the Spring."[42] Yet Dickinson may have singled out this conventional hardship in order to communicate a pain that would otherwise not be appreciated, namely the "woe" of being denied the pleasures of reading, "the only [woe] that ever made [her] tremble." Unlike Rousseau, who cheerfully kept his books locked away as he strolled through the bowers of the Île de St-Pierre, or, in a more ironic vein, Goethe's Werther who, fleeing society, implored his friend Wilhelm not to send him any volumes from his library (save for his edition of Homer), Dickinson trembles at the thought of being denied her reading material. Rather than longing for an immediate encounter with the world, she shudders at the thought of negating mediation, of losing sight of the way. For her, a life consigned to immediacy would be a life wasted in the wilderness.

In the end, Dickinson was released from her cold prison and allowed to reopen her bibliophile passion. The note to Lyman continues:

> Well do I remember the music of the welcome home. It was at his office. He whistled up the foxhounds. He clapped and said 'Sesame'. How my blood

42. Emily Dickinson to Lavinia Dickinson, May 1864 (no. 289) in Dickinson, *Letters*, 1: 430.

> bounded! Shakespear was the first; Antony & Cleopatra where Enobarbus laments the amorous lapse of his master. Here is the ring of it.
>
> > "heart that in the scuffles of
> > great fights hath burst the
> > bucke on his breast"
>
> then I thought why ~~touch~~ clasp any hand but this. Give me ever to drink of this wine. Going home I flew to the shelves and devoured the luscious passages. I thought I should tear the leaves out as I turned them. Then I settled down to a willingness for all the rest to go but William Shakespear. Why need we Joseph read anything else but him[43]

The terrifying fermata has yielded to a new and exciting overture of welcomed music. Having once commanded his patient's will to lie "down" for the sake of a cure, the master physician now summons up the "foxhounds," signaling them to resume the hunt. With instinctual, intensely corporeal language, she describes how she at once picked up on the scent and targeted Shakespeare, the only "wine" that would satisfy her bloodthirsty desire, flying to the shelves like a hawk and devouring the delectable flesh. Her bounding bloodlust nearly rips the binding to shreds. In her impulsive recounting—if we can trust Lyman's fidelity to Dickinson's script—the "buckle" burst by Antony's passion is rendered as "bucke," which further recalls, in a rather brilliant *lapsus*, the image of Actaeon, transformed into a stag and torn apart by his hounds.

The cited words, replete with internal rhyme and alliteration, are "luscious"—pleasing, gratifying, delicious—ostensibly because they are already loved, already known. A hunting dog must know its prey. That is, Dickinson is not reading simply for content, for discovering new information or learning new plots, but rather re-reading for the ringing, resonant pleasure held between the covers. The passages continue to nourish her, because they are never entirely digested, processed, and incorporated. The books are decidedly not dispensable, because the hunger is never sated. And the verbal flesh instantly revivifies, feeding her poetic drive to produce the anapestic pulse of "Give me ever to drink of this wine"—a prancing line that vividly evokes the chase. It was perhaps Dickinson's especially sharp ear that caused her to attribute the opening lines of Shakespeare's play falsely to Enobarbus rather than Philo, insofar as it

43. Sewall, *The Lyman Letters*, 76.

more readily creates the sonically rich, anapestic phrase "Enobarbus laments the amorous lapse."[44] The idea of touch is too weak for representing this kind of lapse, which is better served, given the phonic resemblance, by the emended "clasp." Appreciation for poetic effects may allow for some indifference to the plot's details, but it does not altogether neglect the intent of the text. As many scholars have noted, Dickinson persistently identified with Antony and his mad passion for the Egyptian queen.[45]

Remaining with the text presented here, one immediately observes how her impetuous reading of Shakespeare is linked to the Roman general's erotic intoxication. The fervor with which she tears open the book's bindings is analogous to the "heart [. . .] that burst the buckle" on Antony's breast. It is the kind of imagined coincidence that Georges Poulet describes in his essay on "Criticism and the Experience of Interiority," which also employs tropes of opening.

> Take a book, and you will find it offering, opening itself. It is this openness of the book which I find so moving. A book is not shut in by its contours, is not walled-up as in a fortress. It asks nothing better than to exist outside itself, or to let you exist in it. In short, the extraordinary fact in the case of a book is the falling away of the barriers between you and it. You are inside it; it is inside you; there is no longer either outside or inside.[46]

Through the medium of language, the consciousness of the reader merges spiritually with the consciousness represented in the text. A closed circuit is achieved, by which external reality melts away. For Poulet as well, this act of reading transmutes into a scene of predation.

> As soon as I replace my direct perception of reality by the words of a book, I deliver myself, bound hand and foot, to the omnipotence of fiction. I say fare-

44. Cf. Marianne Noble, "The Sublimity of *Hamlet* in Emily Dickinson's Poem, 'He Fumbles at Your Soul,'" in *Shakespeare and the Culture of Romanticism*, Joseph Ortiz, ed. (Surrey: Ashgate, 2013), 121–38; here 122.

45. See Judith Farr, *The Passion of Emily Dickinson* (Cambridge: Harvard University Press, 1998), 170–76; and Páraic Finnerty, *Emily Dickinson's Shakespeare* (Amherst: University of Massachusetts Press, 2006), 140–60.

46. Georges Poulet, "Criticism and the Experience of Interiority," in *The Structuralist Controversy: The Languages of Criticism & the Sciences of Man*, Richard Macksey and Eugenio Donato, eds. [1970] (Baltimore: Johns Hopkins University Press, 2007), 56–72; here 57.

> well to what is, in order to feign belief in what is not. I surround myself with fictitious beings; I become the prey of language.[47]

The same holds for the experience described by Dickinson: descending upon the text like a famished raptor, she becomes enraptured. Again, the book's content functions as a container, a "frigate" that carries the devouring reader off to "lands away." With such opportunities for rapture occasioned by her Shakespeare, the wide-eyed poet is willing to cry "avaunt" to all other tomes. The way is the life.

47. Poulet, "Criticism and the Experience of Interiority," 58.

4

Implications of Citation

Specifically as a repetition of language, citation entails an act of speaking that is, at the same time, an act of listening, or an act of writing that also involves an act of reading. Despite these conjoined efforts, citational practice tends to privilege one aspect over the other, which, in turn, signals how language itself is believed to operate. The speaker who assumes the role of an assured agent of language generally implements citation as an instrument for communicating a thought, while the one who listens to language tends to regard the cited words themselves as the generative source of thought and concepts. Insofar as a citation is a repetition, one could specify the former case as a *repetitio sententiarum* (a repetition of thoughts), which presumes language to be *a posteriori*, and the latter as a *repetitio verborum* (a repetition of words), which instead takes language to be *a priori*. In the first case, the one who cites appeals to another's words in order to clothe a thought already formulated, while in the second case, the one who cites receives another's words in which thought is believed to be incarnate.

This distinction is particularly acute in the alternative approaches that obtain when comparing the citational practices of that oddest couple of the late eighteenth century, Immanuel Kant and Johann Georg Hamann. In the starkest terms, whereas Kant reaches for language in order to transmit his thinking, Hamann abides with language as the determinant origin of the content of thought. The implications of these opposing presuppositions, however, point well beyond considerations of linguistic functions and instead strike at the very core of what counts as the Enlightenment, touching on and complicating fundamental questions of metaphysics, theology, and, ultimately, human nature.

Originally published in the December 1784 issue of the *Berlinische Monatsschrift*, the principal organ for the free-thinking of the Berlin Enlightenment, Kant's famous *Response to the Question: What Is Enlightenment?* (*Beantwortung der Frage: Was ist Aufklärung?*) not only provides one of the most important and memorable definitions of the European movement, but also, already in its opening lines, broaches crucial issues regarding the form and function of citations in philosophical discourse.

> Enlightenment is man's exit from his self-incurred immaturity [*aus seiner selbstverschuldeten Unmündigkeit*]. Immaturity is the incapacity [*Unvermögen*] to use one's own understanding without the guidance of another [*ohne Leitung eines anderen zu bedienen*]. This immaturity is self-incurred if its cause is not lack of understanding, but lack of resolution and courage to use it without the guidance of another [*ohne Leitung eines anderen zu bedienen*]. *Sapere aude!* Have courage to use your own understanding! is therefore the motto [*Wahlspruch*] of the Enlightenment.[1]

Kant's decision to appropriate a tagline from Horace's *Epistles* (1.2) is, at the very least, intriguing. Despite the call to apply one's understanding "without the guidance of another"—a qualification that Kant apparently feels compelled

1. Immanuel Kant, *Beantwortung der Frage: Was ist Aufklärung?* [1784] in, *Gesammelte Schriften*, 8: 33–42, here 33. "Aufklärung ist der Ausgang des Menschen aus seiner selbstverschuldeten Unmündigkeit. Unmündigkeit ist das Unvermögen, sich seines Verstandes ohne Leitung eines anderen zu bedienen. Selbstverschuldet ist diese Unmündigkeit, wenn die Ursache derselben nicht am Mangel des Verstandes, sondern der Entschließung und des Muthes liegt, sich seiner ohne Leitung eines anderen zu bedienen. *Sapere aude!* Habe Muth, dich deines eigenen Verstandes zu bedienen! ist also der Wahlspruch der Aufklärung." ["An Answer to the Question: What Is Enlightenment?" in Kant, *Political Writings*, H. Reiss, ed., H. B. Nisbet, trans. (Cambridge: Cambridge University Press, 1991), 54–60, here 54.]

to repeat verbatim—he allows philosophy to be guided by a classical citation: *sapere aude!* The resolution to be intellectually self-sufficient, to abandon one's "self-incurred immaturity" (*selbstverschuldete Unmündigkeit*), is expressed by borrowing a phrase from an ancient poet. The exhortation to think for oneself is prescribed by an external source. The courageous independence of one's intellect is shown to be strikingly dependent. The plea for autonomy—for release from tutelage, for authenticity—curiously relies, still, on prior authority. Is it Kant's own anticipated feelings of "guilt" (*Schuld*) that causes him to cite himself, to repeat the phrase *without the guidance of another*? Can this act of autocitation redeem him from the charge of reliance or dependency, a charge based on his turn to Horace's *sapere aude*?

Apparently without blinking, Kant emerges from the condition of immaturity (*Unmündigkeit*)—he graduates from the position of an underage child who has no voice or mouth (*Mund*)—by becoming a mouthpiece of poetic tradition or even by allowing tradition to speak *for him*, here in a text that explicitly challenges all the institutions and authorities that act as *Vormünder*, as *guardians* or *advocates* who dare to speak in the people's stead.

> That by far the greatest part of mankind (including the entire fair sex) should consider the step toward maturity [*Mündigkeit*] not only as difficult but also as highly dangerous: those guardians [*Vormünder*] already take care of it, they who have kindly taken upon themselves the task of supervision.[2]

As a legal term, *Unmündigkeit* denotes the incapacity for self-representation exemplified by the case of children, yet is also applicable to the insane, the senile, and—as Kant points out—women. Powerful institutions infantalize the populace by portraying independent thinking as something highly precarious and frightening. They strive to convince society that entrance into self-reliance should be restricted to those accompanied by a legal guardian. In Kant's rating system, too, Enlightenment is decidedly for mature audiences only. However, what distinguishes the philosopher's project is the desire to encourage every citizen to grow up—to examine, judge, and speak *for oneself*. Thus, Kant rails

2. Kant, *Was ist Aufklärung?*. "Daß der bei weitem größte Teil der Menschen (darunter das ganze schöne Geschlecht) den Schritt zur Mündigkeit, außer dem daß er beschwerlich ist, auch für sehr gefährlich halte: dafür sorgen schon jene Vormünder, die die Oberaufsicht über sie gütigst auf sich genommen haben." *Gesammelte Schriften*, 8: 54.

against the "laziness and cowardice" that causes the majority to "remain immature [*unmündig*]," long after they have naturally come of age. Nonetheless, as already indicated, Kant does not hesitate to import language from other sources. He not only cites natural law or *naturaliter maiorennes,* but also, more emphatically, a poet. He lets Horace be his spokesman, even if only in passing. With one hand, he decries the "rules and formulas," that mechanically operate as "the foot-cuffs of perpetual immaturity," while, with the other hand, he cites a poetic formula, implicitly footnoted, making it moreover into the slogan of autonomy, into the very motto or *Wahlspruch* of the Enlightenment, seemingly unaware of any contradiction or irony.[3]

All the same, it really should come as no surprise that Kant expresses even the notion of intellectual independence by means of a Latin quotation. Since antiquity, thinkers have been drawn to the pithy utterance, the concise maxim, the well-coined phrase. Modern writers, from the Renaissance of Machiavelli and Montaigne straight through to Kant's eighteenth century and beyond, inherited the ancients' inclination to harvest key insights, precepts, and viewpoints from the poetic tradition, not out of "laziness" or "cowardice," but rather in order to communicate their own positions with concision and cogency. For Quintilian there is an obvious, authoritative value in the "maxims of poets" (*sententiae poetarum*):

> For not only are speeches full of maxims from the poets, but also the books of philosophers, who, though they believe everything to be inferior to their own precepts and writings, have not disdained to draw on [*repetere*] the authority from great numbers of verses.[4]

Poetic turns of phrase lend authority to philosophical disquisitions. Even those thinkers most skeptical of public opinion were captivated by the forcefulness of the apothegm, the proverb, and the gnomic utterance, appreciating their potential contribution to thoughtful reflection. In Plato's *Protagoras,* for instance, Socrates expresses admiration for the Spartans' capacity to philosophize:[5]

3. Kant, *Was ist Aufklärung?, Gesammelte Schriften,* 8: 33–34.

4. Quintilian, *Institutio oratoria.* "nam sententiis quidem poetarum non orationes modo sunt refertae sed libri etiam philosophorum, qui quanquam inferiora omnia praeceptis suis ac litteris credunt, repetere tamen auctoritatem a plurimis versibus non fastidierunt" (5.11.39).

5. On the tension between intellectual autonomy and heteronomy in the *Protagoras,* see Charles L. Griswold, "Relying on Your Own Voice: An Unsettled Rivalry of Moral Ideas in

> For if anyone is willing to associate with the most ordinary Lacedaemonian, he will find him for the most part to appear ordinary in his speech; but then by chance, at some point in the conversation, all at once, like a skillful lancer, he hurls forth a valuable remark, brief and condensed, so that his interlocutor appears no better than a child.[6]

Socrates goes on to attribute to Spartan ingenuity the seminal maxims of "know thyself" and "nothing in excess," which were inscribed on the Temple to Apollo at Delphi, in order to demonstrate how the first philosophers exhibited this "laconic brevity" (βραχυλογία Λακωνική, 343b). Kant's nomination of *sapere aude* as the very motto of the Enlightenment belongs precisely to this venerable tradition of appropriating the efficacy of a succinct dictum. Indeed, how better to emerge from childish *Unmündigkeit* than by reducing one's formidable *Vormünder* to the level of helpless children!

Of course, Socrates' irony in this passage should not be overlooked. Elsewhere, for example in the *Gorgias*, he militates against the kind of sophistry that cleverly piles on terse poetic citations in the course of a refutation—a practice that he dismisses as a dubious method for discovering the truth (*Gorgias*, 471e–472a). Nonetheless, as in the *Ion*, Socrates cannot deny the sheer force of poetic recitation, which derives its magnetic power from the divine Muses (*Ion*, 536a). Moreover, one need only recall the Delphic dictum, "Know thyself" and the central, motivating role it played in Socrates' philosophical mission.

In drawing from the Horatian source, Kant apparently wants to enlist this kind of power. His usage does not necessarily imply dependence as much as it recalls a notion of authorship that regards the *auctor* not only as the creator or originator of discourse but also as the one who preserves prior *auctoritas*, granting it continued existence or even a kind of permanence by vouching for its veracity or present relevance. By evoking the Latin imperative—*sapere aude!*—

Plato's *Protagoras*," *Review of Metaphysics* 53: 2 (1999): 283–307. For an examination of the Spartans' reputed brevity in speech, see Ephraim David, "Sparta's *Kosmos* of Silence," in *Sparta: New Perspectives*, in Stephen Hodkinson and Anton Powell, eds. (London: Duckworth, 1999), 117–46; and Eric David Francis, "Brachylogia Laconica," *Bulletin of the Institute of Classical Studies* 38: 1 (1991–93), 198–212.

6. Plato, Protagoras. "εἰ γὰρ ἐθέλει τις Λακεδαιμονίων τῷ φαυλοτάτῳ συγγενέσθαι, τὰ μὲν πολλὰ ἐν τοῖς λόγοις εὑρήσει αὐτὸν φαῦλόν τινα φαινόμενον, ἔπειτα ὅπου ἂν τύχῃ τῶν λεγομένων, ἐνέβαλεν ῥῆμα ἄξιον λόγου βραχὺ καὶ συνεστραμμένον ὥσπερ δεινὸς ἀκοντιστής, ὥστε φαίνεσθαι τὸν προσδιαλεγόμενον παιδὸς μηδὲν βελτίω" (342 d–e).

Kant can hardly be charged with dogmatism. On the contrary, he strives to reveal a fundamental, universal trait of human intellectual courage, reminding his readers of what Horace already knew, hoping to reawaken a spirit of independent inquiry that is otherwise silenced by the Church, the State, and other oppressive institutions. Against these intimidating sovereigns, Kant summons Horace to marshal a counterforce, to inspire intellectual self-sufficiency and autonomy. The philosopher, therefore, does not succumb to power as much as he draws it to his side; and this alignment of power entails reciprocal effects: in the course of legitimizing his own discourse by means of citation, Kant also establishes Horace's legitimacy for the Enlightenment. That is, we are dealing with the transference and maintenance of power, one that confirms the authority cited, while empowering the author who cites.[7]

This conjoined power enhances philosophical presentation and has consistently contributed to its clout and validity. As Aristotle notes in his *Metaphysics,* quotation is one of three viable methods for granting a discourse credibility and currency: "Some people do not accept statements unless you express them mathematically; others, unless by way of examples; while others deem that one call in a poet as a witness (*martyra*)."[8] Along with mathematical proofs and paradigmatic illustrations, poetic quotations find their place in ancient philosophical discussions precisely as items that recipients "deem valuable" (ἀξιοῦσιν), like the "valuable remark" (ῥῆμα ἄξιον) that Socrates found so impressive among the Spartans.[9] Should a philosopher strive to ascertain and impart knowledge, he would be expected to deal directly with the anterior body of *sophia* displayed by the poets. Accordingly, for an audience steeped in poetic culture, it is worthwhile to summon a poet's voice, either for points of verification or contestation.

Aristotle's verb for invoking, introducing, or calling in—*epagesthai* (ἐπάγεσθαι)—a term almost perfectly replicated in the modern German *anführen,* engages the metaphor of calling someone in as a witness before a judg-

7. Peter Pütz, "Autorität durch Wiederholung: Von der Herrschaft des Zitats." *Autorität der/in Sprache: Literatur, Neue Medien,* Jürgen Fohrmann, ed. (Bielefeld: Aisthesis, 1999), 694–704, here 695.

8. Aristotle, *Metaphysica,* Werner Jaeger, ed. (Oxford: Clarendon Press, 1957). "οἱ μὲν οὖν ἐὰν μὴ μαθηματικῶς λέγῃ τις οὐκ ἀποδέχονται τῶν λεγόντων, οἱ δ᾽ ἂν μὴ παραδειγματικῶς, οἱ δὲ μάρτυρα ἀξιοῦσιν ἐπάγεσθαι ποιητήν" (995a7–8).

9. On the value and function of poetic quotations in ancient philosophy, see Stephen Halliwell, "The Subjection of Muthos to Logos: Plato's Citation of the Poets," *Classical Quarterly* 50: 1 (2000), 94–112.

ing party, of summoning a person in court to provide testimony. The juridical image is further operative in the Latin *citare*, which is composed from the perfect passive participle of *ciere* (*to cause to move, stir, drive, or shake*) and cognate with the Greek *kinein* (κινεῖν, *to put in motion*). A passage cited is one that has been called to appear, made to move from one context to another, perhaps even shaken loose from its initial setting. This kinetic energy is not always amenable to control—the citation as attestant or testifier always stands in a position to become a hostile witness. This possibility is grounded in the fact that the testimony adduced by citation can never be entirely absorbed by the new incorporating text. In addition to the synchronic axis (how the citation relates to the present discourse), there is also the diachronic axis (how the citing text relates back to the cited discourse); and the energy that is ignited by the friction between the synchronic and the diachronic, between repetition and difference, derivation and innovation, also stands to disrupt the adoptive context.[10]

In Kant's essay, the potential disruption is signaled by the verbal intrusion of the citation, which is both lexically and typographically marked. In hitting upon the italicized phrase *sapere aude*, the person who reads Kant's piece encounters an opening that leads away from the text at hand and toward prior sources. Needless to say, the first step onto this intertextual path would be to consult, with or without Kant's sanction, the initial usage, namely the second poem from Horace's first book of *Epistles*. Here, the poet attempts to persuade Lollius Maximus, a young student of rhetoric, to devote himself to the Homeric poems as a repository of moral philosophical precepts. Rather than waste one's youth on the pursuit of wealth and pleasure, like Penelope's suitors, one should devote serious time to studying the principles of virtue and wisdom by way of exemplary poetry, before it is too late:

> dimidium facti qui coepit habet: sapere aude:
>
> incipe. qui recte vivendi prorogat horam,
> rusticus exspectat dum defluat amnis: at ille
> labitur et labetur in omne volubilis aevum.
>
> *Epist.* 1.2.40–4[11]

10. Cf. Stefan Morawski, "The Basic Function of Quotation," in *Sign, Language, Culture*, C. H. van Schooneveld, ed. (The Hague: Mouton, 1970), 690–705, here 692.

11. Horace, *Opera*, H. W. Garrod, ed. (Oxford: Oxford University Press, 1901), 208.

> He who begins has half the deed done: dare to be wise:
> begin! He who postpones the hour of living rightly,
> is like the farmer who waits for the river to run off; but the river
> flows past and will flow, rolling along for all time.

Horace's eminently quotable bid (*sapere aude*) itself follows on the heels of proverbial wisdom: *dimidium facti qui coepit habet*, which faithfully translates the Greek adage, Ἀρχὴ δέ τοι ἥμισυ παντός, an utterance that would continue its career in most European languages: for instance, in the French (*Il est bien avancé, qui a bien commencé*), the German (*Frisch gewagt ist halb gewonnen*), or the English (*Once begun is half done*). In Horace's epistle, it is this gnomic keenness that characterizes the poet's advice as especially paternal and direct.

Returning to Kant's usage, what the initial poetic context reveals is that *sapere aude* should be understood in a moral and not a cognitive sense. In Horace's poem, the command refers to the careful study of epic poetry, and not, as Kant implies, a resolute rejection of dogmatic guidance. Kant's exhortation, calling for the intellectual emancipation from the "guidance of another," contrasts with Horace's original recommendation, which promotes Homer as a moral advisor of virtue. It is noteworthy that Horace recommends the reading of poetry and not philosophy for moral instruction. Although both Horace and Kant allude to hesitation and childishness, the philosopher's admonition—"dare to be wise": "dare to know," "dare to have the courage to use your own understanding"—is addressed to someone who lacks scientific curiosity, while the poet's encouragement, "dare to study true wisdom," is aimed at the hedonistic procrastinator, who, like a foolish rustic, refuses to cross the river until the waters run dry (*rusticus exspectat dum defluat amnis*).

In summoning the phrase *sapere aude*, Kant may have been motivated by Pierre Gassendi, who, a century earlier, had already refitted Horace's admonition to express a modern appeal for free inquiry. Gassendi, who imprinted all his books with the Horatian line, enlisted the phrase to argue explicitly *against* virtue, which the scientist regarded as conformity to a norm. For Gassendi, himself a precursor of the Enlightenment, *sapere aude* should inspire the boldness required for the fearless application of critical reason.[12] The same intention is discernible in an earlier text that Kant published a year before the *Aufklärung* essay,

12. For an overview of modern adoptions of the Horatian motto, see Franco Venturi, "Sapere aude!" *Revista storica italiana* 71 (1959), 119–28.

namely his *Prolegomena zu einer jeden künftigen Metaphysik* (*Prolegomena to Any Future Metaphysics* [1783]), which also includes a reference to Horace's epistle. In the introductory pages, Kant addresses philosophers who have hitherto been reluctant to pose the simple question, "whether such a thing as metaphysics is at all possible?"[13] According to Kant, the reason philosophers have hesitated to ask this fundamental question is that, by inquiring into the possibility of a science, one implicitly doubts its actuality. For Kant, this sheepishness is yet another instance of the cowardice that obstructs the establishment and elaboration of sound metaphysics. "The reader who thinks for himself" (*der selbstdenkende Leser*) must not cower in apprehension, for the demand to form the foundations of any future metaphysics will not disappear merely by neglecting to cross the treacherous waters of doubt. To illustrate, Kant appends a footnote that simply cites the simile from Horace's epistle: *rusticus exspectat* ("the farmer waits").[14]

In essence, Kant uses Horace's words to express his own ideas. He employs Horace's utterance without full regard for the initial act of utterance—the *énonciation* is subordinated to or dissolves into the *énoncé*. This verbal appropriation clearly correlates to the free use of reason: the capacity to repurpose or even abuse an inherited quotation corresponds to the rational autonomy that Kant champions throughout his piece. As a consequence, Kant reduces the intrusion of the quoted text to a minimum. A reader may or may not stammer at the sudden appearance of a poetic citation in Kant's philosophical exposition; the point is that this reader is expected to move past the interruption without further ado, to continue reading Kant's essay rather than pause and reach for an edition of Horace's *Epistles*. To be sure, Kant repeats Horace's language, but it is specifically a repetition of an idea, a *repetitio sententiae*, an idea, moreover, that Kant himself aims to steer with rational, sovereign control. To this end, the signified—that which is presented as ideational content—must take precedence over the initial form that voiced the signifiers; the voice (*vox*) and its words (*verba*) must yield to the thought expressed in words or the *sententia*.[15] Kant is more concerned with communicating a thought than with transmitting the discourse that mediates the thought. Although necessary for transmission, Kant's exposition relies

13. Kant, *Prolegomena zu einer jeden künftigen Metaphysik* [1783]. "[. . .] ob auch so etwas als Metaphysik überall nur möglich sei?" *Gesammelte Schriften*, 4: 255.

14. Kant, *Prolegomena*, *Gesammelte Schriften*, 4: 257.

15. For further discussion, see Antoine Compagnon, *La seconde main, ou le travail de la citation* (Paris: Seuil, 1979), 149.

on the principle of the vanishing medium: once the idea is received, the discourse itself can be disposed. A writer who is simply content to repeat words, to insert into his or her text a *repetitio verborum*, is, at least in Kant's assessment, as foolish as an underage child or a farmer waiting for the river to drain out.

It is precisely this kind of foolishness or childishness that we discover in the work of Kant's neighbor in Königsberg, his rather difficult friend, Johann Georg Hamann. Hamann's writings, which are often regarded as documents of a counter-Enlightenment, are indeed notoriously obscure, dense, and abstruse, at once pious and humorous, ironic and bawdy, perplexingly digressive and saturated with countless allusions and citations from the Bible, Greco-Roman antiquity, and European letters. As Goethe famously quipped, when reading Hamann, "one must completely rule out what one normally means by understanding."[16] The difficulty of Hamann's work may be summarized as a steadfast refusal to follow the principle of the vanishing medium. For Hamann, discourse, which is bound to a unique historical and cultural context, is never simply dispensable. The words of the discourse—that is, the concrete *verba*—possess value in themselves. Hamann's writings are replete with citations because citations are examples of language that are not exhausted in their original enunciation. They persist beyond their initial purpose, having broken free of the primary communication, while still retaining the qualities of their provenance. This liberation from and continuation of the first communicative context is the earmark of poetic discourse, which is thereby distinguished from the ordinary speech that treats language as a perishable commodity.[17] As we shall see, Hamann's approach reveals a disavowal on Kant's part: Kant cites Horace to lend a certain value to his own discourse, yet he does so by enforcing the dissolution of the poetic medium—a medium that is, in fact, the very source of the value he wishes to exploit. In striving to make his own new thought visible, Kant must render the old initial discursive situation invisible. The fate of Lollius's moral education from Horace's epistle should have no bearing on

16. Johann Wolfgang von Goethe, *Aus meinem Leben: Dichtung und Wahrheit. Werke*, Erich Trunz, ed., vol. 9 (Munich: Deutscher Taschenbuch Verlag, 1981): "muß man durchaus auf das Verzicht tun, was man gewöhnlich Verstehen nennt" (515). For an excellent overview of Hamann's early reception, see Oswald Bayer, ed., *Johann Georg Hamann: Der hellste Kopf seiner Zeit* (Tübingen: Attempo, 1998).

17. Cf. Gian Biagio Conte, *The Rhetoric of Imitation: Genre and Poetic Memory in Vergil and Other Latin Poets*, C. Segal, ed. (Ithaca: Cornell University Press, 1986), 41. I borrow the phrase "perishable commodity" from Conte.

Kant's project of enlightenment. In contrast, Hamann insists on savoring the discourse itself, indulging in its depth and opacity. His starting point is the starting point for every devout Christian: *In principio erat Verbum*. Rather than follow the principle of the vanishing medium, Hamann attends to the principal medium, the human *verba*, which he takes to be analogous to the redemptive *Verbum*.

The contrast between Kant's and Hamann's practices of citation is especially pronounced in their exchange from 1759, regarding Kant's proposal to collaborate on a physics primer for children—a project that Kant had hoped would lure his friend back to the side of enlightened free thought and thus temper the religious fanaticism that Hamann had been exhibiting since his recent major conversion in London.[18] At first, Kant plotted with Hamann's employer, Johann Christoph Berens, who was equally troubled by their friend's extreme religiosity, and suggested that Hamann translate portions of d'Alembert and Diderot's *Encyclopédie*—a proposal that Hamann flatly dismissed. Kant subsequently replied with the children's physics project. This time, Hamann's interest was sparked.

In his idiosyncratic fashion, Hamann entertains the plan, while assuming an altogether playful, whimsical tone. In his first letter in response to Kant, before inscribing any greeting, Hamann opens with an epigraph from Horace's *Odes*:

> ——ah! miser,
> Quanta laboras in Charybdi
> Digne puer meliore flamma!
> *Carm.* 1.27.18–20[19]

> ——ah! wretched one,
> how much you labor in Charybdis
> a boy worthy of a better flame!

18. On the proposed project to collaborate on the physics book for children, see Reiner Wild, "Natur und Offenbarung: Hamanns und Kants gemeinsamer Plan zu einer Physik für Kinder," *Geist und Zeichen: Festschrift für Arthur Henkel zu seinem sechzigsten Geburtstag*, Herbert Anton, Bernhard Gajek, and Peter Pfaff, eds. (Heidelberg: Winter, 1977), 452–68; Hans Graubner, "Physikotheologie und Kinderphysik: Kants und Hamanns Plan zu einer Physik für Kinder in der physikotheologischen Tradition des 18. Jahrhunderts," *Johann Georg Hamann und die Krise der Aufklärung, Acta des fünften internationalen Hamann-Kolloquiums*, Bernhard Gajek and Albert Meier, eds. (New York: Lang, 1990), 117–45; and John R. Betz, *After Enlightenment: The Post-Secular Vision of J. G. Hamann* (Oxford: Wiley-Blackwell, 2009), 84–87.

19. Cited from Johann Georg Hamann, *Zugabe zweener Liebesbriefe* [1763], in *Sämtliche Werke*, 6 vols., Josef Nadler, ed. (Vienna: Herder, 1949–57), 2: 369.

Hamann, too, shakes some lines out of their initial context to speak to new circumstances. Whereas Horace's ode teases a young man wounded by a disastrous love affair, Hamann applies the verses to lament the vain labors of his friend, who, he suggests, is being drawn down into the horrifying whirlpool of philosophical rationalism.[20] The epigraph implies that Kant is the *miser puer*, the wretched boy who fancies himself to be mature enough to brave the monstrous maelstrom. Horace interestingly evades mentioning Charybdis's twinned threat, Scylla, and instead speaks of a "better flame." What, then, would represent this improved love affair for Hamann? Moreover, would this erotic investment be without danger or would it be but another monster posing as a blessing? Given Hamann's insistence on Christian conversion, the alternative to the frightening whirlpool of pure reason might well be understood as religious faith, as an open engagement with God, which is not, of course, achieved without sacrifice and therefore risk.

In addition to staging a structured dilemma, and emphatically unlike Kant's own use of citation, which passes over the initial discursive situation, Hamann allows Horace's erotic setting to impinge upon and color his message. Tellingly, when Hamann publishes his first two replies to Kant, he titles them specifically as *Zugabe zweener Liebesbriefe* ("Two extra love-letters" [1763]). That is to say, in contrast to Kant's citational practice, Hamann *invites* the reader to consult Horace's erotically driven poem.[21] He does not neglect the original *énonciation* in favor of a more amenable *énoncé*, but rather allows it to intrude, to cause an interruption, to transform his consideration of a scholarly proposal into a personal love letter. Rather than gloss over the consequences of his citation's provenance, Hamann gives free rein to the ramifications of performing a *repetitio verborum*. It takes a boy to know one.

In starting the letter proper, Hamann maintains the amorous context while brusquely shifting metaphors, not without sarcasm: "The benefactors of your merits would shrug their shoulders in pity, if they knew that you went about pregnant with a children's physics book."[22] The guiding image, which relates

20. Cf. Betz, *After Enlightenment*, 84–85.

21. On Hamann's engagement with sexuality in relation to his general theories of language and knowledge, see Gwen Griffith-Dickson, "God, I, and Thou: Hamann and the Personalist Tradition," in *Hamann and the Tradition*, Lisa Marie Anderson, ed. (Evanston: Northwestern University Press, 2012), 55–66.

22. Hamann, *Zugabe zweener Liebesbriefe*. "Die Gönner Ihrer Verdienste würden vor Mitleiden die Achseln zucken, wenn sie wüßten, daß Sie mit einer Kinderphysick schwanger giengen" (2: 369).

authorship to childbearing, in addition to transfiguring the addressed philosopher from a miserable adolescent to an expectant mother, also alludes to that key philosophical tradition instigated in Plato's *Symposium*, where Diotima, in her famous account of Eros, distinguishes the two alternate drives for achieving immortality. In Diotima's view, of course, "all men are pregnant": some seek to reproduce corporeally, while others strive to engender virtue and prudence by means of educating the youth (*paideuein* [παιδεύειν], 209c). By portraying Kant as someone pregnant with an educational treatise, Hamann either preserves Diotima's distinction between somatic and soulful reproduction or cleverly allows both interpretations to converge.

The letter eventually reveals Hamann's main point. He points to the difficulty of writing for children, which he claims would require transforming oneself into a child, for only a childish author could communicate in a language understandable by children. Hamann then asks if Kant is truly up to this bold task.

> To manage to receive praise from the mouth of children and infants!—To take part in this ambition and taste is no *ordinary* business, which one must begin not by *stealing colored plumes*, but rather by a voluntary relinquishing of all superiority in age and wisdom and renouncing all vanity. A philosophical book for children, therefore, would necessarily appear as simplistic, foolish, and tasteless as a *divine* book written for mankind. Now test yourself: Do you have enough heart to be the author of a simplistic, foolish, and tasteless theory of nature? Take heart, for then you are also a *philosopher for children*. Vale et sapere AUDE![23]

Unlike Kant's underage or *unmündige* cowards, Hamann's children and infants explicitly have a "mouth." Is Kant capable of receiving praise "from the mouth [*Mund*] of children"? Hamann compares the proposed physics book for chil-

23. Hamann, *Zugabe zweener Liebesbriefe*. "Sich ein Lob aus dem Munde der Kinder und Säuglinge zu bereiten!—an diesem Ehrgeiz und Geschmack Theil zu nehmen, ist kein *gemeines* Geschäfte, das man nicht mit dem *Raube bunter Federn*, sondern mit einer freywilligen Entäußerung aller Überlegenheit an Alter und Weisheit, und mit einer Verläugnung aller Eitelkeit darauf anfangen muß. Ein philosophisches Buch für Kinder würde daher so einfältig, thöricht und abgeschmackt aussehen müssen, als ein *Göttliches* Buch, das für Menschen geschrieben. Nun prüfen Sie sich, ob Sie so viel Herz haben, der Verfasser einer einfältigen, thörichten und abgeschmackten Naturlehre zu seyn? Haben Sie Herz, so sind Sie auch ein *Philosoph für Kinder*. Vale & sapere AVDE!" (2: 372).

dren to the Christian Gospel, the "*divine* book written for mankind." Thus, in considering Kant's proposal, which the philosopher had hoped would rekindle his friend's allegiance to the Enlightenment, Hamann stays true to his religious convictions, resorting to a reflection on the Christian mystery of divine kenosis and incarnation, of God's self-humiliation, his loving condescension to mankind. For Hamann, the philosopher who is willing to accommodate his scientific approach to the level of children is analogous to the God who voluntarily descended to a less dignified state, to the God who subjected himself to "a voluntary relinquishing of all superiority." The proposed project—a children's book of physics—would hardly be a testament to the accomplishments of rational investigation, but would rather appear as "simplistic, foolish and tasteless" as the Christian Gospel was initially received: To recall the words from Paul's First Epistle to the Corinthians, "for the Jews a stumbling block [σκάνδαλον] and for the Greeks foolishness [μωρίαν]" (1 Cor. 1:23). Does Kant have the "taste" to be so "tasteless," the *Geschmack* to be so *abgeschmackt*? Certainly, this would be "no *ordinary* business." Here, Hamann engages the primary meaning of *sapere* ("to taste") and asks if Kant would *dare to savor* what common sense finds insipid?

Throughout his writings, Hamann repeatedly had recourse to Paul's verse from First Corinthians. In fact, they are inscribed on his tombstone in Münster, in the Latin Vulgate translation:

> nos autem praedicamus Christum crucifixum Iudaeis quidem scandalum gentibus autem stultitiam, ipsis autem vocatis Iudaeis atque Graecis Christum Dei virtutem et Dei sapientiam, quia quod stultum est Dei sapientius est hominibus et quod infirmum est Dei fortius est hominibus (1 Cor. 1:23–25)
>
> But we preach Christ crucified, for the Jews a stumbling block and for the Greeks foolishness, but for those who have been called, both Jews and Greeks, Christ is the strength of God and the wisdom of God, because the foolishness of God is wiser than men and the weakness of God is stronger than men. (NKJV)

Hamann's closing imperative, lifted from Horace—*sapere aude*—thus provokes Kant to dare to savor the oxymoronic scandal of the Incarnation and thereby learn to acknowledge a foolishness that is wiser (*sapientius*), to dare to convert his mouth to a child's mouth, in brief, to sense in his own mouth a Eucharistic economy of salvation that reason may judge to be immature, while, in fact, it exhibits an even higher maturity.

Hamann responds to Kant's proposal with another proposal: Is the philosopher willing to humble himself in this manner or does he merely want to *take all the credit* (in German: "sich mit fremden Federn schmücken" ["to adorn oneself with borrowed plumes"])—like the jackdaw of the Aesopian fable who proudly flaunts himself, dressed with the plumage of other birds? Can rationalism ever be anything other than a vain philosophical practice that tries to pass off poetic quotations as one's own material, as if it had been written with one's own *quill* (*Feder*)? Hamann, too, borrows plumes and quills from other songbirds, but he does so in a decidedly different way, not as someone who proudly *speaks* as an assured agent of language, but rather as someone who speaks by *listening* to language.

Hamann frames his letter to Kant with two citations from Horace, who is thus brought in to bear witness to some truth. He begins with an epigraph from Horace's *Odes* and concludes with a line lifted from Horace's *Epistles*. Hardly a rustic sap "who waits for the river to run off," Kant is obliquely depicted as a lovesick boy who bravely plunges into the whirlpool of rational inquiry. Yet Hamann seems to suggest that, although the philosopher struggles with one monster, he neglects to deal with another, perhaps more worthy opponent. Falling between Scylla and Charybdis, Kant is "miserable," avoiding one danger, while exposing himself to a greater call. In this love letter, Hamann implies that Kant is "worthy of a better flame," a love that would shipwreck his reasoned course. Is the philosopher ready to swallow this difficult truth? For Hamann, the fact that Kant would propose to write a children's book is encouraging; it inspires his love. For "he who begins has half the deed done."

From this early exchange with Kant straight through to his *Metakritik über den Purismum der Vernunft* (*Metacritique on the Purism of Reason*) of 1784, Hamann insisted on the messy materiality of language, fully recognizing that every *repetitio sententiarum* is necessarily a *repetitio verborum*. This insistence is verified by Hegel's assessment: "Hamann's writings do not *have* a peculiar style as much as they *are* style through and through."[24] Hegel points here to the inseparability

24. Georg Wilhelm Friedrich Hegel, "Hamanns Schriften." *Werke*, 20 vols., Eva Moldenhauer and Karl Markus Michel, eds. (Frankfurt a. M.: Suhrkamp, 1971), 11: 275–352. "Hamanns Schriften *haben* nicht sowohl einen eigentümlichen Stil, als daß sie durch und durch Stil *sind*"

of form and content, word and idea, which not only motivates Hamann's use of citation beyond purposes of legitimization or ornamentation, but also corresponds to Hamann's primary article of faith. For Hamann, it is vitally important to regard the incarnation of the Logos, as understood in Christian doctrine, not as mere embodiment or possession but rather as a perfect coincidence of the divine and the human. Consistently throughout his writings, Hamann warns against any slippage into Nestorianism, which sharply distinguishes between the god and the man. He also militates against Docetism, which fails to grasp the human depth of the Incarnation. As Chalcedonian orthodoxy would establish, Christ did not merely *have* a human body, he *was* a human body, just as ideas do not simply *have* words to express them but rather *are* words, firmly grounded in historical and cultural situations, just as Hamann's writings do not simply *have* style but rather *are* style through and through.[25]

In Hamann's hands, citation rests on Trinitarian doctrine and thereby serves as a weapon against what he perceives as the antihistorical position of the Enlighteners.[26] In his *Sokratische Denkwürdigkeiten* (*Socratic Memorabilia*), addressed to Kant and Berens and published in 1759, Hamann confesses his faith in the final paragraph:

> If it is true that God Himself, as it reads in the *good confession* which he made before Pilate; if it is true, I say, that God Himself became man and came into the world, *that he might bear witness to the truth*: if so, then it would require no omniscience to foresee that he would not escape from the world as well as Socrates, but rather would die a more humiliating and more cruel death than the *parricide of that most Christian king*, Louis the *Well-Beloved*, who is a great-grandchild of Louis the *Great*.[27]

(281; emphasis in text). Hegel's review of Hamann first appeared in the *Jahrbücher für wissenschaftliche Kritik*, October and December 1828.

25. On the importance of Trinitarian doctrine for Hamann's theory of language, see Josef Nadler, *Johann Georg Hamann: Der Zeuge des Corpus Mysticum* (Salzburg: Müller, 1949), 252–53.

26. Hamann is quite explicit on this point in his *Hierophantische Briefe* (1774), *Sämtliche Werke* 3: 83–85.

27. Hamann, *Sokratische Denkwürdigkeiten* [1759], in Hamann, *Sämtliche Werke*. "Ist es wahr, daß GOtt Selbst, wie es in dem *guten Bekenntnisse* lautet, das er vor Pilatus ablegte; ist es wahr, sage ich, daß GOtt Selbst, *dazu* ein Mensch wurde und *dazu* in die Welt kam, *daß er die Wahrheit zeugen möchte*: so brauchte es keine Allwissenheit vorher zu sehen, daß er nicht so gut wie ein Sokrates von der Welt kommen, sondern eines schmählichern und grausameren Todes sterben würde, als der *Vatermörder des allerchristlichen Königes*, Ludwich des *Vielgeliebten*, der ein Urenkel

There is much that is notable about these concluding lines of Hamann's peroration, which rashly moves from Christ's interview with Pilate and the pronouncement of divine condescension to a pair of comparisons that shifts from the expected to the startling. Although it was not uncommon to correlate Socrates' martyrdom with Christ's Passion, the subsequent connection to the torture and cruel execution of the would-be assassin, Robert François Damiens, amounts to an associative tailspin. It is this manner of thinking that Kant would find particularly troubling, an adventurousness that borders on recklessness. Yet, for Hamann, linking the Crucifixion to a regicide's excruciating persecution forms exactly the kind of coincidence of opposites that Hamann found especially appealing, for it forcefully expresses the conjunction of an antithetical pair that confounds any "reasonable" abstraction. The same effect obtains here, in the stylistic breach that occurs when sublime theological references yield to an appended and rather mundane account of the lineage of Louis XV.[28] The audacious foolishness of Hamann's verbal assemblages testifies to the truth of divine condescension. Indeed, understood specifically as a man "came into the world, *that he might bear witness to the truth*," Christ—as the Word Incarnate, as the amalgam of the highest and the basest, the divine and the mortal, the synchronic and the diachronic—is, at least for Hamann, the greatest, most powerful citation of all.

Strikingly, Hamann concludes this critique of Enlightenment, dedicated to Kant and Berens—the two men who actively attempted to win him back to the side of Reason—with a rapid listing of three death sentences: the executions of Socrates, Christ, and Damiens. By summoning these figures on the death row of history, Hamann would seem to call attention to the lethal power of authorities. This gesture surprisingly anticipates the implicit problem discernible in Kant's later essay on *Aufklärung*, where the philosopher denounces the need for a *Vormund* only to install himself as an authoritative representative for the masses. In presuming guardianship for the masses, Kant unavoidably poses as the sovereign judge, who fatally decides on what does and does not count as Enlightenment. What, then, to refer to the preface of Kant's first *Critique*, would differentiate the philosopher from the "despotic authority" to whom all must

Ludwich des *Grossen* ist" (2: 82; emphasis in text). [James C. O'Flaherty, *Hamann's Socratic Memorabilia: A Translation and Commentary* (Baltimore: Johns Hopkins University Press, 1967), 184.]

28. Cf. O'Flaherty, *Hamann's Socratic Memorabilia*, 79.

submit?[29] Hamann already appears to warn against the consequences, should the masses refuse to assent to this reeducation program. Fairly or unfairly, in a highly suggestive fashion, Hamann modulates his interrogation of core Enlightenment beliefs into a blatant assignment of guilt.

Culpability would continue to color Hamann's engagement with the strongest intellectual beliefs of his century. Twenty-five years later, in 1784, upon reading Kant's *Aufklärung* essay, Hamann composed a long letter to his close friend Christian Jacob Kraus, an explicitly enlightened political theorist who once counseled Frederick the Great, taught practical philosophy and mathematics, and was Kant's colleague at Königsberg. While expressing his indebtedness to Kraus for having sent him the most recent copy of the *Berlinische Monatsschrift* in which Kant's essay appeared, Hamann took the opportunity to address the philosopher's provocative thesis—that is, to offer his own "response" to Kant's *Response to the Question* concerning the nature of Enlightenment, presumably in the hope that his reply would somehow reach Kant's desk. As usual, Hamann cannot resist adopting the persona of comic foolishness:

> *Clarissime Domine Politice!*
>
> Since my old stiff bones are hardly suitable any longer for peripatetic philosophy, and since I reach my moments of labyrinthine strolls not always *before* but also on occasion between the table *ab ouis ad poma*, I must therefore have recourse to a *macaronic* goose-quill to bestow to you my thanks for the enclosed *Berlinische Christmonath* in *cant-style*, which the comical [*komische*] historian of comical [*komischen*] literature has rendered in *Kantian style per* e like an *Asmus cum puncto*.[30]

29. Kant, *Kritik der reinen Vernunft* [1781], *Gesammelte Schriften*, 3: ix.

30. Hamann to Christian Jacob Kraus, December 18, 1784, in Johann Georg Hamann, *Briefe*, Arthur Henkel, ed. (Frankfurt a. M.: Insel, 1988). "*Clarissime Domine Politice!* Weil meine alten steifen Knochen zur peripatetischen Philosophie kaum mehr taugen, und meine Augenblicke zu labyrinthischen Spatziergängen nicht immer *vor* sondern auch zuweilen zwischen der Tafel *ab ouis ad poma* eintreffen; so muß ich schon zu einem *maccaroni*schen Gänsekiel meine Zuflucht nehmen, Ihnen meinen Dank für den beykommenden Berlinschen Christmonath im *cant-style*, den der komische Geschichtsschrieber der komischen Litteratur *per* e wie ein *Asmus cum puncto* durch *Kantschen Styl* gegeben, zu übermachen" (145; emphasis in text). The English translation, slightly modified, is by Brian Jacobs, "Self-incurrence, Incapacity, and Guilt: Kant and Hamann on Enlightenment Guardianship," *Lessing Yearbook* 28 (1996), 147–61. Jacobs provides a full translation of Hamann's letter on pp. 155–61.

The citational energy of these lines is impossible to contain or comprehend fully. Already with the Latin greeting (*Clarissime Domine Politice*, "Most brilliant master politician"), Hamann combines the touted *clarity*, in superlative mode, with the implicit *domination* and *political governance* of the *Aufklärung*. From the start, Hamann regards Kant's reply to the question concerning Enlightenment as little more than a justification of Frederick the Great's policies. Insofar as he considers the Prussian king the true authority behind Kant's claims to philosophical autonomy, Hamann refrains altogether from assuming an authoritative tone, choosing instead to embrace the "cant-style" (written in English), which he recently learned about in Karl Friedrich Flögel's *Geschichte der komischen Literatur* ("History of comical literature," 1784). Flögel provides two possible derivations for the English term *cant*, both from the seventeenth century: either it was introduced by the courtiers of Charles II, who in their contempt for solemnity "affected wantonness [*Ausgelassenheit*] in morals and language such as an unbound, ungrammatical baseness of expression"—that is, they emulated the kind of laxity that one finds in *song* (*cantus*); or, according to Richard Steele, it alludes to the Scottish clergyman, Andrew Cant, who was said to have preached to his uneducated congregation in low dialect.[31] Hamann delights in reading Flögel "*per* e" as a *Flegel* (a *churlish cad*), especially in the way this "comical historian" allows the e to be *omitted* (*ausgelassen*) in translating the English *cant-style* with the German *Kantischer Styl*—a sign of the author's own cheerful *Ausgelassenheit* ("jolly exuberance"). Flögel, the knowledgeable historian, would therefore be another *Asmus*, a common abbreviation for Erasmus, the erudite scholar of the Reformation, or the pseudonym of the German poet and journalist, Matthias Claudius; an *Asmus*, however, *cum puncto*, with a point that should be made, serious enough, but not without humility; for Hamann makes his point by putting a dot on the first vertical stroke of the letter *m* in order to expose the "ass" (*asinus*) in the discourse, reminiscent of the way a Hebrew scribe adds vowel points, but also recalling that the Christian savior entered Jerusalem on an ass. That Kant himself willingly assumed the cant-style is evident enough in the other essay that he published in the previous, November issue of the *Berlinische Monatsschrift*, his *Idee zu einer allgemeinen Geschichte in weltbürgerlicher Absicht* ("Idea for a universal History with a cosmopolitan Intent"), in which the philosopher accommodates his language to the lowly register of the *Weltbürger*.

31. For some of these glosses on Hamann's language, see Arthur Henkel's notes, in Hamann, *Briefe*, 400–2. Henkel cites the relevant passage from Flögel's *Geschichte* on p. 401.

Too old to travel peripatetically to Kraus's home or office, and too indifferent to enter into Aristotelian or Peripatetic logic, Hamann remains at his table and takes up his macaronic-goose-quill (maccaroni*schen Gänsekiel*) to express his labyrinthine thoughts in a style that churlishly mixes terms from different languages—food for thought, *ab ovis ad poma*. Already in his opening remarks, Hamann has Horace in mind. While the phrase *ab ovis ad poma* ("from eggs to apple") generally denotes an entire meal (as in English "from soup to nuts"), it derives from Horace's *Satires*:

> Omnibus hoc vitium est cantoribus, inter amicos
> ut numquam inducant animum cantare rogati,
> iniussi numquam desistant. Sardus habebat
> ille Tigellius hoc. Caesar, qui cogere posset,
> si peteret per amicitiam patris atque suam, non
> quicquam proficeret; si collibuisset, ab ovo
> usque ad mala citaret "io Bacche!"
>
> *Satires*, 1.3.1–7, in Horace, *Opera*, 141

> All singers have this fault, among friends
> they are never inclined to sing when asked,
> yet unbidden they never stop. That Sardinian
> Tigellius was like this. If Caesar, who would be able to force him,
> should beg him by his father's friendship and his own,
> he would not accomplish anything; but if it should please him, from
> the egg
> to the apple he would call out "Io Bacche!"

Hamann's cant therefore begins before he mentions it explicitly. He is precisely like one of those singers (*cantores*) who refuse to sing on demand, yet, unbidden, will never stop *calling out* (*citare*), citing one source after the next. Like the poet Tigellius, who would dismiss even a request from Caesar, Hamann pays little heed to earthly authority. Instead, somewhat like an ass, he continues to pour out authoritative citations, perhaps in order to watch authority get *shaken* (*citus*).

> Along with *Sapere aude!* belongs *Noli admirari!* ["Do not wonder!"], which comes from the very same source. *Clarissime Domine Politice!* You know how

> much I love our Plato and how much I like to read him; I also want to allow myself, but *cum grano salis,* to delight in his guardianship [*Vormundschaft*] as the guide of my own *understanding,* without worrying about a self-incurrence [*Selbstverschuldung*] through a lack of *heart.*[32]

Perhaps Hamann recognizes Kant's citation of *sapere aude* as a citation from his own letter from 1759, where he provoked the philosopher to "dare to savor" a foolishness that is wiser (*sapientius*)? In any case, unlike Kant, Hamann sees no opposition between adhering to external guardianship and developing one's own understanding. If enlightened reason demands thinking in incorporeal abstractions—if it requires tarrying in some make-believe realm of Platonic ideas—then the "self-incurred immaturity" that Kant vilifies can be embraced worry-free, insofar as it allows the thinker to have his passions, to have his *heart.* The command *sapere aude,* which Kant translates as "Have courage to use your own understanding!" reaches back to the same Horace who dissuades us from admiration or wonder—*Noli admirari!*

For Hamann, there is nothing to admire in any enlightenment that issues imperatives like *sapere aude.* The unresolved problem that Kant fails to fathom—appealing to an authoritative spokesman (Horace) to instruct how we might be free from heteronomous authority—is already discernible in the command itself. By *following* the advice, "Dare to think for yourself," you are already not thinking for yourself. Accepting the principle already violates it.[33] Hamann, again, appears to suggest that one thinks for oneself not by pretending to think as an authority unto oneself, but rather by acknowledging that one always thinks in specific words—in the materiality of language—that necessarily predates one's existence. Apart from God, there is no original, absolute source, entirely free from a context that forms it and formulates it: neither Kant as a rational subject, who must borrow his motto from Horace, nor Horace, who may have borrowed his verse from another. Hamann may simply be suffering from a lapse of memory or he may be making yet another point: the famous opening of Horace's *Epistle* 1.6 does not read *Noli admirari* but rather *Nil admirari*:

32. Hamann, *Briefe*. "Zum *Sapere aude!* gehört auch aus eben derselben Qvelle das *Noli admirari! Clarissime Domine Politice!* Wie sehr ich unsern Plato liebe und wie gern ich ihn lese wißen Sie[;] auch will ich mich seiner Vormundschaft zur Leitung meines eigenen *Verstandes,* doch *cum grano salis* gefallen laßen, ohne eine Selbstverschuldung durch Magel des *Herzens* zu besorgen" (145).

33. Cf. Jacobs, "Self-incurrence, Incapacity, and Guilt," 152.

Nil admirari prope res est una, Numici,
solaque quae possit facere et servare beatum.
Epistles, 1.6.1–2, in Horace, *Opera*, 212

To marvel at nothing is almost the one thing, Numicius,
And the only thing that can make and keep someone blessed.

Is Hamann simply confused? Or is he not, rather, eager to have his addressee hear Horace's advice as itself a quotation from Catullus, and, moreover, as an asinine dig at Kant's notorious bachelorhood?

Noli admirari quare tibi femina nulla,
  Rufe, velit tenerum supposuisse femur,
non si illam rarae labefactes munere uestis
  aut perluciduli deliciis lapidis.
laedit te quaedam mala fabula, qua tibi fertur
  ualle sub alarum trux habitare caper.
hunc metuunt omnes, neque mirum: nam mala ualde est
  bestia, nec quicum bella puella cubet.
quare aut crudelem nasorum interfice pestem,
  aut admirari desine cur fugiunt.
Catullus, *Carmina*, 69, p. 88

Do not wonder why no woman,
  Rufus, wishes to place her soft thigh beneath you,
not even if you should weaken her with a gift of rare clothes
  or with the delights of a pellucid gemstone.
What hurts you is a certain bad story, which claims
  that under the valley of your armpits a wild billy-goat lives.
This is what everyone fears; and no wonder: for it's really an evil
  beast, and no pretty girl wants to sleep with it.
Therefore either kill this cruel plague of noses,
  or cease to wonder why they flee.

Hamann, who later on explicitly states in his letter to Kraus that his three daughters would not react kindly to Kant's dismissal of the "entire fair sex," may be citing Horace incorrectly in order to adduce Catullus's harsh imperative, which could subsequently remind Königsberg's most famous bachelor that he has a body—a body that announces its bestial presence to everyone with a nose. This recollection thus serves as an oblique cue to Kraus, that he should "not marvel" at his colleague Kant (*noli admirari*), because his philosophy, in the final assessment, offers nothing worthy of admiration (*nil admirari*). Recognizing that alone would keep one "blessed."

There is, in Hamann's assessment, nothing whatsoever to admire in Kant's main argument, which insists on the "incapacity to use one's own understanding without the guidance of another" as "self-incurred immaturity." On the contrary, denying the guidance of another is the greater immaturity, insofar as it deludes the subject of language to believe in himself as the original source of his thinking. Furthermore, what justifies judging any "incapacity" as a source of "guilt" (*Schuld*)? If there is any guilt to be assigned, it should, rather, fall on the man of enlightenment himself:

> But who is this undetermined *other*, who appears twice anonymously? [. . .] The answer: the wretched guardian (*Vormund*), who must implicitly be understood as the correlate of the immature one. This is the man of death. Self-incurred guardianship and not immaturity.[34]

A century and a half before Adorno and Horkheimer, Hamann provides his own dialectic of Enlightenment by identifying the man of reason as the man of death. The one who preaches the universal light of reason is in fact the guilty party, the one who willfully incurs guardianship for himself. In Hamann's view, he is the one who is lazy and cowardly, someone who dubiously hides behind anonymity. As Hamann goes on to suggest, the guilt-laden *Vormund* is complicit with political authorities, like the authority of the enlightened despot Frederick the Great, who claims to emancipate his people but only through thorough oppression, implementing the voice of Reason by silencing voices that are deemed to be undignified, like "the entire fair sex" that Kant singles out.

34. Hamann, *Briefe*. "Wer ist aber der unbestimmte *andere*, der zweymal anonymisch vorkommt? [. . .] Antwort: der leidige Vormund, der als das *correlatum* der Unmündigen *implicite* verstanden werden muß. Dies ist der Mann des Todes. Die selbstverschuldete Vormundschaft und nicht Unmündigkeit" (146).

> In what then does the *incapacity* or *guilt* of the falsely accused immature one consist? In his own laziness and cowardice? No, in the blindness of his guardian, who passes himself off as seeing, and, for precisely this reason must be responsible for all guilt.[35]

The enlightened guardian is blind because he thinks in abstractions, tearing language away (*abstrahere*) from lived experience, believing excessively in his own rational capacities and thus neglecting his heart—in sum, believing that he is not a human being in the flesh. In Hamann's opinion, Kant misleads others and misleads himself in insisting that one thinks *through* language rather than thinking *in* language. As he famously formulates it elsewhere: "Even if I were as eloquent as Demosthenes, I would yet have to do nothing more than repeat one word three times: reason is language, *logos*."[36] To be human—to be mortal—is to understand that the mind cannot be detached from the heart, that the distinction of soul and body is falsified by their true indistinctness in incarnate being; and similarly, that the division of meaning and expression, content and form, is overridden by their true indivisibility in the incarnate *logos*, which is no less human, no less mortal. As Hamann recommends in his *Metacritique of the Purism of Reason*, Kant should be faulted or accused for rigorous analytical dualism: "Certainly one should conclude from so many analytical judgments on a gnostic hatred of material or even a mystical love for form."[37]

For Hamann, the latent Gnosticism of Kant's analyses, which deduce pure intuitions of space and time, tries to dupe his readers into accepting the absurd possibility of a discarnate existence, something that this philologist of the flesh will not tolerate. In his notes entitled "Philological Ideas and Doubts," Hamann heartens his own readership to follow a much different guide:

35. Hamann, *Briefe*. "Worinn besteht nun das *Unvermögen* oder die *Schuld* des fälschlich anklagten unmündigen? In seiner eigenen Faulheit oder Feigheit? Nein, in der Blindheit seines Vormundes, der sich für sehend ausgiebt, und eben deshalb alle Schuld verantworten muß" (146).

36. Hamann to Johann Gottfried Herder, August 10, 1784, in Hamann, *Briefwechsel*, Walther Ziesemer and Arthur Henkel, eds., 8 vols. (Frankfurt a. M.: Insel, 1955–1975): "Wenn ich auch so beredt wäre, wie Demosthenes, so würde ich doch nicht mehr als ein einziges Wort dreymal wiederholen müssen: Vernunft ist Sprache, λόγος" (5: 177).

37. Hamann, *Sämtliche Werke*. "Zwar sollte man aus so manchen analytischen Urtheilen auf einen gnostischen Haß gegen Materie oder auch eine mystische Liebe zur Form schließen" (3:285).

> Every philosophical contradiction and the whole historical puzzle of our existence, the impenetrable night of its *terminus a quo* and *terminus ad quem*, is resolved and explained by the primal message of the Word made flesh.[38]

Although for Hamann the doctrine of Incarnation represents above all a theological truth, it equally applies to human existence, which thinks in the flesh. As he expresses it in a letter to Friedrich Hartknoch: "But the *pudenda* of our nature hang together with the chambers of the heart and brain so precisely, that too strict an abstraction of such a natural bond is impossible."[39] Rather than traffic in ideas stripped of a body, Hamann allows the flesh to come out of cowardly hiding, so as to reveal that every *repetitio sententiae* is necessarily a *repetitio verborum*, that the free use of our reason, which demands the subordination of language to thought, invariably entails a lethal abstraction, one that is at fault, insofar as it divorces the mind from the body. For Hamann, daring to know would indeed be fatal, should it fail in daring to savor the incarnate truth.

38. Hamann, *Philologische Einfälle und Zweifel* [1776], in *Sämtliche Werke*. "Aller *philosophische* Widerspruch und das ganze *historische* Räthsel unsrer *Existenz*, die undurchdringliche Nacht ihres termini a quo und termini ad quem sind durch die *Urkunde* des *Fleisch gewordenen Wortes* aufgelöst" (3: 192).

39. Hamann to Friedrich Hartknoch, July 24, 1784, in *Briefe*. "Doch die *Pudenda* unserer Natur hängen mit den Cammern des Herzens und des Gehirns so genau zusammen, daß eine zu strenge *Abstraction* eines so natürlichen Bandes unmöglich ist" (113).

My dear friend, now where I can see again the teeming brood of philologists of our day up close, where I must daily observe the whole of their mole-like efforts, their swollen cheek pouches and their blind eyes, their joy over the captured worm and their indifference towards the true, indeed the urgent problems of life, and not only in the young brood, but also in their fully-grown elders: then it appears ever more comprehensible to me that both of us, if we otherwise only remain true to our genius, will not walk our life's journey without multiple challenges and obstructions.

—Friedrich Nietzsche to Erwin Rohde, November 20, 1868[1]

5

The Mountain and the Molehill

Philology has long been treated with condescension, even among those who would identify themselves as members of the guild. The critique is fairly consistent: In its unflagging attentiveness to written texts from the past, philologists all too readily limit themselves to excessive formalism and debilitating antiquarianism. Philology's adherence to the minutiae of written discourse, its concentration on the complex and historically contingent ways by which meaning has been produced and conveyed, distracts the scholar from the truth, value, and applicability of the meanings transmitted. By endlessly scrutinizing the forms

1. "Mein lieber Freund, jetzt wo ich wieder das wimmelnde Philologengezücht unserer Tage aus der Nähe sehe, wo ich das ganze Maulwurfstreiben, die vollen Backentaschen und die blinden Augen, die Freude ob des erbeuteten Wurms und die Gleichgültigkeit gegen die wahren, ja aufdringlichen Probleme des Lebens täglich beobachten muß und nicht nur an der jungen Brut, sondern an den ausgewachsenen Alten: da kommt es mir immer begreiflicher vor, daß wir beide, falls wir nur sonst unserm Genius treu bleiben, nicht ohne mannichfache Anstöße und Quertreibereien unsern Lebensweg gehen werden." Friedrich Nietzsche to Erwin Rohde, November 20, 1868, in Nietzsche, *Briefwechsel: Kritische Gesamtausgabe*, 24 vols., Giorgio Colli and Mazzino Montinari, eds. (Berlin: de Gruyter, 1975–2004), 1/2: 344.

and functions of verbal language, philologists neglect what is most important in their own world, their own age, and their own lives. They look too closely at the mechanics of language and thereby overlook their present sociopolitical and personal circumstances. Like moles, they burrow ever deeper into their manuscripts and critical editions, into their grammars and lexica, barely lifting their heads to take in what is taking place all around them. They gorge themselves on books and yet remain morally blind. They read the words of the past without recognizing what these words are communicating to them and what they should communicate to their students.

At the age of twenty-four, Nietzsche expressed these complaints to his "dear friend," Erwin Rohde, who, like him, was studying classical philology under Friedrich Wilhelm Ritschl in Leipzig, where, incidentally, Nietzsche had cofounded the students' Philological Society. Friend to friend, philologist to philologist, the doctoral candidate is typically questioning the field in which he is training. He is appalled by the sclerotic nature of his advisors and fearfully recognizes how their appearance may be an image of what he will become in a matter of years. Also typically, he accuses his profession of being obstructive, insofar as it misconstrues the means for the end, the way for the life. He has come to realize that philology's excessive attentiveness to verbal form is concerned more with *how* a text functions than with *what* the text says. Stumbling over one word after the other, philology causes us to get stuck along the way, preventing us from ever reaching the desired destination of meaning. Philology invites condescension whenever it attends to written discourse as if it were a collection of material things rather than a series of transparent signs. Instead of reading through the words, philologists look at them, examining them and measuring them, assessing their historical characteristics or judging their correctness. Nietzsche's youthful interest in philosophical "genius"—both his own and the genius of the authors who spoke to him—disparages such roadblocks. He disdains the "multiple challenges and obstructions"—the *mannichfache Anstöße und Quertreibereien*—that hold him up. Instead, he wants to follow the textual passages all the way to the vivid ideas and vital insights to which they lead; he wants to turn the words into deeds, the *logoi* into *erga*. Words should be digested and processed, but his laborious colleagues simply stuff their cheeks, unable to swallow.

For Nietzsche, however, it is not merely the blind laboriousness of his teachers and peers that is problematic. Philology further disappoints because its scriptural devotion fails to offer a true vision of ancient Greek culture. Already at this point in his career, he laments how classical pedagogues invariably settle for an antiquarianism that proffers conventional, anemic models for imitation. Instead, they should employ their skills to present textual materials with the kind of difficulty that would instigate active engagement. Nietzsche therefore rejects any philological approach that reads merely to read rather than reading to live. In his letter to Rohde, he invokes the long-standing ideal that defines philosophy in its ethical sense as an *ars vivendi*—an "art of living," a *Lebenskunst*. In contrast, the "teeming brood of philologists" are a hyper-professionalized, self-serving lot, who care little for any such appeals. As a result, philology has become anti-philosophy. In their "indifference" toward the present, they have supplanted "the true, indeed urgent problems of life [*Probleme des Lebens*]" with mere problems of reading—*Probleme des Lesens*. Consequently, the philological "way of reading," a perverse *Lesensweg*, stands to obstruct him as he makes his way along his "life's journey" or *Lebensweg*. The one way appears to block the other.

The distaste that Nietzsche expresses in this letter was arguably colored by some degree of embarrassment or even self-loathing, feelings that were likely exacerbated by the young man's visit, just over one week before, at the Ritschls' home, where he had the opportunity to meet in person that most heroic of German tone-poets, Richard Wagner. In his previous letter to Rohde, Nietzsche described the inspiring evening in loving detail. Wagner held court in the city of his birth, performing passages from *Die Meistersinger* before dinner and after. There was talk of Schopenhauer, aesthetics, and the ineptness of German opera companies. Together, presumably when Ritschl was out of earshot, they poked fun at the university professors and their *beckmesserisch* pedantry. So "rare and stimulating" was the experience, so "joyous," that Nietzsche, the following day, confessed his inability to get back "on the old track [*im alten Gleise*]."[2] Derailed by this fateful accident, and reflecting on the ideas and enlivening force of Wagner's monumental genius, the once industrious student now viewed the piles of books and papers that cluttered his and his cohort's desks as little more than molehills.

A mere six months later, on May 28, 1869, when Nietzsche had to stand before the faculty at Basel to give his inaugural lecture as a newly appointed professor of classical philology, he dutifully stepped up to the occasion and,

2. Nietzsche to Rohde, November 9, 1868, in Nietzsche, *Briefwechsel*, 1/2: 355–41.

without any qualms, defended his discipline against its detractors: "Where does one not find them, the mockers, who are always ready to deliver a blow to the philological 'moles.'"[3] Without ever letting on that he is in fact a mocker among moles, Nietzsche underscores the need to rehabilitate the "species" to which he belongs, one that is persistently accused of "swallowing dust *ex professo*" and ridiculed for "burrowing about and chucking up [*aufwirft*] for the eleventh time the same clod of earth chucked up [*aufgeworfen*] ten times before."[4] Admittedly, philologists "raise" (*aufwerfen*) too many questions, which, according to a popular folk etymology, would confirm their identity as *Maulwürfe*, as the "moles" who "chuck" (*werfen*) clods of earth with the mouth (*Maul*). How can one get on with the business of reading, while being assaulted with an endless barrage of muddying questions? And Nietzsche admits that the discipline of philology, with its ceaseless hairsplitting, carping, and fuss, has had to withstand the dismissive attitudes of a public, which is incapable of understanding and appreciating such meticulous labor.

As one would expect on such an occasion, Nietzsche readily dismisses this line of attack: "For opponents of this sort, however, philology is merely a useless, harmless, and inoffensive pastime, an object of laughter and not of hate."[5] The young professor thereby preemptively exonerates himself of any serious charge. Even if the views expressed in the letter cited above were made public—even if he were exposed as one of those mockers who shamelessly wrote off philologists as blind *Maulwürfe*—he could excuse his behavior as a healthy exercise, laughing at one's own profession from within rather than assaulting it from without. And Nietzsche does not conceal the fact that such enemies are real and truly lethal:

> In contrast, there is a wrathful and unbounded hatred of philology wherever an ideal as such is feared, where modern man in jubilant admiration falls down

3. The speech was subsequently published as *Homer und die klassische Philologie* (1869); in *Werke in drei Bänden*, Karl Schlechta, ed. (Munich: Hanser, 1966), 3: 155–74. "Wo trifft man sie nicht, die Spötter, die immer bereit sind, den philologischen 'Maulwürfen' einen Hieb zu versetzen" (156).

4. Nietzsche, *Homer und die klassische Philologie*. "Geschlecht, das das Staubschlucken *ex professo* treibt, das die zehnmal aufgeworfene Erdscholle noch das elfte Mal aufwirft und zerwühlt (156).

5. Nietzsche, *Homer und die klassische Philologie*. "Für diese Art von Gegnern ist aber doch die Philologie ein freilich unnützer, immerhin harmloser und unschädlicher Zeitvertreib, ein Objekt des Scherzes, nicht des Hasses" (156).

> to worship himself, and where Hellenism is looked upon as a viewpoint that has been superseded and is therefore rather uninteresting.[6]

In contradistinction to those who merely mock philology's persnickety concern with the verbal form of texts from classical antiquity, there are those who more insidiously call into question the very content of this material, eager to consign it to the dustbin of obsolescence. In rehearsing his own version of the *Querelle des anciens et des modernes,* Nietzsche takes a stand against those who champion the present as having far surpassed antiquity in its admirable achievements. Nietzsche has approached the university podium prepared to do battle: to save philology from the barbarism of the present. But to do so, he must also save philology from the philologists. In his assessment, the war must be waged on two fronts: against the modernist "curse of ridiculous and Scythian bad taste" as well as against the classicist-pedagogical inclination to petrify thinking, to cause "annihilation by means of the fearfully beautiful Gorgon head of the classical."[7]

In Nietzsche's view, both threats must be countered by reuniting the two tendencies that have torn philology from within and have thereby rendered it weak: the tendency toward "art" (*Kunst*), which teaches that "life is worth living" (*das Leben ist wert gelebt zu werden*); and the tendency toward "science" (*Wissenschaft*), which teaches that "life is worth knowing" (*das Leben ist wert erkannt zu werden*). If classical philology is to survive, it must constantly aim to reconcile these otherwise conflicting desiderata—a reconciliation that requires the unifying vision of philosophy. Philosophy alone can incorporate Nietzsche's métier, the weakness of which "lies in the many-sided character, in the lack of a conceptual unity [*begrifflichen Einheit*], in the inorganic aggregate state [*unorganischen Aggregatzustande*] of heterogeneous scientific activities, which are bound together only by the name 'Philology.'"[8] Philosophy, under-

6. Nietzsche, *Homer und die klassische Philologie.* "Dagegen lebt ein ganz ingrimmiger und unbändiger Haß gegen die Philologie überall dort, wo das Ideal als solches gefürchtet wird, wo der moderne Mensch in glücklicher Bewunderung vor sich selbst niederfällt, wo das Hellentum als ein überwundener, daher sehr gleichgültiger Standpunkt betrachtet wird" (157).

7. Nietzsche, *Homer und die klassische Philologie.* "[. . .] vor dem Fluch lächerlicher und skythischer Geschmacksverirrungen und vor der Vernichtung durch das furchtbar-schöne Gorgonenhaupt des Klassischen [. . .]" (157).

8. Nietzsche, *Homer und die klassische Philologie.* "Die Ursache liegt in dem vielspältigen Charakter derselben, in dem Mangel einer begrifflichen Einheit, in dem unorganischen Aggregatzustande verschiedenartiger wissenschaftlicher Tätigkeiten, die nur durch den Namen 'Philologie' zusammengebunden sind" (157).

stood as an *ars vivendi*, will be able to breathe life into this inorganic or lifeless conglomeration.

Thus, by the end of his lecture, Nietzsche will offer his own "confession of faith" (*Glaubensbekenntnis*), pronounced as an optimistic inversion of a claim first formulated by Seneca. In *Epistle* 108, the Roman Stoic had complained of present-day philosophy students, who were exceedingly devoted to the verbal form of speeches and texts and thereby neglected to acknowledge the import of the message contained therein. Seneca's lament is simple: *philologia facta est quae philosophia fuit*—"What was once philosophy has become philology."[9] Similarly, for the young Basel classicist, studying mere words for the sake of words and caring little or not at all for the philosophical demands these texts imposed were inclinations that he believed were symptomatic of the decadence of his age—a baneful trend that he hoped to reverse; hence his inverted citation from Seneca:

> *Philosophia facta est quae philologia fuit* ("What was once philology has become philosophy"). What ought to be expressed by this is that every philological activity should be surrounded and enclosed by a philosophical worldview, in which everything individual and isolated evaporates as something objectionable, and only what is whole and consistent endures.[10]

Debased for too long as an object of condescension, philology is poised for redemption, but only when it is has been organized by philosophy. The philosophical worldview will allow each atomistic part of philological busywork to work together in producing a body of knowledge, including aesthetic knowledge, demonstrating that a life worth knowing is also a life worth living. The mole-like obsession with petty, disparate particulars must be made morally useful through more capacious insight. Moreover, the individual, divisive positions among scholars, their risible infighting, must be coordinated into a collective vision. For this future anti-Christian, at least at this early stage in his career, God does not hide in the details. Individual pieces must dissolve into a coherent, organic

9. Seneca, *Ep.* 108.23, *Ad Lucilium epistulae morales*, 2 vols., L. D. Reynolds, ed. (Oxford: Oxford University Press, 1987–89).

10. Nietzsche, *Homer und die klassische Philologie*. "*Philosophia facta est quae philologia fuit.* Damit soll ausgesprochen sein, daß alle und jede philologische Tätigkeit umschlossen und eingehegt sein soll von einer philosophischen Weltanschauung, in der alles Einzelne und Vereinzelte als etwas Verwerfliches verdampft und nur das Ganze und Einheitliche bestehen bleibt" (174).

whole, a textual corpus that speaks with power and relevance. Varying technical approaches must work together in concert, producing a *Gesamtkunstwerk* that only a transcendent philosophical view can achieve.

However, what precisely is this miraculous philosophical worldview? And is it effective? Does it achieve what the young philologist *cum* philosopher wants it to achieve? Certainly, at least up to and including *The Birth of Tragedy* (1872), the interconnections and mutual support of art and science are a persistent theme in Nietzsche's work—what he names in the opening sentence of the *Tragedy* book as "aesthetic science" (*ästhetische Wissenschaft*). Yet in reading the main body of the Basel lecture, one is immediately struck by the fact that Nietzsche has chosen the "Homeric Question" as his primary case study—a somewhat problematic decision, insofar as the debate over the authorship of the ancient epics not only divided the unitary identity of the poet, but also ultimately caused the reading public to protest against philological institution. Perhaps, in a singular act of bravado, the freshly appointed professor—one who received the position before he received his doctorate and before he submitted a *Habilitation*—chose a particularly thorny topic to demonstrate his scholarly prowess. If he could integrate philology's classicist and historicist pursuits as they pertained to the Homeric Question, then he would decisively prove the viability of his philosophical program. At any rate, in adducing this particular issue, Nietzsche appears to draw an analogy between doubts concerning the authorial unity of the epics and doubts concerning the unity of philology. Yet how sound is this analogy?

The scholarly debate was initially ignited by Friedrich August Wolf, whose *Prolegomena ad Homerum* (1795) persuasively argued that the *Iliad* and the *Odyssey* could not be the work of a single author, but rather were the compiled product of oral recitations across the centuries. As a dutiful philologist, Nietzsche is compelled to accept the hard evidence of previous historical scholars who deny the single-author theory, even though, ever since Wolf published his thesis, this conclusion inspired the wrath of poets and philhellenists across the German States. As Nietzsche points out, Schiller dismissed the idea as scandalously barbaric, while Goethe, who at one time enthusiastically attended Wolf's lectures incognito, ultimately recanted his support on poetic grounds:

> Scharfsinnig habt Ihr, wie Ihr seid,
> Von aller Verehrung uns befreit;
> Und wir bekannten überfrei,
> Dass Ilias nur ein Flickwerk sei.

Mög' unser Abfall niemand kränken;
Denn Jugend weiß uns zu entzünden,
Dass wir ihn lieber als Ganzes denken,
Als Ganzes freudig ihn empfinden.[11]

Ingenious as you are, you have
Freed us from all adoration;
And we confess quite freely indeed,
That the Iliad is but a patchwork.

May our renunciation offend no one;
For youth knows how to inflame us,
That we would rather think it a whole,
And as a whole joyously sense it.

Although recognizing the validity of Wolf's historical-scientific method and appreciating its promise of enlightenment, which "freed us from all adoration," Goethe's artistic sensibility could not allow the disintegration of the Homeric epics into mere "patchwork." Implicit in Goethe's opposition between patchwork and wholeness is a theory of genius, which, as David Wellbery has shown, consistently plays a unifying role across Goethe's *œuvre*: "The genius engenders; he does not sew or suture, does not stitch together parts or fragments already given."[12] The genius, being whole and consistent in himself, creates in a unified gesture of pure act a work of art that exhibits a fluid continuity that suffers no breaks, no cuts. By demonstrating how the *Iliad* and the *Odyssey* were compiled across centuries by means of an oral tradition, Wolf undermined this conception of the genius. Like Goethe and Schiller, Nietzsche believes too much in art to rob the Homeric epics of their genial power; but he is also too much a philologist to dismiss the linguistic-scientific evidence to the contrary. In the end, he must designate the figure of Homer as an "aesthetic judgment," as a theoretical image or philosophical construct that has oriented millennia of readings.[13] This

11. Cited in Nietzsche, *Homer und die klassische Philologie*, 160.

12. David Wellbery, *The Specular Moment: Goethe's Early Lyric and the Beginnings of Romanticism* (Stanford: Stanford University Press, 1996), 126.

13. On the ramifications of Nietzsche's conclusion, see James Porter, *Nietzsche and the Philology of the Future* (Stanford: Stanford University Press, 2000), 62–69.

orientation is thus a demonstration of how philological research, if "surrounded and enclosed" within the compass of philosophy, can produce a body of knowledge that would convince us that life is worth living. In brief, Nietzsche provides his audience an illustration of how meticulous work on textual materials can contribute to—rather than destroy—a classicizing perspective.

Nietzsche's central example would then seem capable of demonstrating the underlying philosophical unity that can organize the variegated and disparate nature of philological work—scientific work, which had been divisive from the perspective of both poetic creation and reception. He shows how a historicist approach to language is not incompatible with the aesthetic intention to formulate classical ideals. However, despite these valiant efforts, the recourse to a *philosophical* solution—for "Homer" is nothing more than an "aesthetic judgment"—appears to constitute a failure for both scientific historicists and cultural classicists alike. Nietzsche's solution solves nothing, but only exacerbates the tension between two irresolvable positions. By extension, the two distinct parts of his inaugural speech—on philology's internal heterogeneity and the Homeric Question—remain desperately disparate, where "everything individual and isolated" resists the promised evaporation. In the end, the young philologist is just another mole "burrowing about and chucking up for the eleventh time the same clod of earth chucked up ten times before."

Fresh on the scene, the young professor is in a rush to push forward his agenda; yet philology invariably slows everything down. A constant source of discontent, it aspires to become—to possess or be possessed by—philosophy. On the level of performance, and at cross-purposes with its intention, Nietzsche's essay reveals philology to be *philo-philosophy*, an activity that expresses the unattainable desire for a desire for wisdom. This desire is unattainable, because philology instigates ceaseless toil, which threatens to be emphatically meaningless, particularly when it obsesses excessively over the means of conveying the message, when it expends all its nervous energy on the verbal vehicle and thereby impedes the arrival of sense. To be sure, Nietzsche explicitly strives to militate against this mole-like activity. The way meaning is transmitted, although important and even necessary, should in no way block the destination. Unless philology is "surrounded and enclosed by a philosophical worldview," unless it allows itself to be oriented by the task at hand, it risks leaving the message by the wayside. Philology, therefore, must learn to *contain* its tendency to question language, so that language can accomplish what it is ostensibly designed to accomplish: namely, to bear meaning, to deliver safely and soundly the significant *content* with which it has been charged. Philology should be employed to refine the text's transparency, so as to free meaningful content from its mediation. Should it fail to do so—should it fail to contain its proclivity to interrogate the means of meaning—it risks instilling the kind of dissatisfaction that Nietzsche forcefully expresses. The philologist's *discontent* is the failure (*dis-*) to restrain or hold together (*con-tenere*) his desire to raise textual questions, the failure to deliver content, to transmit what is held together in language. To remedy this problem—both in terms of language's mission and in terms of the philologist's unnerving activity—Nietzsche believed it would be sufficient to supplant philology with philosophy, and to do so without any further delay. *Philosophia facta est quae philologia fuit.* Yet can this rushed call for a cure achieve anything other than underscore the severity of the dis-ease?

Many of the traits that would be cause for the debasement of philology in modernity are already discernible at its institutional origin in Alexandrian culture of the third and second centuries BCE. Nietzsche never tired of casting blame on the "Alexandrian man" who sheepishly hid from the ebullience of life. Although Alexandrian society conferred considerable honor and prestige to the title *philologos*, disparagement was not uncommon, especially among the philologists themselves. The notoriously prolific historian Timaios of Tauromenion, who, according to Polybius, made "such a parade of minute accuracy," was viciously branded Epitimaios ("fault-finder");[14] while the polymathy of Eratosthenes, director of the library at Alexandria, earned him the pejorative nickname of Pentathlos ("jack of all trades") as well as Bēta ("second"), presumably because the breadth of his erudition compromised his ability to master any single field. Whereas earlier, in the Platonic dialogues, the term *philologos* simply denoted the man who, like Socrates, took pleasure in speeches, the serious study of written discourse—the tireless scrutiny and punctilious criteria that characterized the work of Alexandrian critics—could easily be dismissed as tedious hairsplitting, ceaseless infighting, or obsessive bookishness out of touch with real-life circumstances. The affect implicit in *philologia* as a loving fondness for discourse easily translated into a longing for the word at the expense of the world.

The social ramifications came to the fore especially during the Roman Re-

14. Polybius, 12.4a, *The Histories: Books 9–15*, W. R. Paton, trans. (Cambridge: Harvard University Press, 2011), 350–51.

public, where *philologi* and the *grammatici* were generally freed Greek slaves, hired by patrician families to educate their sons. As might be expected, these foreign scholars or migrant workers would at times come under severe attack in the Roman Senate, which feared their pedagogical influence. Placing the young minds of the nobility into the hands of plebian teachers threatened to capsize the hierarchies of power that organized civil life in the Republic.[15] Cato the Elder was especially suspicious of Hellenic intervention within the Republic and therefore deprecated the practice of allowing Greek slaves to have so great a power over the children of Rome. He drew on common stereotypes, depicting *philologi* as "Asiatic," as effeminate idlers, who dissuaded the Roman youth from a life of virtuous action and manliness.[16] To demonstrate his concern, he is reported to have persuaded his son to quit his studies in Greek language.[17] With the spread of Roman power following the great military victories in the East and the annexation of Macedonia in 168 BCE, the capital witnessed increasing waves of Graecophone rhetoricians, grammarians, and philosophers, to the point where the Senate proposed banishing them from the city in 161 BCE.[18]

Centuries later, now at the height of the Roman Empire, Seneca voiced concern over the deleterious effect of philological obsession in an epistle that would well serve as a source for anyone wishing to cast blame on mole-like scholars who blindly dig for the sake of digging. *Epistle* 108 opens by addressing explicitly the problem of haste:

> What you are asking about is one of those matters that pertain to knowing [*scire*] only in order that you may know [*ut scias*]. Yet nonetheless, because it is pertinent, you are in a hurry and are not willing to wait for the books containing [*continentes*] the entire part of moral philosophy, which I am arranging for you right now. I shall send them out [*expediam*] immediately; but first I shall

15. Ingo Gildenhard, *Paideia Romana: Cicero's Tusculan Disputations* (Cambridge: Cambridge University Press, 2007), 28–34.

16. See Johannes Christes, "Texte im Elementarunterricht als Träger sittlicher Werte in republikanischer Zeit," in *O tempora, o mores! Römische Werte und römische Literatur in den letzten Jahrzehnten der Republik*, Andreas Haltenhoff, Andreas Heil, and Fritz Heiner Mutschler, eds. (Munich: Saur, 2003), 51–68.

17. Pliny the Elder, *Naturalis historia*, 29.14 [*Natural History*, vol. 8, *Books 28–32*, W. H. S. Jones, trans., Cambridge: Harvard University Press, 1963, 190–93].

18. Suetonius, *De grammaticis et rhetoribus*, 25.1, in *Suetonius*, vol. 2, J. C. Rolfe, trans. (Cambridge: Harvard University Press, 1914), 418–19.

> write how this desire to learn [*cupiditas discendi*], which I see burning in you, ought to be directed, so that it may not impede itself [*ne ipsa se inpediat*].[19]

Seneca's addressee, Lucilius, is in a rush. His lust for knowledge for the sheer sake of knowledge (*scire . . . ut scias*) makes him exceedingly impatient, unwilling to wait for the books of moral philosophy that his teacher is presently composing. The disciple's impatience therefore puts the Stoic master in a rather difficult position, compelled to interrupt his writing in order to write. The urgent request disturbs the project that aims to "contain the whole part" (*continentes totam . . . partem*), maybe to the degree where the whole may disintegrate into parts or to the point where the teacher's will to contain is broken. At any rate, Seneca will impart a lesson that should help regulate the young man's ardor, without restraining his own tendency to exploit the specific resources of language: Seneca shall expedite (*expediam*) the books, lest the "desire to learn" (*cupiditas discendi*) may impede (*inpediat*) the path of learning itself.

With the intention of directing a proper course of study—one that takes its time to absorb everything that philosophy teaches—Seneca provides an illustration of his own days as a pupil. He contrasts his steady engagement at the time with those whom he pejoratively identifies as *inquilinos*—a term used to designate those of foreign birth, aliens or migrants who simply occupy a place (*incolare*) without belonging there. These intruders almost illegally inhabit the citadel of philosophy, not because of any real civil status but rather because they attend lectures apparently for the wrong reason.

> Certain people come to hear and not to learn, just as we are led into the theater for the sake of pleasing the ear with a speech, a song, or a play. You will see that this class comprises a large part of the listeners, for whom the philosopher's school [*philosophi schola*] is merely a lounging-house of idleness [*deversorium otii*]. They do not act in order to remove any faults or to accept some rule for living [*legem vitae*], by means of which they may examine their habits; but rather they fully enjoy the amusement of the ears. Still, some even

19. "Id de quo quaeris ex iis est quae scire tantum eo, ut scias, pertinet. Sed nihilominus, quia pertinet, properas nec vis expectare libros quos cum maxime ordino continentes totam moralem philosophiae partem. Statim expediam; illud tamen prius scribam, quemadmodum tibi ista cupiditas discendi, qua flagrare te video, digerenda sit, ne ipsa se inpediat" (*Ep.* 108.1).

> arrive with writing tablets, not to record the subject matter [*res*] but the words [*verba*], which they can pass along to another with as little profit as they have when they hear them.[20]

Seneca faults the passive listener, the one who fails to take the lesson to heart and instead indulges in the rhetorical, formal aspects of the presentation. Rather than consume and digest what they are fed, they relish in it. In showing more interest in *how* something is said rather than *what* is said, they neglect to discover their own "faults" (*vitia*) and thereby overlook the "rule for living" (*legem vitae*), which in itself is the gravest of vices. By opting to "enjoy fully the amusement of the ears" (*oblectamento aurium perfruantur*), they decline to use the knowledge furnished and apply it morally. The vicious penchant to treat words as an object to be enjoyed (*frui*) supplants the virtuous will to receive them as instructions to be used (*uti*).

The conventional distinction between ideas (*res*) and the words (*verba*) that convey them articulates Seneca's main point. In his view, the true hearers are those who are ravished and stirred by the beauty of the subject matter and not merely by the sound of empty words—*Rapit illos instigatque rerum pulchritudo, non verborum inanium sonitus* (*Epistle* 108.7). The ideational content deserves more attention than its verbal formulation. Seneca laments the fact that today more than ever the import of philosophical discourse has degenerated into a useless longing for pretty vacuous sounds. Teachers mistakenly "teach us how to debate, not how to live" (*nos docent disputare, non vivere*); and pupils are eager "to cultivate not their souls but their wit" (*non animum excolendi sed ingenium*)—in sum, "what was once philosophy has now become philology"—*quae philosophia fuit facta philologia est* (*Epistle* 108.23). Values have been inverted. And reversing this reversal is, as we have seen, precisely the task that Nietzsche assumes in his professorial role.

Seneca continues his epistle by offering another illustration, a short line from Vergil, which should help us distinguish between a truly philosophical

20. "Quidam veniunt ut audiant, non ut discant, sicut in theatrum voluptatis causa ad delectandas aures oratione vel voce vel fabulis ducimur. Magnam hanc auditorum partem videbis cui philosophi schola deversorium otii sit. Non id agunt ut aliqua illo vitia deponant, ut aliquam legem vitae accipiant qua mores suos exigant, sed ut oblectamento aurium perfruantur. Aliqui tamen et cum pugillaribus veniunt, non ut res excipiant, sed ut verba, quae tam sine profectu alieno dicant quam sine suo audiunt" (*Ep.* 108.6).

reading and one that is merely philological. As if to save time—his addresee is, after all, in a rush—Seneca quotes only a hemistich, taken from Vergil's *Georgics* (3.284): *fugit inreparabile tempus* ("time flies irreparably"). How would this line be received? The scholar (*grammaticus*), Seneca argues, would certainly not interpret it in view of its philosophical significance—he would not take the message to heart and realize that time is short, that we must wake up and achieve what we must achieve. Rather, he would comment pedantically on how Vergil always employs the verb *fugere* when speaking of the rapidity of time. The grammatical reading would not take Vergil at his word; he would not heed the verse as an urgent warning against procrastination, but instead would take his time accumulating parallel passages and semantic glosses. Here, *how* Vergil expresses a thought overrides *what* the expression should communicate.

Seneca's illustration, however, does not leave things so straightforward. In citing Vergil's *tempus fugit*, the philosopher clearly harks back to his letter's opening paragraph, which described his addressee's pressing request for philosophical instruction. Apparently, as someone who understands that life is short, that time flees irreparably, Lucilius is already thinking philosophically; he recognizes that there is no time to spare. The young man's disruptive urgency demonstrates that he has already learned the lesson from the *Georgics*, well before his teacher enjoined him to take Vergil at his word.

Seneca, who suffers from old age (*senectus*), has even less time on his hands. He is eager to complete his tractates on moral philosophy, but must interrupt his work in order to gratify his pupil's burning need. He assures Lucilius that he will send the books to him immediately at least once he has finished his epistolary reply. Such pauses would seem to be perfectly responsible but also contradictory: Seneca is willing to stop writing in order to write. The master's plans to *expedite* the volumes are delayed by his concern that his student will be *impeded*—a concern that conversely impedes the philosopher's own desire to work expeditiously.[21]

As we have seen, the essential guidance that Seneca furnishes is one that promotes a philosophical—that is, *nonphilological*—approach to texts. This core teaching is formulated at the epistle's conclusion, but only after the philosopher has finished discussing at length a number of textual examples and how they are variously read:

21. My interpretation here is indebted to Thomas Schestag's brilliant reading of Seneca's epistle, which he shared with me in manuscript.

> But that I, too, while doing something else, may not slip into the role of philology or grammar, I advise that listening to and reading philosophers must be drawn toward bringing forth a blessed life, that we should not chase after archaic or artificial words and wanton tropes [*translationes*] and figures of speech, but rather seek beneficial precepts and elevated, courageous utterances which should at once be translated [*transferantur*] into fact [*rem*]. We should thoroughly learn in such a way that what were words [*verba*] may become deeds [*opera*].[22]

Seneca's message is clear: What was philology will become philosophy, but only when what were words become "deeds" or "works" (*opera*)—when the verbal messages are taken to heart and acted on in real life. To avoid slipping into philological dawdling, one must ignore the seductive sheen of "wanton tropes" (*translationes inprobas*) and instead let the words be actively "translated" (*transferantur*) into what they represent. Philosophy is operational, moving quickly past the impediments of philological tarrying. The call to work—to reflect philosophically and thereby acquire the "blessed life" (*beata vita*)—should be read against the foil of the prior disparagement of the *inquilini*, the nonphilosophical sorts who attend lectures for the sheer delight they afford the ear and thereby turn the "philosopher's school" (*philosophi schola*) into a "lounging-house of idleness" (*deversorium otii*).

Seneca recognizes all too well the seductions of philological tarrying. He has to catch himself from slipping into distraction. Through a sheer act of will he redirects the course of words, including above all his own words. Verbal transference remains inevitable, yet it is the philosopher's mission to make sure that words are carried across (*transferantur*) along the profitable path of referentiality and not allowed to bear wantonly on more words, on more transferred turns of phrase (*translationes*). Still, the philosophical mission is almost impossible to carry out thoroughly. For example, Seneca's word for "school" (*schola*) is a loanword from Greek that comes dangerously close to the *otium* explicitly denounced. Indeed, the term *scholē* primarily denotes "leisure" or even "idleness,"

22. "Sed ne et ipse, dum aliud ago, in philologum aut grammaticum delabar, illud admoneo, auditionem philosophorum lectionemque ad propositum beatae vitae trahendam, non ut verba prisca aut ficta captemus et translationes inprobas figurasque dicendi, sed ut pro futura praecepta et magnificas voces et animosas quae mox in rem transferantur. Sic ista ediscamus ut quae fuerint verba sint opera" (*Ep.* 108.35).

in opposition to the word for "business" or "occupation," which is formed by an alpha-privative: *ascholia*. The verb from which *scholē* is derived—*scholazein*—means "to have spare time," "to be unrushed," "to cease working" and therefore "to have the leisure" to study. Seneca wants his disciples to attend *school*, to take the time out to devote oneself to education, but somehow with an eye to leave scholarship behind and begin the work of living. In order to transmit any lesson, Seneca has to halt its transmission, spending a rather long time on poetic words, read at one's leisure. To take Seneca's Vergilian example, one must stop to hear the words *tempus fugit* in order to flee the words and act on them. It would appear that the only way for a reader to attend philosophically to what the words say would be to stop reading and start living, before time runs out. Yet this prescription invariably—irreparably—gets stuck in a double bind. The philosopher is commanded at once to read and not to read. As long as one meditates leisurely on the phrase *tempus fugit*, one is not obeying what the phrase expresses, yet the phrase can never be obeyed unless it is first read. Work is always undermined by the unworking of language.

According to Seneca, the philologist fails to flee the page. He is unlike the philosopher because he loves words as objects to be enjoyed rather than used. And yet it is precisely for this reason that the philologist would appear to escape the double bind that traps the philosopher, who must read in order to stop reading and start living. Philologists are not burdened by this aporia because they read in order to read. While Seneca is in too much haste to cite more of Vergil, the philologist has the time to look deeper. Seneca suppresses much of the couplet, but he cannot prevent the reader from consulting the primary text.

> sed fugit interea, fugit inreparabile tempus,
> singula dum capti circumvectamur amore.
>
> *Georgics* 3.284f

> but it flies meanwhile, it flies irreparable time,
> while we, captivated by love, linger around each detail.

Here, the poet closely resembles the grammarian, who lingers lovingly around every verbal detail. Strikingly, at one point in the epistle, Seneca, a poet in his own right, reformulates the philosophical call with the imperative: *Quod fugit occupandum est*—"What flees must be seized" (*Epistle* 108.27). Bearing this recommendation in mind, one begins to think that it is perhaps the scholar's inclination to linger lovingly that better attends to the philosophical call. In tarrying with singularities, captivated by the love for the word, the philologist stands to seize what flees, if only because he realizes that the words do not flee the page. Words, like the word *fugit*, take the time to occupy Vergil's line twice, surrounding and enclosing what takes place "in the meantime" (*interea*). Although on the level of the message the flight of time cannot be "retrieved" or "restored" (*inreparabile*), on the level of the word it clearly is retrievable: *fugit* *interea* *fugit*. What if the scholar's *occupation* with words, always somehow untimely, is a kind of work more effective than work?

In disrupting the text's continuity so as to listen to the word as a discontinuous voice, philology could be said to approximate a musical sensibility. The lesson—or rather, nonlesson—of this kind of philology would eventually dawn upon Nietzsche, the former aspiring musician, who ultimately found more than enough time to pause and thus give pausing its due:

> Philology is namely that venerable art [*jene ehrwürdige Kunst*], which begs of its votaries [*Verehrer*] one thing above all: to go aside, to take time, to become still, to become slow—it is a goldsmith's art and connoisseurship of the *word* which has nothing but delicate, cautious [*vorsichtige*] work to do and achieves nothing if it does not achieve it *lento*. But for precisely this reason it is more necessary than ever today, by precisely this means does it attract and enchant us most strongly, in the midst of an age of 'work', that is to say, of hurry, of indecent and perspiring hastiness [*Eilfertigkeit*], which wants to 'get everything done' [*fertig werden*] at once, including every old or new book: — this art does not so easily get anything done, it teaches to read *well*, that is to say, to read slowly, deeply, looking cautiously before and aft [*rück- und vorsichtig*], with hidden agendas [*Hintergedanken*], with doors left open, with delicate eyes and fingers . . .[23]

23. Friedrich Nietzsche, 1887 "Preface" to *Daybreak: Thoughts on the prejudices of morality* [1881/1887], R. J. Hollingdale, trans. (Cambridge: Cambridge University Press, 1997), 5 (translation modified); *Morgenröthe*, in KSA, 3: 17: "Philologie nämlich ist jene ehrwürdige Kunst, welche von ihrem Verehrer vor Allem Eins heischt, bei Seite gehn, sich Zeit lassen, still werden, langsam werden—, als eine Goldschmiedekunst und -kennerschaft des *Wortes*, die lauter feine vorsichtige Arbeit abzuthun hat und Nichts erreicht, wenn sie es nicht lento erreicht. Gerade damit aber ist sie heutige nöthiger als je, gerade dadurch zieht sie und bezaubert sie uns

Regarding philology as an "art" and no longer as a science or discipline finally allows Nietzsche to redefine its practitioners as devotees prepared to perform the duties expected of them. "With delicate eyes and fingers," they attend to the service of words rather than enlist words into the hurried service of communicative meaning. On the basis of rushed productivity, their slowness might be regarded as sluggishness, yet from the perspective of philology it is clearly a "good": for "it teaches to read *well* [gut *lesen*]." Proceeding with caution—*Vorsicht*—philologists assume the Epimethean and Promethean roles of peering backward and forward—*rück- und vorsichtig*—which render any completion of sense *provisional*, expressing "hidden agendas" (*Hintergedanken*) that penetrate into the substance of the words that lie "behind the thoughts"—*hinter den Gedanken*—delving into the substrate of meaning that leaves all work unfinished, incomplete, *unfertig*. "In the midst of an age of 'work,'" Nietzsche the philologist proposes a method of idleness, a *désœuvrement* that actively unworks the compulsion to "get everything done" and close up shop. He does so by leaving doors ajar and keeping his ears open. A critic of the times that are frantically fueled by instrumental reason, he resets the tempo to *lento* in order to rein in the industrial and industrious horsepower that rushes to some definitive goal.

Nietzsche's more mature stand on philology, which persistently informs his moral philosophical escapades, was clearly born, like his idea of tragedy, "out of the spirit of music."[24] In an early autobiographical sketch, written while still a student in Leipzig, the decision to take up classical philology is explicitly based on a resolution to stifle hopes of becoming a composer:

> Since my ninth year I was drawn most strongly to music; in those fortunate circumstances in which one does not yet recognize the limits of one's talents and considers everything that one loves to be attainable, I had written down countless compositions and acquired a more than dilettantish knowledge of music theory. Only in the last period of my life at Pforta, in correctly under-

am stärksten, mitten in einem Zeitalter der 'Arbeit,' will sagen: der Hast, der unanständigen und schwitzenden Eilfertigkeit, das mit Allem gleich 'fertig werden' will, auch mit jedem alten und neuen Buche:—sie selbst wird nicht so leicht irgend womit fertig, sie lehrt *gut* lesen, das heisst langsam, tief, rück- und vorsichtig, mit Hintergedanken, mit offen gelassenen Thüren, mit zarten Fingern und Augen lesen . . ." (emphasis and ellipses in text).

24. For a comprehensive overview of Nietzsche's life-long engagement with music, see Georges Liébert, *Nietzsche and Music*, David Pellauer and Graham Parkes, trans. (Chicago: University of Chicago Press, 2004).

> standing myself, did I give up all my artistic plans; and from that point on Philology entered into the gap that consequently opened up.[25]

While granting some postadolescent exaggeration, the passage reveals a quality that persists across Nietzsche's written work. Here, the silencing of music has left a "gap" (*Lücke*) or perhaps a gaping wound that only the study of words could patch. It would be, of course, only a partial healing, one that would never entirely remedy what would never cease from festering. The interruption of music, which yields place to classical philology, should be taken as an extended fermata that resounds long after the final chord is struck.

It is not at all difficult to see how the realm of music continues to exert an intoxicating fascination for the pastor's orphan, particularly after his adoption into Richard Wagner's home, attempting to correct what the philologist comes to characterize as his profession's deafness. Again, musical sensitivity consists in having an ear for the "break":

> That one must not be in doubt about the rhythmically decisive syllables, that one experiences the break [*Brechung*] with any excessively severe symmetry as deliberate and attractive, that one lends a subtle and patient ear to every *staccato* and every *rubato*, that one figures out the meaning in the sequence of vowels and diphthongs and how delicately and richly they can be colored and change colors as they follow each other—who among book-reading Germans has enough good will to acknowledge such duties and demands and to listen to that much art and purpose in language? In the end, one simply does not 'have the ear for that.'[26]

25. Nietzsche, KGA 1/5: 52–53: "Zur Musik nämlich fühlte ich schon seit meinem neunten Jahre den allerstärksten Zug; in jenem glücklichen Zustande, in dem man noch nicht die Grenzen seiner Begabung kennt und alles, was man liebt, auch für erreichbar hält, hatte ich unzählige Compositionen nieder geschrieben und mir eine mehr als dilettantische Kenntniß der musikalischen Theorie erworben. Erst in der letzten Zeit meines Pförtner Lebens gab ich, in richtiger Selbsterkenntniß, alle künstlerischen Lebenspläne auf; in die so enstandene Lücke trat von jetzt ab die Philologie."

26. Nietzsche, *Beyond Good and Evil: Prelude to a Philosophy of the Future*, Walter Kaufmann, trans. (New York: Vintage, 1966), §246, 182; "Dass man über die rhythmisch entscheidenden Silben nicht im Zweifel sein darf, dass man die Brechung der allzustrengen Symmetrie als gewollt und als Reiz fühlt, dass man jedem staccato, jedem rubato ein feines geduldiges Ohr hinhält, dass man den Sinn in der Folge der Vocale und Diphthongen räth, und wie zart und reich sie in ihrem Hintereinander sich färben und umfärben können: wer unter bücherlesenden Deutschen ist

Throughout his philosophical career, Nietzsche applies his "third ear" to those verbal breaks in the history of values, to the "detached notes" and "robbed time"—"every *staccato* and every *rubato*"—that punctuate and puncture dogmatic systems. It is this musical sensitivity that transforms Nietzsche's idiosyncratic approach to philology into an art of interruption, always ready to give pause, always willing to hearken to the voice behind the words, to the "vowels and diphthongs" that do not signify in the strict sense but are for this very reason all the more meaningful; for the message is incarnate in the medium. Adhering to this presemantic yet meaningful phenomenon, Nietzsche alludes to the imperative of his fathers' Redeemer—"He who has ears to hear, let him hear!"[27]

The case of tragedy remains exemplary for Nietzsche, insofar as it proves to be a testing ground for the ear. For in Nietzsche's well-known view, tragedy stages the conflict between the voice and the word, maintaining the difficult tension between Dionysian music and Apollonian form, between choral song and individualized dialogue, before it is silenced by Platonism, before it is suppressed beneath the demands of a resolving *pax philosophica*. In *The Birth of Tragedy*, Nietzsche refers to an aspect of persistent, resonant idleness: "The ecstasy of the Dionysiac state with its annihilation of the usual limitations and borders of existence contains, for as long as it lasts, a *lethargic* element, into which all personal experiences from the past plunge."[28] In other words, Apollonian form, which will eventually give rise to logical schematism, sets the terms that the raving god would break. As Nicole Loraux stresses, Nietzsche's account of the birth of tragedy reveals the "mourning voice" that resounds as something *interminable*, something repetitive and nonappeasable, a shrill tone that thereby "diverts, rejects, or threatens [. . .] the obligations and prohibitions constituting the ideology of the

gutwillig genug, solchergestalt Pflichten und Forderungen anzuerkennen und auf so viel Kunst und Absicht in der Sprache hinzuhorchen? Man hat zuletzt eben 'das Ohr nicht dafür'" (*Jenseits von Gut und Böse*, KSA 5: 189).

27. The phrase occurs multiple times in the Synoptic Gospels, primarily in the "Parable of the Sower" (Mark 4:9, Matt. 13:9, and Luke 8:8), but also in the "Parable of the Wheat and Tares" (Matt. 13:43), in Jesus's comments on the role of John the Baptist (Matt. 11:15), and in the figures of light under a basket (Mark 4:23) and tasteless salt (Luke 14:35). The significance of this line is discussed further below.

28. Nietzsche, *The Birth of Tragedy and Other Writings*, Ronald Speirs, trans. (Cambridge: Cambridge University Press, 1999), 40 (translation modified); "Die Verzückung des dionysischen Zustandes mit seiner Vernichtung der gewöhnlichen Schranken und Grenzen des Daseins enthält nämlich während seiner Dauer ein *lethargisches* Element, in das sich alles persönlich in der Vergangenheit Erlebte eintaucht" (KSA 1: 56).

city-state."[29] For Loraux, whereas civic discourse tends to limit grief, channeling or sublimating lamentation into the persuasive arguments of the funeral oration, tragedy allows the wailing to continue to be heard. It recalls what the state works to forget. Concerned precisely for this voice, ever alert to the sufferings of Dionysus, Nietzsche raises philology's resistance to a musical pitch. His work with words unworks the work of mourning, so that the mourning itself never fades off entirely. As an art of breaking free from the precipitous drive of discourse, philology sides with the breaks that tragedy consistently registers. When others gather their things and head for the exit, satisfied with the feeling that everything has been understood, that all the terms have fallen into place, Nietzsche stays put in the theater, unwilling—like every slow reader—to move on.

Over time, then, Nietzsche learned to embrace the mole-like efforts of philology, which he had once ridiculed. In a succinct aphorism from 1880, Nietzsche notes: "The blind mole comes from a stock of good eyesight—The effect of darkness on the optic nerves."[30] Now, it is the patient burrowing of this nocturnal creature that provides a strategic model for undermining the metaphysical and moral systems that have weakened and mortified human history. In 1886, while he was at work on *On the Genealogy of Morality*, Nietzsche interrupted his merciless explorations to write a preface to *Daybreak*, which first appeared in 1881—an account of the genealogist's method from the field:

> In this book one finds a "subterranean" at work, someone drilling, mining, undermining. One can see him, provided that one has eyes for such work of depth—, how he moves forward slowly, prudently, with gentle inexorability, without showing too much of the hardship that goes along with any long privation of light and air: one could even call him content with this dark work. Does it not seem that some faith is leading him on, that some solace is compensating him? That perhaps he wants to have his own long darkness, something incomprehensible, hidden, enigmatic, because he knows what he will also have: his own morning, his own redemption, his own dawn? [. . .] Certainly, he will turn back: do not ask him, what he wants down there, he

29. Nicole Loraux, *The Mourning Voice: An Essay on Greek Tragedy*, Elizabeth Trapnell Rawlings, trans. (Ithaca: Cornell University Press, 2002), 26.

30. Nietzsche, *Nachlaß*, 1880. "Der blinde Maulwurf stammt vom gut sehenden ab—Wirkung der Dunkelheit auf die Sehnerven" (KSA 9: 109).

> himself will tell you, this apparent Trophonius and Subterranean, when he once again has "become man." One thoroughly unlearns how to keep silent, when one has been a mole, when one has been alone, like him—.[31]

Like a mole—and therefore like a philologist—Nietzsche digs deeply, penetrating through the sediments of history, in order to reach the dubious bases for our moral codes and laws. His eyes accustomed to the dark, he can see where others cannot.[32] Yet we can see him and appreciate his work only "provided we have the eyes for such work of depth." This *katabasis* does indeed have as its ultimate aim a desire to communicate, even if it will be a communication that perfectly reverses the one imparted by the Platonic philosopher: Whereas the philosopher in the *Republic*'s Allegory of the Cave ascends to the light and then must return to the darkness in order to share his enlightenment, Nietzsche's mole-like philologist descends into the dark, promising to return to the light in order to share something "incomprehensible, hidden, enigmatic." What was philosophy must become philology, if only to encourage a ceaseless search into the very foundations of knowledge; for what we know matters little if we cannot evaluate how we know it. Here, the *Maulwurf*, who "chucks up" (*aufwirft*) clods of earth and "raises" (*aufwirft*) too many questions—the figure that was once an object of derisive laughter—now performs a crucial task. The philologist, ever a mole, will also undergo a renewed "incarnation" (*Menschwerdung*)—

31. Nietzsche, *Morgenröthe*:

> In diesem Buche findet man einen "Unterirdischen" an der Arbeit, einen Bohrenden, Grabenden, Untergrabenden. Man sieht ihn, vorausgesetzt, daß man Augen für solche Arbeit der Tiefe hat—, wie er langsam, besonnen, mit sanfter Unerbittlichkeit vorwärts kommt, ohne daß die Not sich allzusehr verriete, welche jede lange Entbehrung von Licht und Luft mit sich bringt: man könnte ihn selbst bei seiner dunklen Arbeit zufrieden nennen. Scheint es nicht, daß irgendein Glaube ihn führt, ein Trost entschädigt? Daß er vielleicht seine eigne lange Finsternis haben will, sein Unverständliches, Verborgenes, Rätselhaftes, weil er weiß, was er auch haben wird: seinen eignen Morgen, seine eigne Erlösung, seine eigne Morgenröte? . . Gewiß, er wird zurückkehren: fragt ihn nicht, was er da unten will, er wird es euch selbst schon sagen, dieser scheinbare Trophonios und Unterirdische, wenn er erst wieder "Mensch geworden" ist. Man verlernt gründlich das Schweigen, wenn man so lange, wie er, Maulwurf war, allein war—. (KSA 3: 11; my translation)

32. For a provocative reading of the figure of the *Maulwurf* in the history of philosophy, see David Farrell Krell, "Die philosophische Wühlarbeit bei Kant, Hegel und Nietzsche," *boundary 2*, vol. 9 (1981), 155–67. On the metaphorological implications, see Karlheinz Stierle, "Der Maulwurf im Bildfeld: Versuch zu einer Metapherngeschichte," *Archiv für Begriffsgeschichte* 26 (1982), 101–43.

wenn er erst wieder "Mensch geworden" ist ("when he once again has 'become human'")—and thereby evangelize his own "redemption." The mole becomes flesh and dwells among us.

Nietzsche's renewed engagement with philology, testing out the resonances underground, can no longer be viewed as opposed to life, but rather as a source of vitality, insofar as it eliminates the moralizing prejudices and dogmas that have restricted life for so long. And when his keen eyes are not probing the subterranean depths, undermining and disturbing the historical groundwork of moral constructions, when instead, he finds himself in mountainous regions far above the world—for example, "6000 feet beyond mankind and time"[33]—his mind is struck by sublime thoughts. Two distinct trajectories are therefore in play. Whereas the mole-like activity of philology sends Nietzsche *downwards* into the depths of genealogical exploration, the vision of a future philosophy drives him *upwards* into dizzying climes. Thus, in Nietzsche's *Also sprach Zarathustra* (1883), the prophet is portrayed as someone who "enjoyed his spirit and his solitude" in the mountains for ten long years, quite familiar with bright, lofty ideas, yet also as someone who must *condescend* in order to share his vision with those capable of receiving it, just like the sun that "sets" (*untergeht*) every night in order to illuminate the underground. That Zarathustra is a religious founder who embarks on his mission at thirty years of age and communicates his teaching primarily in parables, already suggests similarity with the condescending figure of Christ, even if Zarathustra represents views "in place of" (*anti*) Christianity. Like Christ, who descended from heaven, and like the philologist, who reemerged from the depths of language, "Zarathustra wants to become man (*Mensch werden*) again."[34] The path downward and the path upward come together in Zarathustra's "incarnation" (*Menschwerdung*).

Two interrelated ideas in particular take hold of Zarathustra during the time spent on high: the revelation that "God is dead" and the enigmatic Thought of Eternal Return. In the autobiographical account from *Ecce Homo* (1888), Nietzsche relates how the latter idea occurred to him suddenly in August 1881, high in the Alps, near the village of Sils Maria in the Swiss Engandin—the very idea that, if we take Nietzsche at his word, provided the singular inspiration for his *Zarathustra*: It is "the fundamental conception of the work, the Thought of Eternal Return [*der Ewige-Wiederkunfts-Gedanke*], this highest formula of affir-

33. Nietzsche, *Ecce Homo*, KSA 6: 335.

34. Nietzsche, "Zarathustras Vorrede," in *Also sprach Zarathustra*, KSA 4: 11–12.

mation, which can ever be reached."[35] It is a thought moreover that seizes the flight of time, otherwise irreparable, which invites a heroic affirmation of life.

This singular epiphany is described in the third part of *Also sprach Zarathustra,* in the section titled "On the Vision and Riddle" (*Vom Gesicht und Räthsel*). Here, we find the prophet arduously climbing along a rocky path, "trampling over the stone [*den Stein zertretend*], which caused his foot to slip," ever "upwards" (*aufwärts*) to the highest peak. The ascent is not without struggle:

> Upwards: —defying the spirit who dragged his foot downwards (*abwärts*), dragged it towards the abyss (*abgrundwärts*), the spirit of gravity, my devil and arch-enemy. Upwards: —although he sat on me, half dwarf, half mole (*Maulwurf*); lame; making lame; dripping lead into my ear, leaden thoughts into my brain.[36]

The struggle is internal, a *psychomachia,* with two inclinations battling over Zarathustra's soul: the will to ascend countered by a dwarfish, mole-like instinct that pulls him toward the depths. Like a philologist, who makes everything *difficult* (*schwer*), this adversarial "spirit of gravity" (*Geist der Schwere*) rides upon the philosopher's shoulders and weighs him down, taunting the desire for loftiness:

> "O Zarathustra," he whispered mockingly, syllable by syllable; "you philosopher's stone [*Stein der Weisheit*]! You threw yourself up high, but every stone that is thrown must — fall! [. . .] Sentenced to yourself and to your own stoning (*Steinigung*): O Zarathustra, you threw the stone far indeed, — but it will fall back on *yourself*!"[37]

35. Nietzsche, *Ecce Homo*. "Die Grundconception des Werks, der Ewige-Wiederkunfts-Gedanke, diese höchste Formel der Bejahung, die überhaupt erreicht werden kann" (KSA 6: 335).

36. Nietzsche, *Also sprach Zarathustra*. "Aufwärts: —dem Geiste zum Trotz, der ihn [den Fuß] abwärts zog, abgrundwärts zog, dem Geiste der Schwere, meinem Teufel und Erzfeinde. Aufwärts: —obwohl er auf mir sass, halb Zwerg, halb Maulwurf; ahm; lähmend; Blei durch mein Ohr, Bleitropfen-Gedanken in mein Hirn träufelnd" (KSA 4: 198).

37. "Oh Zarathustra, raunte er höhnisch Silb' um Silbe, du Stein der Weisheit! Du warfst dich hoch, aber jeder geworfene Stein muss — fallen! [. . .] Verurtheilt zu dir selber und zur eignen Steinigung: oh Zarathustra, weit warfst du ja den Stein, — aber auf *dich* wird er zurückfallen!" (KSA 4: 198)

As the Spirit of Gravity, the *Maulwurf* knows that no matter how high an idea may be thrown (*geworfen*), it always falls back to the ground. Even with the most sublime ambition, climbing ever upwards (*aufwärts*), even with the most elevated determination, there is always another question, another problem "to be raised" (*aufgeworfen*). The philologist knows much about problems, how every *problēma* is a stone "thrown in front" (*pro* + *beblēmenon*), obstructing the climber's path. All too readily, the "stone of wisdom" (*Stein der Weisheit*)—a wisdom that should be set in stone—becomes a missile used in the philosopher's own "stoning." Perhaps it is philology alone that can save philosophy from *petrification* (*Versteinerung*)?

Nietzsche's parable proceeds to relate how the mole-like dwarf eventually fell silent and how this silence—analogous to the silence of Dostoevsky's Christ—tormented the prophet bent on ascent: "His silence oppressed me [. . .]. I climbed, I climbed, I dreamed, I thought."[38] Finally, Zarathustra plucked up the "courage" (*Muth*) to confront the fiend once and for all. "Courage [. . .] is the best slayer, courage, which attacks (*angreift*): which slays even death."[39] Attuned to the German text, one might hear how Zarathustra *grasps* and *understands* (*greift* and *begreift*) the situation and how he has the *courage* (*Muth*) or even perhaps a myth (*Mythos*) that, by employing *concepts* (*Begriffe*), is capable of *attack* (*Angriff*). At any rate, Zarathustra summons the courage to put the oppressive protests to rest, yet not without hesitation: "In such a saying, however, there is a lot of ringing play (*klingendes Spiel*). He who has ears, let him hear (*Wer Ohren hat, der höre*)!"[40] Zarathustra has the courage to proceed along the stony path, yet something continues to be bothersome, a ringing in the ear (*Klingeln im Ohr*). Despite the fact—or perhaps precisely because—he has lead in his ears, Zarathustra dips down into Christian Scripture: "He who has ears to hear, let him hear!" What do we learn when we listen more closely? When we dig a little deeper?

The phrase occurs in all three of the synoptic Gospels, used by Jesus to conclude the Parable of the Sower, for example in Luke 8:

38. "Sein Schweigen aber drückte mich [. . .]. Ich stieg, ich stieg, ich träumte, ich dachte" (KSA 4: 198).

39. "Muth aber ist der beste Todtschläger, Muth, der angreift: der schlägt noch den Tod todt" (KSA 4: 199).

40. "In solchem Spruche aber ist viel klingendes Spiel. Wer Ohren hat, der höre" (KSA 4: 199).

"A sower went out to sow his seed. And as he sowed, some fell by the wayside; and it was trampled down, and the birds of the air devoured it. Some fell on rock; and as soon as it sprang up, it withered away because it lacked moisture. And some fell among thorns, and the thorns sprang up with it and choked it. But others fell on good ground, sprang up, and yielded a crop a hundredfold." When He had said these things He cried, "He who has ears to hear, let him hear!" (Luke 8:5–8 [NKJV])[41]

The *way* this tale of the word's insemination is told already attracts the ear. Most translators have therefore tried to retain the particularities of the verbal form. In addition to the polyptoton of the conclusion (Ὁ ἔχων ὦτα ἀκούειν ἀκουέτω [*ho echōn ōta akouein akouetō*]; *qui habet aures audiendi audiat* [Vulgate]; *Wer Ohren hat, zu hören, der höre* [Luther]; *He who has ears to hear, let him hear* [NKJV]), there is the striking use of assonance, alliteration, and polyptoton of the incipit (Ἐξῆλθεν ὁ σπείρων τοῦ σπεῖραι τὸν σπόρον αὐτοῦ [*exēlthen ho speirōn tou speirai ton sporon autou*]; *exiit qui seminat seminare semem suum*; *Es ging ein Säemann aus, zu säen seinen Samen*; *A sower went out to sow his seed*). Emphasis is placed therefore on the way the parable is verbally formulated, even though, on the level of content, the "way" (*hodos, via, Weg*) is precisely where the seed will *not* flourish, just as it will not flourish "upon rock" (*epi tēn petran, supra petram*); or "among thorns" (*en mesōi tōn akanthōn, inter spinas*). Only when the seed is sown into "good ground" (*eis tēn gēn tēn agathēn, in terram bonam*) will it bear profitable "fruit" (*karpon, fructum*). However one might understand the meaning of this "good ground," it is clear that the Word in itself is not sufficient, insofar as it relies on fruitful reception.

Similarly, the parable is not sufficient, which is why Jesus subsequently offers to his disciples a clarifying interpretation. To them, his intimate friends, "it

41. The SBL Greek New Testament reads: Ἐξῆλθεν ὁ σπείρων τοῦ σπεῖραι τὸν σπόρον αὐτοῦ. καὶ ἐν τῷ σπείρειν αὐτὸν ὃ μὲν ἔπεσεν παρὰ τὴν ὁδόν, καὶ κατεπατήθη καὶ τὰ πετεινὰ τοῦ οὐρανοῦ κατέφαγεν αὐτό. καὶ ἕτερον κατέπεσεν ἐπὶ τὴν πέτραν, καὶ φυὲν ἐξηράνθη διὰ τὸ μὴ ἔχειν ἰκμάδα. καὶ ἕτερον ἔπεσεν ἐν μέσῳ τῶν ἀκανθῶν, καὶ συμφυεῖσαι αἱ ἄκανθαι ἀπέπνιξαν αὐτό. καὶ ἕτερον ἔπεσεν εἰς τὴν γῆν τὴν ἀγαθήν, καὶ φυὲν ἐποίησεν καρπὸν ἑκατονταπλασίονα. ταῦτα λέγων ἐφώνει· Ὁ ἔχων ὦτα ἀκούειν ἀκουέτω. And in the Vulgate: "exiit qui seminat seminare semen suum et dum seminat aliud cecidit secus viam et conculcatum est et volucres caeli comederunt illud et aliud cecidit supra petram et natum aruit quia non habebat humorem et aliud cecidit inter spinas et simul exortae spinae suffocaverunt illud et aliud cecidit in terram bonam et ortum fecit fructum centuplum haec dicens clamabat qui habet aures audiendi audiat."

has been given to know the mysteries of the kingdom of God, but to the rest it is given in parables, that 'Seeing they may not see, and hearing they may not understand'" (Luke 8:10 [NKJV]). Apparently, neither the outsiders, who hear the parable, nor the insiders, the disciples who also hear the parable and yet are about to receive a supplemental interpretation, have the ears to hear what the parable is attempting to proclaim, its *kērygma*. Moreover, before telling his closed circle what the parable means, Jesus alludes to the Book of Isaiah, where God commands the prophet to "blind the heart of the people [. . .] lest they see with their eyes, and hear with their ears" (Isaiah 6:10). The passage, cited in all three of the synoptic Gospels, is severe. As we have seen, it appears as the injunction pronounced by Emily Dickinson's doctor who, in preventing her from reading, "might as well have said, 'Eyes be blind', 'heart be still.'"[42] Just as the God of the Hebrew Bible sent His prophet, so Jesus communicates in parables in order to "blind the heart of the people" (Vulgate: *excaeca cor populi huius*). In hearing only the manifest parable, the outsiders are condemned to remain outside, which is precisely where the disciples would be if Jesus did not offer them the key to the latent "mysteries." The privileged inside is created by the very act of providing this latent sense.[43] Even if the initiates do not have the ears to hear, they have the benefit of an explanation from the Word Incarnate, who Himself embodies the literal-carnal words of the parable and the figurative-spiritual words of the interpretation.

With the following explanation, Jesus heals His disciples' blindness and deafness. The terms from the Vulgate are included for further clarity:

> "Now the parable is this: The seed is the word of God. Those by the wayside (*secus viam*) are the ones who hear; then the devil comes and takes away the word out of their hearts, lest they should believe and be saved. But the ones on the rock (*supra petram*) *are those* who, when they hear, receive the word with joy; and these have no root, who believe for a while and in time of temptation fall away. Now the ones *that* fell among thorns (*in spinis*) are those who, when they have heard, go out and are choked with cares, riches, and pleasures of life,

42. Emily Dickinson to Joseph Lyman, in Sewall, *The Lyman Letters*, 76.

43. This role of interpretation in the Parable of the Sower, particularly as it relates to outsiders and insiders, is the major theme in Frank Kermode, *The Genesis of Secrecy: On the Interpretation of Narrative* (Cambridge: Harvard University Press, 1979).

> and bring no fruit to maturity. But the ones *that* fell on the good ground are those who, having heard the word with a noble and good heart, keep *it* and bear fruit with patience." (Luke 8:11–15 [NKJV])

Everyone, then, has ears to hear the word of God—ὁ λόγος τοῦ θεοῦ, *verbum Dei*—yet the contingencies of reception limit the opportunities for this word to flourish, for this divine seed or *semen*—this *logos spermatikos*—to be fertile, to disseminate further, from one generation to the next. The implicit problem with this explanation, however, is that it too, precisely because it is expressed verbally, would require a further explanation. Interpretations of words are themselves composed of words, which are presumed to have a manifest form and latent content. Hermeneutics breeds hermeneutics. A number of lessons may be drawn. First, exclusive attention to the "way" prevents the vital message from spreading, because too much time spent "along the way" gives the devil opportunity to steal the word from the heart. Second, transforming the word into solid rock may last for a while, but, having no "roots," the seed ultimately caves to temptation. And finally, exposing the word to the "cares, riches, and pleasures of life" denies the seed sufficient nourishment. In sum, the way is exceedingly *problematic*, whether it causes distraction, petrification, or competing demands. Moreover, that the way is problematic is an even greater problem, for in order to receive the message, one must attend to the way the message is transmitted. Even the good path that leads to the word's fructification must first "hear" it. The way is beset with problems, but it is a path that must be traveled.

The Gospel account in Luke underscores how both the meaning and the means are emphasized: "When he was saying (*legōn, dicens*) these things, he cried (*ephōnei, clamabat*), 'He who has ears to hear, let him hear!'" Here, a distinction appears to be made between the message, transmitted by participial forms of *speaking* (*legōn, dicens*), and the medium, conveyed by indicative forms of *vocalizing* (*ephōnei, clamabat*). We recall Augustine's gloss on John 3:30, cited in chapter 3, where he distinguishes between the *voice* (*vox*) that is merely *crying* (*clamans*) and the *word* (*verbum*) that *speaks* (*dicit*).[44] As Augustine explains, "the voice precedes the Word," just as the Baptist—a *vox clamans in deserto*—announced the advent of Christ, and yet "makes possible the understanding of the Word." As in the Seneca epistle, the point is that one must depart from the way by adhering to the way. In listening to the way, one learns to leave the way

44. Augustine, Sermon 288, cited in Dolar, *A Voice and Nothing More*.

behind—an achievement, however, that is possible only by listening. The two distinct modes—marked by the dual verbal forms of speech and voice, speaking and crying—must cohere, just as the two distinct natures, human and divine, cohere in the *coincidentia oppositorum* that is Christ, the way and the life. Should one pay exclusive attention to the way, the seminal message will never take root.

Nietzsche's Zarathustra, who cites from the Parable of the Sower ("Wer Ohren hat, der höre!")—Zarathustra, who suffers from a ringing in the ear—struggles to ascend to the idea, but is obstructed by many rocky problems: not only the slipperiness of the stony path, but also his obstinate desire to discover the "philosopher's stone" (*Stein der Weisheit*), which leads to his own "stoning." One may therefore focus on the specific problem, in Jesus's parable, of seed that falls "upon rock" (*supra petram*), for it may include, provided we have ears to hear it, the ecclesiological determinations of the Word as pronounced by the Church—the Church, which, as we hear elsewhere, will be built "upon the rock" (*super hanc petram*) that is Peter. As the Vulgate renders it: *Tu es Petrus et super hanc petram aedificabo ecclesiam meam* ("You are Peter, and upon this rock I shall build my church," Matthew 16:18 [NKJV]). As a rock, Peter is a sturdy foundation, the very basis of the Church, an unshakeable, secure support for the institution. In giving Simon the fisherman the name of Peter, Jesus confers this consolidating role and baptizes his disciple into the service of securing the Church and thereby securing salvation. And Peter wants to be this rock, proud to know that the Church will be built *super hanc petram*. He is entirely content with the identity that he obtains from his Messiah, always eager to demonstrate his loyalty, to uphold his duty to safeguard the message of redemption. Yet can the inseminating word bear fruit *super hanc petram*?

The adamant foundation that Peter represents is precisely what is undermined and rendered weak by the burrowing of moles that are blind to the message. As we know, Peter, precisely in his obstinacy, is not always innocent of violence. The account of Jesus's arrest in the Garden of Gethsemane, which marks the beginning of the great Passion, serves as a fitting illustration. In the version recorded in the Gospel of John, when the Roman soldiers arrive with the temple priests, it is Peter who hastily draws his sword and cuts off the right ear of the high priest's servant, Malchus. This rash and violent act works as foil against the superior calmness of Jesus, who has already courageously accepted his fate. *Mitte gladium in vaginam!* Jesus orders in the Vulgate: "Put your sword into its sheath! Shall I not drink the cup which my Father has given me?" (John 18:11 [NKJV]). In the report provided by Luke, Jesus lays his hand upon the servant's wound and heals it, making this event the last miracle the Messiah performs before the Resurrection (Luke 22:51). It would also count as the only miracle that remedies something human-inflicted. Throughout his ministry, Jesus heals the blind and the cripple, he exorcises demons and even raises Lazarus from the dead—but repairing the ear of Malchus corrects an ill wrought by human violence alone. The uniqueness of the episode attests to its strangeness. Why, indeed, the ear? A lunge at the chest, a swipe at the arm, a slash across the belly, would all be expected—but an attack on the ear begs credibility. As a mimetic representation, it disrupts one's sense of verisimilitude.

Unless, of course, the episode comprises an allegory, something more intellectual than referential—specifically, an allegory that pertains to the problem of security: how audible experience, how the very act of listening, poses a threat to security projects of all sorts, including those that aim to determine knowledge and truth, which have arguably motivated metaphysics since its inception. As Philippe Lacoue-Labarthe has shown, in Plato's *Republic*, philosophy must convert audible experience into a *vision*: the "listeners," as Socrates explains and as Lacoue-Labarthe emphasizes, must possess the "antidote" or *pharmakon* of "knowledge" or "sight"—for in Greek, "to know" means "to have seen" (*oida*); mimesis must be "specularized"; "one must correct the (vulnerable) hearing with sight."[45] The guardians, educated in the "internal and external protection of the State" (101), must train their sights on the Ideal precisely by being cured of audition. If the stability of the polis and the soundness of the citizenry are to be maintained, the guardians must essentially cut off their ears.

As for the Gospel story, Peter, armed with his sword, behaves very much like a faithful *phylax*, ready to defend his ideal, if not his philosopher-king. But Jesus renounces this prophylactic mode and chides his disciple—"Do you think that I cannot appeal to my Father, and he will at once send me more than twelve legions of angels?" (Matthew 26:53 [NKJV]). Jesus chooses not to call upon his own security forces, which would be unfruitful or infertile, and instead orders Peter to revaginate his weapon. Jesus's rebuke and what follows would seem to attempt to remind Peter that he is still also Simon or Shimon, a name from the Hebrew word for hearing. In the Jewish tradition, the word resonates most immediately with *Shema*, the first word (and title) of the prayer from Deuteronomy (6:4) that ought to be recited at the beginning and end of each day: *Shema*

45. Philippe Lacoue-Labarthe, "Typography," in *Typography: Mimesis, Philosophy, Politics*, Christopher Fynsk, trans. (Cambridge: Harvard University Press, 1989), 100–101.

Yisrael (שְׁמַע יִשְׂרָאֵל)—"Hear, O Israel, the Lord our God, the Lord is one." Is it possible that in desiring to be the secure foundation of the Church, Peter wants to forget or suppress his past life as Shimon, as a Hebrew listener? Is it not the case that he ignores his first name as one might ignore a haunting melody? Is this why he wants to slice off the ear of Malchus, the high priest's servant, why he wants to prevent all Hebrew listening, to cut away all Hebrew ears, including perhaps his own? If Peter were a good listener, he might have heeded the words of the Parable of the Sower, which explains how the seed that falls *supra petram* has no roots and invariably withers.

Peter the auricide appears to be a symptom of denial and phonophobia. Jesus, who willingly accepts the imminent Passion, had already prophesied that Peter's certainty would be shaken, that his rock-hard commitment would suffer and fall into vulnerability, precisely by denying his relationship to his teacher. "Truly, I say to you, the cock will not crow, till you have denied me three times" (John 13: 38 [NKJV]). In John's account, the scene is explicitly linked to the mutilation in the garden: "One of the servants of the high priest, a kinsman of the man whose ear Peter had cut off, asked, 'Did I not see you in the garden with him?' Peter again denied it; and at once the cock crowed" (John 18:26–27 [NKJV]). At sunrise, at the time when the *Shema* is to be pronounced, Peter is compelled to attend to the ringing in his ears, to remember that he is still Shimon and not simply a rock, not simply an identity chiseled, as it were, into stone.

One could go on along these burrowed trails, which rhizomatically prevent any text from constructing a secure body of knowledge, pulling down every thought and every dream that tries to ascend to unimpeachable heights. As the mole-like dwarf reminds Zarathustra, every stone, no matter how high it has been thrown, always falls to the ground. Every hardened resolution, every stone—be it the "philosopher's stone" or the "rock" upon which the Christian Church was built—strives toward elevation by coopting elements and fragments that compose the resolution, while also sowing the seeds of its collapse. The point would appear to insist on maintaining both trajectories: the integrative ascent toward the Word and the disintegrating descent back to the words: From *logos* to *logos*, and back. The notion that "the road up and down are one and the same" (ὁδὸς ἄνω κάτω μία καὶ ὡυτή), accredited to Heraclitus,[46] seems to address this dynamic interaction, which limits either extreme: saving words

46. Heraclitus, Fr. 60, in G. S. Kirk, J. E. Raven, and M. Schofield, eds., *The Presocratic Philosophers* (Cambridge: Cambridge University Press, 1957), 188.

from senseless, aimless rummaging, while preventing the Word from lifeless, bloodless petrification. Is that what Nietzsche's text wants us to hear?

Returning to the *Zarathustra* chapter, "Vom Gesicht und Räthsel" ("On the Vision and Riddle"), we read that, after the prophet has silenced the silent dwarf by means of deadly courage, he happens upon a "gateway [*Thorweg*] with two faces [*Gesichter*]":

> "See this gateway! Dwarf!" I continued: "It has two faces. Two paths [*Wege*] come together here: no one has yet followed them to the end. This long lane back: it lasts an eternity. And that long lane leading out—that is another eternity. They contradict each other, these paths; they simply snub each other: — and here, it is at this gateway where they come together. The name of the gateway is written above: 'Moment' [*Augenblick*]."[47]

The prophet had resolved to kill off the bothersome dwarf, but the mole-like creature cannot be written off so readily. The sudden appearance of the gateway causes Zarathustra to pause and forget his anger. As we soon learn, it is an epiphany: the very "moment" where he will be struck by the idea of "eternal return."

Rather than discuss this text, in relation to other descriptions in *Zarathustra* and in *The Gay Science* (*Die fröhliche Wissenschaft* [1882]), it is sufficient to note that here, in the *Zarathustra* episode, the *arrival* or *Ankunft* to this "fundamental conception" of the *Ewige-Wiederkunft* is in fact the meeting of two "ways" (*Wege*).[48] Perhaps they can be identified in accordance with Heraclitus's

47. "Siehe diesen Thorweg! Zwerg! sprach ich weiter: "der hat zwei Gesichter. Zwei Wege kommen hier zusammen: die gieng noch Niemand zu Ende. Diese lange Gasse zurück: die währt eine Ewigkeit. Und jene lange Gasse hinaus — das ist eine andre Ewigkeit. Sie widersprechen sich, diese Wege; sie stossen sich gerade vor den Kopf: — und hier, an diesem Thorwege, ist es, wo sie zusammen kommen. Der Name des Thorwegs steht oben geschrieben 'Augenblick'" (KSA 4: 199–200).

48. The scholarship on Nietzsche's concept is vast, beginning with Heidegger's Nietzsche seminars, held from 1936 to 1940: Martin Heidegger, *Nietzsche*, vol. 1 (Pfullingen: Neske, 1961) [*Nietzsche*, vol. 1, David Farrell Krell, trans. (San Francisco: HarperCollins, 1991)]. See also Pierre Klossowski, *Nietzsche et le cercle vicieux* (Paris: Mercure de France, 1969) [*Nietzsche and the Vicious Circle*, Daniel W. Smith, trans. (Chicago: University of Chicago Press, 1997)]. Comprehensive and insightful discussions include Günter Abel, *Nietzsche: Die Dynamik der Willen zur Macht und die ewige Wiederkehr*, 2nd ed. (Berlin: de Gruyter, 1998). See also James Winchester, *Nietzsche's Aesthetic Turn: Reading Nietzsche after Heidegger, Deleuze, and Derrida* (Albany: SUNY Press, 1994); Oliver Dier, "Die Verwandlung der Wiederkunft," *Nietzsche-Studien* 30 (2001), 133–74; and Melanie Shepherd, "Affirmation and Mortal Life: Nietzsche's Eternal

image of the *anabasis* and *katabasis*, which, being "one and the same," may provide the model for Nietzsche's thought of "the eternal return of the same." Yet whereas the Heraclitian image suggests a single road, which one may travel either upwards or downwards, Nietzsche emphasizes that there are two distinct ways, contradicting each other and snubbing each other for eternity. Even if Nietzsche will later admit, with his qualifying emphasis, that, "Zarathustra's lesson *could* have also been taught by Heraclitus," we are struck with the fact that, in *Zarathustra*, each way leads to another way.[49] The image of the *single* road implies that the part or fragment of the journey—sometimes up, sometimes down—presupposes an *a priori* whole, which can thus be broken into stages; while the image of *two* different roads, even though they meet for a moment, implies that the fragment is prior, that any whole is a constructed ideal, and thereby forever under threat of failure.[50] Here, an important contrast can be made with the Christian Parable of the Sower, which distinguishes between the means and the meaning, the transmitting voice and the transmitted *logos*, the way and the destination. In the *Zarathustra* episode, there is no destination, no ultimate meaning, not even one that might be qualified or compromised by a pull back down to the mediating form. This absence of meaning, this *nihilism*, is precisely what Nietzsche consistently affirms. It is an affirmation, moreover, that boldly differentiates him from the European nihilists, from the "last men" mired in moral apathy and incapable of striving because there is nothing for which to strive. Whereas the nihilists (like Dostoevsky's Ivan) renounce a world without meaning, Nietzsche embraces it, dancing.[51]

The "Vision" (*Gesicht*) of the episode's title leads to a gateway with two contradictory "faces" (*Gesichter*). Although gates are for passing through and roads are for traveling toward a destination, the goal here is simply the gate and the ways. While reflecting on this vision, "frightened by his own thoughts and hid-

---

Return and the Death of Zarathustra," *Philosophy Today* 55 (2011), 22–36, which includes useful bibliography.

49. Nietzsche, *Ecce Homo*. "Diese Lehre Zarathustra's *könnte* zuletzt auch schon von Heraklit gelehrt worden sein" (KSA 6: 313; Nietzsche's emphasis).

50. The a priori status of the fragment plays a significant role in Maurice Blanchot's important readings of Nietzsche. See Blanchot, "Nietzsche et l'écriture fragmentaire," in *L'entretien infini* (Paris: Gallimard, 1969), 227–55. In Gilles Deleuze's reading, the primary tension in Nietzsche's thought is the one that obtains between "active" and "reactive" forces: Deleuze, *Nietzsche and Philosophy*, Hugh Tomlinson, trans. (New York: Columbia University Press, 1983), 40.

51. See David Rowe, "The Eternal Return of the Same: Nietzsche's 'Value-Free' Revaluation of All Values," *Parrhesia* 15 (2012), 71–86.

den agendas [*vor meinen eigenen Gedanken und Hintergedanken*]" (KSA 4: 201), Zarathustra is interrupted a second time, now by the howling of a dog. The vision, or perhaps even the ideal, of collapsing all time into a single *Augenblick*—this thought or hidden agenda, which is the product of his *own* mind (*meinen eigenen Gedanken und Hintergedanken*)—is disturbed by an intrusive sound from the outside. Yet the prophet's "thought ran back," as if to counter this call from an external source, as if to block his ears. Specifically, he thinks of a dog from his childhood, which howled in the same exact way; and he "takes pity" (*es mich erbarmte*, KSA 4: 201), commiserating with the dog he now hears nearby. With this, however, the initial vision vanishes: "Where did the dwarf go now? And the gateway? [. . .] And all the whispering? Was I dreaming, then? Did I wake up?"[52] Zarathustra is disoriented. His thoughts have scattered, and he knows not "where to" (*wohin*).

Without resolving the nature of the preceding vision, Zarathustra has awoken from his own thoughts and resigns himself to the fact that he is entirely alone: a solipsistic, emptied subject. But then, at this point along the way, he discovers a *man* in the flesh: "A young shepherd I saw, writhing, choking, convulsive, with face distorted, and a heavy black snake hung out of his mouth."[53] Despite his own nausea, Zarathustra feels compelled to tear the snake from the young man's throat, to bite it off. Here, we are told, is the explicit "vision" of the title, the "vision" and the "riddle":

> You who delight in riddles! Guess for me this riddle that I once saw, interpret for me this vision [*Gesicht*] of the loneliest man! For it was a vision and a foreseeing: — *what* did I see once in a parable? And *who* is he, who is yet to come one day? *Who* is the shepherd, into whose throat the snake thus crawled? *Who* is the man, into whose throat all that is heaviest, blackest [*alles Schwerste, Schwärzeste*] will crawl?[54]

52. "Wohin war jetzt Zwerg? und Thorweg? Und Spinne? Und alles Flüstern? Träumte ich denn? Wachte ich auf?" (KSA 4: 201).

53. "Einen jungen Hirten sah ich, sich windend, würgend, zuckend, verzerrten Antlitzes, dem eine schwarze schwere Schlange aus dem Munde hieng" (KSA 4: 201).

54. "Ihr Räthsel-Frohen! So rathet mir doch das Räthsel, das ich damals schaute, so deutet mir doch das Gesicht des Einsamsten! Denn ein Gesicht war's und ein Vorhersehn: — *was* sah ich damals im Gleichnisse? Und *wer* ist, der einst noch kommen muss? *Wer* ist der Hirt, dem also die Schlange in den Schlund kroch? *Wer* ist der Mensch, dem also alles Schwerste, Schwärzeste in den Schlund kriechen wird?" (KSA 4: 202).

For a text that persistently sets up each path to lead to yet another path, it is appropriate to answer its questions with more questions. Like Dostoevsky's Inquisitor, Zarathustra asks if this shepherd is the "Coming One." Is this vision, then, an eschatological vision? Is the "Thought of Eternal Return [*Wiederkunft*]" the "Second Coming"—in German: *Wiederkunft*? Is this why Zarathustra speaks in parables, and even cites the Christian Gospels? That the vision is eschatological appears to be certain, underscoring the end of time, the end of history, when all time collapses into a single eternal moment. The Last Judgment falls on mankind, whose end is here envisioned; and the Coming One is the *Übermensch*, who transcends all of mankind's restrictions, limitations, and prejudices. The shepherd whom Zarathustra encounters, the one who jolts him from his own thoughts, may in fact be the "good shepherd," who takes upon himself the vilest, "heaviest and blackest" of mankind's sins—the snake that chokes him, trying to prevent his arrival. Yet this Christ is one who comes, only now that God is dead, now that transcendence has proven to be vacuous. He is the word-in-the-flesh, the way that is also the life, because the Word no longer refers to anything that transcends him.

At the conclusion of the episode, the young shepherd bites off the snake on his own, leaps up as someone transfigured: "someone transformed, someone luminescent, who *laughed!*"—*ein Verwandelter, ein Umleuchteter, welcher lachte!* (KSA 4: 202)—a laughter that Zarathustra has never before heard on earth. Perhaps it is the laughter that he was always longing for, striving and burrowing, erecting and disassembling: the philosopher and the philologist in one. Along these lines, Pierre Klossowski insists that Nietzsche's Thought of Eternal Return be regarded as an initially physiological experience, which only subsequently comes to be articulated through multiple voices—here in *Zarathustra*, in *The Gay Science*, in Nietzsche's notebooks and letters—voices that consequently frustrate integration. In order to derive a body of knowledge from these heterogeneous statements, expressions, and personae, one must dress or even camouflage their carnal source.[55] The preservation of the body, which aims to stabilize and protect the conscious organism, requires an asceticism or a mortification of the flesh that Nietzsche understands as a defusing or depletion of the Will to Power, which constantly strives to discharge energy and not restrain it. The "will of the flesh"—the *voluntas carnis*, as it appears in the Johannine Prologue (1:13)—exceeds all attempts to incorporate it into a stable, immutable body.

55. Klossowski, *Nietzsche and the Vicious Circle*, 56.

Whenever philosophy, in its noble ascent, struggles to establish a sound body of knowledge, philology, in its mole-like descent, gnaws away at the base, causing this statuesque body to tumble.

For this reason, the epiphany at Sils Maria held out to Nietzsche the promise of a transformative moment. As he noted around this time, "If you absorb [*einverleibst*] into yourself the thought of thoughts, then it will transform [*verwandeln*] you."[56] The verb *einverleiben* denotes taking something into one's "living, carnal body" (*Leib*). Although it could well be translated as *incorporate, einverleiben* speaks more to an idea of swallowing, ingestion, and corporeal assimilation: whereby the foreign element taken in does not simply occupy the *body* (*Körper*), but rather is worked into the very texture of the body's flesh. In the *Zarathustra* episode, the concluding "vision and riddle" introduces the young shepherd as figure capable of this *absorption* (*Einverleibung*), biting off the snake, which has halfway crawled into his throat. Upon ingesting this creature of gravity, we see him "transformed": no longer "writhing" and "gagging," but instead, "laughing."

What the shepherd ingests may be the mocking tone of the "Spirit of gravity," the gravity (*Schwere*) that weighs the philosopher-of-the-future down: a burden, a mole-dwarf that rides on the shoulders of one who longs for ascension. By absorbing this figure of "all that is heaviest, blackest" (*alles Schwerste, Schwärzeste*), the integral body of the young man comes to assume the excessive flesh that disintegrates him and thus transforms him into an *Übermensch*, laughing at himself: a Christic figure—one presented in place of (*anti*) the Christ of Christianity.

Whereas Nietzsche regarded the Christ of Christianity as a preacher of revenge and *ressentiment*, encouraging the weak to long for just rewards in an afterlife that is life-negating, Zarathustra comes across as a Christic figure who teaches the delusional nature of this afterlife, its emptiness, for "God is dead." Although the nihilists—the "last men"—have long recognized this evacuation of transcendent meaning, they, like Christians, have renounced the world. In contrast, Zarathustra sees how the *Übermensch* will celebrate life, discovering an endless stream of shifting meanings in this life, on this earth, in this fleshly existence. "Der Übermensch ist der Sinn der Erde"—"The *Übermensch* is the meaning of the Earth."[57] In the wake of God's demise, the *Übermensch* shows how this

56. Nietzsche, Nachlaß 1881. "Wenn du dir den Gedanken der Gedanken einverleibst, so wird er dich verwandeln." KSA 9: 11.

57. Nietzsche, "Zarathustras Vorrede," *Also sprach Zarathustra*, KSA 4: 14.

life proceeds and expands, striving to erect an idol or idea that is always prone to fall. Every thought is subject to mockery. Taking the Prologue of John at its word, this is the teaching of the word-made-flesh—a thoroughly mortal flesh that is not trapped in its idea, that is not immune to collapse: a willful flesh that lives because every pull upwards is matched by a pull downwards. If the Christian Christ is the hypostatic union of the divine and the human, Zarathustra is the union of the striving philosopher and the difficult philologist—a mortal, who cannot ignore the ringing in his ears.

Before he lost his mind entirely, Nietzsche appropriated the words of Pontius Pilate to serve as the title of his autobiography: *Ecce homo*. With this gesture, the philosopher-philologist strikingly presents himself as a Christ—someone "anointed" (*christos*) to proclaim the mysteries of the *Übermensch*—a Christ, whose presence spells the death of God's transcendence. In the foreword to this work, Nietzsche assumes the role joyfully:

> It is a privilege without equal to be a listener here. Nobody is free to have ears for Zarathustra. . . . [. . .] You revere me: but what if your reverence one day *tumbles* [*umfällt*]? Beware lest a statue slay you! [. . .] Now I bid you lose me and find yourselves; and only when you have all denied me will I return to you . . .[58]

58. Nietzsche, "Vorwort," *Ecce Homo*. "Es ist ein Vorrecht ohne Gleichen hier Hörer zu sein; es steht Niemadem frei, für Zarathustra Ohren zu haben . . . [. . .] Ihr verehrt mich: aber wie, wenn eure Verehrung eines Tages *umfällt*? Hütet euch, dass euch nicht eine Bildsäule erschlage! [. . .] Nun heisse ich euch, mich verlieren und euch finden; und erst, *wenn ihr mich Alle verleugnet habt,* will ich euch wiederkehren . . ." (KSA 6: 260–61).

6

Carnal Inscriptions

In her critical biography of Walter Benjamin, which she prepared for the publication of the author's translated essays, *Illuminations*, Hannah Arendt presents a long section on the centrality of collecting for understanding Benjamin's general method:

> It started early with what he himself called his "bibliomania" but soon extended into something far more characteristic, not so much of the person as of his work: the collecting of quotations. (Not that he ever stopped collecting books. Shortly before the fall of France he seriously considered exchanging his edition of the Collected Works of Kafka, which had recently appeared in five volumes, for a few first editions of Kafka's early writings—an undertaking which naturally was bound to remain incomprehensible to any nonbibliophile.)[1]

1. Hannah Arendt, "Walter Benjamin: 1892–1940" [1968] in Benjamin, *Illuminations: Essays and Reflections*, H. Arendt, ed. (New York: Schocken, 1969), 1–58; here, 39.

The passage attempts to establish a causal connection between Benjamin's earlier, somewhat aristocratic passion for book collecting and his later, ostensibly more critical and, at least according to Arendt, "far more characteristic" practice of citation. In Arendt's view Benjamin's "bibliomania," which could be dismissed as a merely aesthetic indulgence, subsequently initiated the politicized acts of retrieving, decontextualizing, and reconfiguring written material. This link is further reinforced by Arendt's editorial choice to place the 1931 essay, *Ich packe meine Bibliothek aus* ("Unpacking My Library"), as the first piece for the present edition, as if this essay in particular, with its loving descriptions of the writer's antiutilitarian relationship to books, provided a key entry-point to Benjamin's work as a whole. Arendt's point is that Benjamin's attraction to old books, his desire to handle volumes that possess the patina of history, is eventually subsumed by the revolutionary act of collecting quotations, that bibliomania is but a species of this broader genus. All the same, the parenthetical remark reminds the reader that, even though Benjamin ultimately expanded his bibliomanic impulses to include the gathering of nearly forgotten quotations, his younger passion for the antiquarian's shop nonetheless persisted.

In terms of Arendt's rhetorical strategy, the use of parentheses makes a point that could just as well have remained unspoken. The persistence of Benjamin's bibliomania emerges as something no longer necessary for the argument at hand. It constitutes an irrelevant relevance, like an embellishment that may contribute to the feel of the exposition without redirecting the explication itself—an aesthetic point that enhances or perhaps supplements the political. Like a broken ellipse, the parentheses marks contain what would or could otherwise be omitted.

Arendt, in other words, is not being elliptical. Rather, she proffers an illustrative anecdote that serves her central argument without the risk of altering its course. The desire to part with five carefully revised volumes of Kafka's writings in exchange for a few slim editions—presumably Rowohlt's 1913 printing of *Betrachtung* and Kurt Wolff's limited editions of *Der Heizer* and *In der Strafkolonie*—is, as Arendt asserts, "incomprehensible," since these texts were perfectly available in the 1935 Schocken collection that Benjamin already owned. Why, indeed, trade in well over a thousand pages of Kafka for a little more than a hundred? For Arendt, we are today in a better position to comprehend Benjamin's incomprehensible mania by consulting any number of texts where he clearly lays out various theories of collecting. For example, in addition to the autobiographical "Unpacking My Library," there is the extended study on Edward

Fuchs and the entire dossier labeled *Konvolut H* of the *Passagen-Werk,* which is devoted to the figure of "the Collector" and thereby also serves a programmatic purpose, insofar as the *Passagen-Werk* is itself composed as a collection. For Arendt, Benjamin's obsession with rare editions is of a piece with his intention to gather what Rémy de Gourmont characterized as "the very detritus of history," to collate materials that have not yet been colonized by the major tradition.[2]

Benjamin's theoretical reflections on collecting may well offer invaluable insights into his impassioned relationship to historical objects, including first editions of his most important authors. Yet these explications would appear to fall short of giving a full account of the possible motivations behind the special case evoked by Arendt, namely the decision to exchange Kafka for Kafka. Should we, in fact, reduce Benjamin's bibliomania to the collecting method exemplified by the *Passagen-Werk*? Are the two acts perfectly congruous? Is the latter simply a radicalized extension of the former, based on the same premises and principles? Or does the fascination for first editions tell us something different about Benjamin as a reader in general and a reader of Kafka in particular? Does Arendt perhaps conflate too quickly the compulsion to acquire rare books and the drive to collect obscure texts? Is the case of Kafka truly as gratuitous as her parenthetical remark may suggest?

Benjamin's decision to exchange a five-volume set of Kafka for a few first editions would be "incomprehensible" but of course only for "nonbibliophiles," that is, only for those who in fact equate reading with *comprehension.* A sane, nonbibliophile reader is presumably indifferent to the book's materiality, someone who regards reading as an act of dematerialization, as an approach that effectively lifts the inked words off the paper page and imports them into the mind. For the nonbibliophile, once the content has been mentally acquired, the book itself is, at least to a certain degree, dispensable. Benjamin's apparently incomprehensible behavior militates against this essentially idealist program of reading. His bibliomania protests against a classical dismissal of the material medium. This dismissal is *idealist* insofar as it marks the *idea* off from its concrete manifestation, privileging the former at the expense of the latter. Presuming the infinite capacities of mental retention, the physical carrier of meaning—the book itself—can ultimately be put to the side. The limitations or the finitude

2. Benjamin inscribes the citation from Rémy de Gourmont as the epigraph to *Konvolut S* of his *Passagen-Werk: The Arcades Project,* Howard Eiland and Kevin McLaughlin, trans. (Cambridge: Harvard University Press, 1999), 543.

of the bound codex—that which binds us madly and lovingly to the pages—yields to the limitless or infinite realm of thought by way of what Plato's Socrates characterized as "the flight into the *logoi*" (*Phaedo* 99e). At that transcendent point, the book itself can be left behind. Volumes can be stored away or sold off. Libraries can be packed up.

When Benjamin attempts to dispense with multiple volumes of Kafka for a few first editions he would seem to confirm this idealist flight path as well as seriously question its validity. In this single gesture of exchange, trading in Kafka for Kafka, he appears to represent an idealist, dematerializing mode of reading as well as renounce it in favor of a more materialist valuation of the book itself. As an idealist he willingly parts with books already read, whose content has been successfully imported into the mind, while as a bibliophile materialist, he seeks out the book as an almost magical object, somewhat like a fetishist who fondles things that exhibit a certain aura well beyond any use value. With one hand he sells off books, while caressing leather bindings with the other.

Benjamin is engaging in at least two distinct philological approaches based on two different conceptions of the book. In other words, for Benjamin, *the book has two bodies*. Historians of the book frequently remind us that every book is always a double object—first, a transparent vehicle of meaning, which is generally the object of literary interpretation; and second, a "manufactured artifact," which is the object of cultural historian.[3] This distinction, however, is rarely related to the epistemological, phenomenological, and even theological presuppositions that motivate it. By adopting Kantorowicz's famous formulation, the book can be regarded as manifesting two distinct corporeal configurations: on the one hand, the book as a body that functions as the material container of immaterial meaning; and on the other hand, the book as a body of flesh, as a singular artifact, in which the content is vitally incarnate in the form and cannot be dissociated from it.[4] Conventional philology attends to the vehicular book and thus expresses love for the word by reading through the corpus and thus anchoring it in the stability of meaning, while the philology of the flesh expresses love for the word by never wanting to part with its material, immanent manifestation.

3. Cf. Cathy N. Davidson, *Revolution and the World: The Rise of the Novel in America* (Oxford: Oxford University Press, 1986), 15; and Karin Littau, *Theories of Reading: Books, Bodies, and Bibliomania* (Cambridge: Polity, 2006), 1–3.

4. Jacques Rancière refers to the incarnation as "the idea of the Book that comes to life," which speaks well to Benjamin's bibliophile passions: Rancière, *The Flesh of Words*, 72.

With the philology of the flesh, the *lector* becomes a *collector*, keeping what has been gathered together "with him" (*secum*), held in his company, indispensably.

Bibliophiles by definition love their books, yet it is important to stress that the idealist or nonbibliophile mode of reading is inimical neither to language nor to the text. On the contrary, one could say that this method is so in love with language that it never wants the words—the *logoi*—to die; and Benjamin clearly understood and exhibited this love for writing. The classical love affair with language may not be bibliophilic, but it is certainly philological, for it, too, betrays a *philia* for the text, a love that strives to redeem the word from material constraints, to unbind it from the bound pages, and to ascribe it instead to the immaterial sphere of the intellect and the immortal tradition of ideas. This dematerializing—classical, idealist—practice describes the philology of the body, insofar as bodies, as Foucault's work demonstrates, serve as objects of discipline, domestication, and identification. Here, the body is explicitly understood as a signifier of the soul. A philologist of the body thus serves the idea, refining the text's transparency, so as to free meaning from base mediation. The philology of the body releases meaning from its mediating vehicle, which is also to say, it removes the text from the circumstances of history and production. It effectively abstracts the book's contents from the concreteness of time. In contrast, the philology of the flesh resists such abstraction. It therefore better characterizes Benjamin's bibliophilia, which can be seen as a self-corrective to any kind of dematerialization, an approach to the book as if it were flesh—a flesh that exceeds the boundaries of the body and is not reducible to it.

Having read all of Kafka, Benjamin can comfortably dispense with the corpus. Yet all the while, there persists a desire for something indispensable, for the material artifacts in which the content inheres—*inseparably*—in the pages' flesh. Benjamin's bifurcated relationship to Kafka's books may remind us of the geometrical figure he once used to describe Kafka's own approach to writing in a well-known letter to Gershom Scholem, reprinted in the *Illuminations* volume as "Some Reflections on Kafka":

> Kafka's work is an ellipse with foci that lie far apart and are determined on the one hand by mystical experience (which is above all the experience of tradition) and on the other by the experience of the modern city dweller.[5]

5. "Kafkas Werk ist eine Ellipse, deren weit auseinander liegende Brennpunkte von der mystischen Erfahrung (die vor allem die Erfahrung von der Tradition ist) einerseits, von der

Benjamin, too, embellishes his statement by means of a parenthetical remark, again appearing as a broken ellipse that fills in what would otherwise have been left out. In other words, Benjamin supplies what others—including, perhaps, Scholem himself—neglect, namely that mystical experience is constituted by tradition or, to use the Hebrew term, *kabbalah*. The impassioned debates over the proper interpretation of Kafka, which span over five years of correspondence between Scholem and Benjamin, essentially turns on Kafka's relation to theology. Although Scholem repeatedly faults his friend for dismissing the theological dimension, Benjamin insists that he fully accepts theological motives in Kafka's work, provided we fill in—even if only parenthetically—what is otherwise omitted.

Benjamin appears to engage two distinct meanings of *Ellipse*, which in German may refer either to the rhetorical *ellipsis* that expresses a *subtraction* of words, or to the geometric *ellipse* that denotes an *addition* of centers. How then does the rhetorical sense relate to the geometric sense? The Greek noun *leipsis* (an "omission," a "minus"), derived from the verb *leipein* ("to leave, forsake, be wanting"), is used to form both *elleipsis* (a "falling short," a "defect") and *ekleipsis* (an "abandonment," a "failing to appear," an "eclipse"). Modern rhetoricians, from the sixteenth century on, frequently conflated *ellipsis* and *eclipsis*, interpreting both as a "leaving out," even though *ellipsis* is clearly formed with the prefix *en-*, thus denoting "an omission in (the discourse, text, or construction)." At any rate, in its syntactic sense, the term comes to signify any abbreviation, lacuna, or omission of words made consciously or not. Although Quintilian preferred to treat ellipsis as an artful figure or trope, modeled on synecdoche, by which "we understand something that is not said" (*quod tacetur accipimus*), he granted that many verbal omissions are little more than vicious barbarisms produced by thoughtless speech or grammatical idleness.[6]

As for the geometric ellipse, one must consult the history of mathematics. According to Plutarch, it was Plato who assigned Menaechmus the mathemati-

---

Erfahrung des modernen Großstadtmenschen andererseits, bestimmt sind." Benjamin to Scholem (Paris, June 12, 1938), in *Briefe*, 2 vols., G. Scholem and T. W. Adorno, eds. (Frankfurt am Main: Suhrkamp, 1978), 2: 760 [*The Correspondence of Walter Benjamin*, G. Scholem and T. W. Adorno, eds., M. R. Jacobson and E. M. Jacobson, trans. (Chicago: University of Chicago Press, 1994), 563].

6. Quintilian, *Institutio oratoria*, 8.6.21. "Quidam synecdochen vocant et cum id in contextu sermonis quod tacetur acipimus: verbum enim ex verbis intellegi, quod inter vitia ellipsis vocatur [. . .]. Mihi hanc figuram esse magis placet."

cian with the task of solving the so-called Delian problem of doubling the cube.[7] Upon consulting the Delphic oracle, the citizens of Delos learned that they must double the cuboid altar to Apollo in order to rid themselves of a horrific plague. Plato interpreted this message as the god's command to cultivate the science of geometry.[8] However, the philosopher was displeased when Menaechmus abandoned number theory and instead turned to mechanical contrivances, namely by cutting a cone to produce the "acute-angled section" that led to the mathematical solution.[9] A century later, when Apollonius of Perga prepared his *Treatise on the Conic Sections,* he named this closed, oblong curve an *elleipsis,* a "falling short," because the figure's "eccentricity" (the ratio of distance between the focus and the directrix) is less than 1. Apollonius designated each of the conic sections with concrete precision: the *parabolē* (an "even comparison or juxtaposition") with an eccentricity equal to 1; the *hyperbolē* (an "overshooting") with an eccentricity greater than 1; and the circle, which is perfectly centered, that is, without any eccentricity.[10]

Independent of geometric analysis, ancient grammarians would come to apply the same terms to denote figurative devices and narrative forms: *hyperbole* ("overstatement"); the *parable* (an equally corresponding "comparison"—in German, *Gleichnis*); and, of course, the *ellipsis,* which designated any verbal "falling short," whether it occurred by contingency or by rhetorical design. Following Quintilian's suggestion to consider the ellipsis as a trope, modern rhetoricians pored over classical texts to locate examples of what George Puttenham characterized as "the Figure of default."[11] Together with other terms derived from *leipein*—primarily *syllepsis* and *prolepsis*—*ellipsis* (or *eclipsis*) was regarded as

7. Plutarch, *Quaestiones convivales,* 8.2.1 (718d) [*Moralia,* vol. 9: *Table-Talk,* Edwin L. Minar, Jr., F. H. Sandbach, and W. C. Helmbold, trans. (Cambridge: Harvard University Press, 1961), 120–21].

8. Plutarch, *De E apud Delphos,* 6.

9. See Proclus's account in *Proclii Diadochi in primum Euclidis elementorum librum,* G. Friedlein, ed. (Leipzig: Teubner, 1873), 111–12; also, Plutarch, *Vita Marcelli,* 14.5. For a comprehensive discussion of the extant sources, with ample bibliography, see George J. Allman, *Greek Geometry from Thales to Euclid* (Dublin: Hodges, Figgis, & Co., 1889), 155–79.

10. Apollonius of Perga, *Treatise on the Conic Sections,* Prop. 1.13. For a complete account, see Thomas Little Heath's introduction to *Apollonius of Perga: Treatise on the Conic Sections* (Cambridge: Cambridge University Press, 1896), xvii–xxx.

11. George Puttenham, *The Arte of English Poesie* (London: Richard Field, 1589), 136. See also Johannes Susenbrotus, *Epitome troporum ac schematum et grammaticorum & rhetorum* (Zürich: C. Froschouer, 1540), 25; and Henry Peacham, *The Garden of Eloquence* (London: 1577), sect. 1.2.2.

a highly effective device, entirely in accordance with "nature." As John Duncan Quackenbos explained in his *Practical Rhetoric* (1896), it could be understood as the very hallmark of genius:

> Art everywhere deals in Ellipsis, the unseen is imagined from the visible. And so it is in nature. Many things in the universe we know only by inference from what is seen—notably nearly one-half of the nearest heavenly body, our moon. "The artist," said Schiller, "is known by what he omits." Likewise in literature, the true artist is revealed by his tact of ellipsis.[12]

In a highly fanciful fashion, then, Benjamin responds to Scholem's elliptical understanding of Kafka's mysticism by reconfiguring the writer's work as an ellipse featuring two foci: There is not one central determinant in Kafka's work, but two. The implicit question that remains is whether, at least according to Benjamin, the two foci that determine Kafka's work as an ellipse also cause it to be elliptical: whether the addition of foci further correspond to a subtraction of sense.

Benjamin appears to answer this question further on in the letter, when he explains that Kafka depicts the central experience of urban fragmentation by way of his familiarity with the mystical tradition, which he acquired not through direct participation but rather through the deficient means of "eavesdropping." The stray sounds he was able to pick up were not intended for his ears. For this reason, Benjamin argues, "Kafka's work represents tradition falling ill":

> Wisdom has occasionally been defined as the epic side of truth. Wisdom is thereby characterized as a property of tradition; it is truth in its haggadic consistency. It is this consistency of truth that has been lost. Kafka was far from being the first to face this fact. Many had accommodated themselves to it, clinging to truth or whatever they regarded as such, and with a more or less heavy heart, had renounced its transmissibility. Kafka's real genius was that he tried something entirely new: he sacrificed truth for the sake of clinging to the transmissibility, to its haggadic element.[13]

12. John Duncan Quackenbos, *Practical Rhetoric* (New York: American Book Co., 1896), 268.

13. "Kafkas Werk stellt eine Erkrankung der Tradition dar. Man hat die Weisheit gelegentlich als die epische Seite der Wahrheit definieren wollen. Damit ist die Weisheit als ein Tradionsgut

Far from being eternal or universal, truth and the tradition that upholds it are subject to time and deterioration. What is true is what is traditionally held to be true. Benjamin is referring specifically to Kafka's retelling of Judaic parables whose truth Kafka himself cannot know for sure. Whereas others cling to a truth that is no longer viable, no longer transmissible, Kafka's genius was to transmit the very failure or ellipsis of truth. He engaged in transmitting a "telling" (*haggadah*) that no longer worked in the service of the religious law and wisdom—the *halakah*—that had always given tales their "consistency."

This notion of transmissibility reaches back to the friends' earlier joint study of the Marburg Neo-Kantian, Hermann Cohen, when Benjamin was a student in Bern in 1918. As Scholem notes in his diaries of the time, "transmissibility as such [*Tradierbarkeit schlechthin*]" can replace the Kantian system insofar as it denotes the system's relation to itself—that is, an utterly singular relation that cannot be encompassed by the tradition itself.[14] Transmissibility, therefore, is tradition's indigestible remnant, something that exceeds the very system it grounds, an excessiveness that Benjamin now brings to bear on his reading of Kafka:

> Kafka's writings are by their nature parables. But that is their misery and their beauty, that they had to become *more* than parables. They do not simply lie at the feet of doctrine, as *haggadah* lies at the feet of *halakah*. When they have crouched down, they unexpectedly raise a mighty paw against it.[15]

To say that Kafka's work is an ellipse is to imply that it does not consist straightforwardly in parables. Although here Benjamin uses the German term *Gleich-*

gekennzeichnet; sie ist die Wahrheit in ihrer hagadischen Konsistenz. Diese Konsistenz der Wahrheit ist es, die verloren gegangen ist. Kafka war weit entfernt, der erste zu sein, der sich dieser Tatsache gegenüber sah. Viele hatten sich mit ihr eingerichtet, festhaltend an der Wahrheit oder an dem, was sie jeweils dafür gehalten haben; schweren oder auch leichteren Herzens verzichtleistend auf ihre Tradierbarkeit. Das eigentlich Geniale an Kafka war, daß er etwas ganz neues ausprobiert hat: er gab die Wahrheit preis, um an der Tradierbarkeit, an dem hagadischen Element festzuhalten." Benjamin to Scholem (June 12, 1938), in *Briefe*, 2.763 [*Correspondence*, 565]; partially cited in Arendt, "Walter Benjamin: 1892–1940," 41.

14. G. Scholem, "Über Kant," Julia Ng, ed., *MLN* 127 (2012), 440–41.

15. "Kafkas Dichtungen sind von Hause aus Gleichnisse. Aber das ist ihr Elend und ihre Schönheit, daß sie *mehr* als Gleichnisse werden mußten. Sie legen sich der Lehre nicht schlicht zu Füßen wie sich die Hagada der Halacha zu Füßen legt. Wenn sie sich gekuscht haben, heben sie unversehens eine gewichtige Pranke gegen sie."

nis for "parable," elsewhere he refers to *Parabel*—the name for the other conic section, the *parabola,* which mathematicians define as having an eccentricity equal to 1. In the rhetorical tradition, the "parable" (παραβολή) denotes a "juxtaposition" or a "comparison by moving from one side to the other," where both sides are equal, where both sides perfectly correspond. Kafka's parables are excessive—"more than parables"—miserably unable to give any adequate version of divine truth or law.[16] The Kafkan parable gives only itself, excessively and beautifully, falling short of veridical correspondence by falling before it. It falls short by exceeding, which is to say: Kafka's work is an ellipse that articulates a fundamental ellipsis.

Benjamin's analysis rehearses an argument that he already developed two years before in his essay *Der Erzähler* ("The Storyteller"), where traditional wisdom is characterized as something that has practical use, and the oral storyteller as someone who thus has "counsel" for his audience. Here, he also refers explicitly to "the epic side of truth" and its modern decline, which coincides with the rise of the novel. For Benjamin, it is the novel's "dependence on the book" that distinguishes it from the story. Whereas the storyteller hands down useful truths based on personal experience, the novelist has no truth to transmit. The "dissemination of the novel" made "possible only with the invention of printing" stems from a novelist in isolation, cut off from the majority of those who will read his book, a solitary writer who has no counsel to give because he himself is uncounseled. Thus, "the novel gives evidence of the profound perplexity of the living."[17]

The novel, whose historical emergence coincides with the invention of the printing press, is therefore a repository of uselessness, disseminated in the form of a reproducible book that transmits material with no relation to traditional wisdom. And the collector of these books indulges in their thingly lack of use value. To approach a printed parable as though it might yield an applicable truth—some moral or some practical advice, some proverbial wisdom or eternal law—is to ignore the book's recalcitrance to tradition. We may believe or even hope that the book is the embodiment of a truth that has been imprinted

16. For further analysis on the implications of Kafka's "inadequacy" or "failure," see Werner Hamacher, "The Gesture in the Name: On Benjamin and Kafka," in *Premises: Essays on Philosophy and Literature from Kant to Celan*, P. Fenves, trans. (Cambridge: Harvard University Press, 1996), 294–336.

17. Benjamin, "The Storyteller," in *Illuminations*, 87.

upon its pages, a truth that is separable from its material transmission, yet what is transmitted may turn out to be nothing but tradition's own systematic failure, nothing but unreadable, incomprehensible flesh.

As for Kafka's work, it is difficult to think of a parable more expressive of this unreadability, more concerned with the incomprehensibility and incomprehensiveness of the flesh, than *In der Strafkolonie* ("In the Penal Colony").[18] The tale is notorious for its gruesome premise and lurid descriptions, for its thematic abuse of language, whereby the Word itself—the word of judgment—is perverted into an instrument of murderous torture. First drafted in October 1914, when Kafka was working on his novel, *Der Proceß* (*The Trial*), the story was revised in 1917, following the author's notoriously vivid public reading at the Galerie Hans Goltz in Munich. Among those in attendance was the Swiss graphologist Max Pulver, who described Kafka's magical effect on his audience:

> A dull fall, confusion in the room, someone carried an unconscious [*ohnmächtige*] woman out. The narrative meanwhile continued. Twice more his words struck people down unconscious. The rows of listeners began to thin out. Some fled at the very last minute, before the poet's vision vanquished [*überwältigte*] them.[19]

Pulver's description, verified by other witnesses, attests to the power of Kafka's text and his delivery: a power (*Macht*) that rendered the weak "unconscious" or entirely "powerless" (*ohnmächtig*); a violence (*Gewalt*) that overpowered (*überwältigte*) those who heard him. Perhaps it was the physical presence of the author that, despite his nonintimidating appearance, contributed to this formidable reaction—a reaction not simply to the words alone but to the words incarnated. Perhaps it was the contrast between Kafka's cool or even clinical

18. As is the case with all of Kafka's work, the secondary literature on *In der Strafkolonie* is dauntingly extensive. For a judicious overview of the primary critical bibliography, see Richard Gray, "Disjunctive Signs: Semiotics, Aesthetics, and Failed Mediation in 'In der Strafkolonie,'" in *A Companion to the Works of Franz Kafka*, James Rolleston, ed. (New York: Camden House, 2002), 213–45.

19. Max Pulver, "Spaziergang mit Franz Kafka," in *Als Kafka mir entgegenkam . . . Erinnerungen an Franz Kafka*, Hans-Gerd Koch, ed. (Berlin: Wagenbach, 1995), 130–35. "Ein dumpfer Fall, Verwirrung im Saal, man trug eine ohnmächtige Dame hinaus. Die Schilderung ging inzwischen fort. Zweimal streckten seine Worte Ohnmächtige nieder. Die Reihen der Hörer und der Hörerinnen beganen sich zu lichten. Manche flohen im letzten Augenblick, bevor die Vision des Dichters sie überwältigte" (132).

delivery and the horrifying nature of the content that proved to be unbearable. However one might speculate, it is certainly credible that a story about a blood-soaked execution carried out by language engraved into human flesh would give rise to the visceral feeling of being tortured by the words themselves. Benjamin, who knew Pulver and was at the time studying in Munich, failed to attend this singular event. Two years later, after some hesitation, Kurt Wolff published the story in 1919 in the limited edition with half brown sheep binding that would decades later attract Benjamin's eye.

In a letter to Wolff, composed one month before the Munich reading, Kafka defends the "embarrassing" or even "painful" (*peinlich*) aspects of the story, comparing it to our own times in general and to the writer's time in particular.[20] This apologia invites readers to regard the narrative as a comparison, to juxtapose its plot with contemporary circumstances and with the circumstances of the writer's own life—that is, to read it as a *parable* (*parabolē*, "comparison," "juxtaposition"). That the story should be read as a parable finds confirmation not only in the author's expressed intention, but also in the narrative form. In contrast to the urban, claustral darkness of *The Trial*, the *Penal Colony* unfolds in the unforgiving light of the tropical desert—*in den Tropen*. The colony is not further identified; it is as nameless as the protagonists, who are only known by their abstract roles: the Officer, the Travelling Explorer, the Soldier, the Condemned Man, and so forth. Human action is thereby reduced to functional anonymity, with each actor being but an organ in the corporate body of colonial justice. The namelessness of the colony and the colonists not only suggests a reduction to instrumentality; it also implies, as Ingeborg Henel has argued, an allegorical intention behind the story: an intellectual argument, rather than a mimetic narrative.[21] The Officer is every "officer," the Travelling Explorer is every one who journeys to experience the foreign, the Condemned Man is every one who has been condemned. Formulated as an allegory, the story aspires to universal applicability. Set in the tropics (*in den Tropen*), the action of these

20. Kafka to Kurt Wolff, Oct. 11, 1916: "[. . .] daß nicht nur sie [die Erzählung] peinlich ist, daß vielmehr unsere allgemeine und meine besondere Zeit gleichfalls sehr peinlich war und ist und meine besondere sogar noch länger peinlich als die allgemeine." Franz Kafka, *Briefe 1902-1924*, Max Brod, ed. (Frankfurt a. M.: Fischer, 1958), 150.

21. Ingeborg Henel, "Kafkas 'In der Strafkolonie': Form, Sinn und Stellung der Erzählung im Gesamtwerk," *Untersuchungen zur Literatur als Geschichte: Festschrift für Benno von Wiese*, Vincent Günther, Helmut Koopmann, and Joachim Krause, eds. (Berlin: Schmidt, 1973), 480–504.

abstract roles would reinforce the existence of a figurative meaning, as if the protagonists themselves were simply "tropes" (*Tropen*) in themselves.

In the foreground, the plot turns—tropically—on two opposing poles, which, at least formally, recall the two foci recognized by Benjamin. On the one hand, there is the Officer, who displays throughout an adherence to a mystical tradition, in which the individual subject is dissolved into a higher, inscrutable power; while on the other hand, there is the Travelling Explorer (*der Forschungsreisende*), a kind of ethnographic researcher who represents a worldview linked to the Enlightenment, one that is grounded in the rationalism of the modern, autonomous subject. The conflict between the Officer and the Explorer corresponds to the conflict between the Old and the New Commandant, neither of whom is ever directly presented in the narrative. The visible antagonism is therefore matched by an invisible antagonism. Both configured pairs—the Officer/Old Commandant and the Explorer/New Commandant—are *focused* on two different notions of truth. Yet, if there are indeed two competing truths at work here, then Kafka's story constitutes a particular kind of allegory or parable—not one whose terms can be easily decoded to reveal a latent sense or a point-by-point comparison, but rather one that yields to multiple possible meanings, including, therefore, the possibility of no meaning at all: an *elliptical* parable that *leaves out* ultimate determination. Again, Kafka hints at such a reading. In a subsequent letter to Kurt Wolff, he confesses: "Two or three pages shortly before the end are shoddy work, their presence points to a deeper flaw, there is somewhere there a worm, which hollows out even the whole of the story."[22] Kafka does not specify further what this "flaw" or "deficiency" (*Mangel*) may be. Yet in pressing Benjamin's insight, one might locate this *ellipsis* to the plot's elliptical form, namely, that the two foci of the narrative—the Officer and the Explorer—somehow contribute to the way the story *falls short* of stable meaning. How then might the work's unworking work?

The initial focus falls to the Officer, who opens the text with a simple declaration: *Es ist ein eigentümlicher Apparat*—"It is a peculiar [or unique] device." The Officer is exceedingly if not perversely fond of this "peculiar" contraption,

22. Kafka to Kurt Wolff, Sept. 4, 1917. "Zwei oder drei Seiten kurz vor ihrem Ende sind Machwerk, ihr Vorhandensein deutet auf einen tieferen Mangel, es ist da irgendwo ein Wurm, der selbst das Volle der Geschichte hohl macht." Kurt Wolff, *Briefwechsel eines Verlegers: 1911–1963*, Bernhard Zeller and Ellen Otten, eds. (Frankfurt a. M.: Fischer, 1966), 45.

which simultaneously serves as a machine of judgment, sentencing and execution. It executes the death sentence by engraving the judgment into the criminal's body, so that that he learns the judgment and sentence as he is about to perish. Again in contrast to Kafka's novel, in the penal colony there is emphatically no *trial*, no legal *process*. "Guilt is always beyond a doubt"—*Die Schuld ist immer zweifellos* (168/145). In the Officer's view, this foregone conclusion forms the very basis for the colonial community. Throughout his description, it is clear that he wants not only to teach the Traveler about the machine's function, but also to situate the device within the cultural and historical context of the colony. As he explains, the machine's "peculiarity" (*Eigentümlichkeit*) consists in its three main parts, which have acquired "popular names" (*volkstümliche Bezeichnungen*): the "bed," upon which the prisoner will be strapped down, naked; the "inscriber" (*Zeichner*), which stretches out above the body; and a moving "harrow" (*Egge*), which hovers over the body and carefully imprints the judgment into the condemned man's flesh. The uniqueness or peculiarity of the device—its *Eigentümlichkeit*—is made comprehensible by the common popularity—*Volkstümlichkeit*—of the parts' labels. This passage from individual peculiarity to shared popularity reflects the Officer's pedagogical intention, which aims to maintain the priority of the community by repressing individual intervention or protest. Hence, the procedure is entirely without process, without any opportunity to deliberate or weigh evidence, to make a counterargument or a viable defense. Moreover, in the Officer's opinion, the word "harrow" is perfectly "suitable" (164), for he believes that the part is indeed comparable to the farming tool with spiked teeth that breaks up recalcitrant clods of earth, transforming the field into fertile, profitable soil and thereby allowing the community to flourish. The peculiar device has replaced the sower who sows his seeds. Although it remains questionable whether anyone has ears to hear the judgment, all have a body to receive it. It is important to stress, however, that the Officer's community-building educational program, which passes from *Eigentümlichkeit* to *Volkstümlichkeit*, militates against the very ideal of an enlightened curriculum, which strives instead to promote and develop the mind of the individual, in order to make the community rationally viable.[23]

23. In his *Pädogogische Schriften*, Friedrich Schleiermacher speaks explicitly about this tension between *Eigentümlichkeit* and *Volkstümlichkeit* in relation to national education. See Schleiermacher, "Einleitung," *Vorlesungen aus dem Jahre 1826*, in *Pädogogische Schriften*, C. Platz, ed. (Langensalza: Beyer, 1902), 35-38.

All in all, then, the Officer regards the apparatus and its social function with profound fondness and admiration, despite the fact that he knows it quite well (*den ihm doch wohlbekannten Apparat*). At least for the Officer, deep familiarity does not preclude adoration. As the Officer explains in his highly didactic mode, the mechanism will work ceaselessly for six hours, at which point there is a glorious transfiguring moment of revelation, when the condemned man finally learns his precise sentence. Knowledge is the fruit of punishment and emerges at the very threshold of death, for the condemned man is not aware of his sentence beforehand. The Officer excitedly anticipates the epiphanic moment:

> But how quiet the man becomes around the sixth hour! The most stupid of them begins to understand. It starts around the eyes and spreads from there. A look that could tempt one to lie down with him under the harrow. Nothing else happens. The man merely begins to decipher the inscription. He purses his lips, as if he is listening. You've seen that it is not easy to decipher the inscription with your eyes, but our man deciphers it with his wounds.[24]

According to the Officer, the body of the condemned man will be transfigured into flesh engraved with the radiant word of the law. The juridical content is not ideational but rather painfully visceral: "It would be useless to pronounce the sentence to him [the criminal]. He will surely learn it on his body [*Leib*]."[25] The judgment is, therefore, the Law made flesh: a flesh that is exposed by the complete laceration of the skin and the complete destruction of the body.[26]

Benjamin suggests that Kafka "eavesdropped" on Jewish tradition; and if one had to identify the verse of Holy Scripture that Kafka picked up for this story,

24. "Wie still wird dann aber der Mann um die sechste Stunde! Verstand geht dem Blödesten auf. Um die Augen beginnt es. Von hier aus verbreitet es sich. Ein Anblick, der einen verführen könnte, sich mit unter die Egge zu legen. Es geschieht ja nichts weiter, der Mann fängt bloß an, die Schrift zu entziffern, er spitzt den Mund, als horche er. Sie haben gesehen, es ist nicht leicht, die Schrift mit den Augen zu entziffern; unser Mann entziffert sie aber mit seinen Wunden." Franz Kafka, "In der Strafkolonie" in *Gesammelte Werke*, 12 vols., H.-G. Koch, ed. (Frankfurt a. M.: Fischer, 1994), 1: 173.

25. "Es wäre nutzlos, es ihm zu verkünden. Er erfährt es ja auf seinem Leib." Kafka, *In der Strafkolonie*, 1: 167.

26. Gerald Bartl thus argues that "traces (of writing) and scars (of the body) become one: the Incarnation of the Logos and the logification of the flesh." Bartl, *Spuren und Narben: Die Fleischwerdung der Literatur im Zwanzigsten Jahrhundert* (Würzburg: Königshausen & Neumann, 2002), 19. To illustrate this key point, Bartl offers an extended reading of Kafka's *In der Strafkolonie*, 191–273.

it would have to be from the Book of Job: "And after my skin is destroyed, this I know, that in my flesh I shall see God" (Job 19:26 [KJV]).[27] Job, who knows his innocence and cannot understand his punishment, looks forward to the opportunity to see and know God, perhaps in order to vindicate himself before God. The promise of redemption rests on the strength of his lacerated skin. Job's incised flesh will confirm God's covenant with humankind, as if his entire body has become the site of circumcision (*brit milah*). So God proclaimed to Abraham: "You shall be circumcised in the flesh of your foreskins, and it shall be a sign of the covenant between Me and you. [. . .] My covenant shall be in your flesh for an everlasting covenant" (Genesis 17:11–14 [NKJV]). As a martyr, Job's wounds bear witness to God's glory; his flesh is a citation (*martys*) of divine authority. The relationship between the incised flesh and the word is explicit in the Hebrew term *milah*, which not only denotes the "circumcision" but also the "word." Just as the male organ of procreation is cut in order to ratify the individual's inclusion in God's covenant, so is the human voice cut or articulated in order to produce meaningful speech.[28] In Kafka's penal colony, the Officer insists that he is performing a sacred task, operating a large writing machine so that the flesh of the condemned may be incorporated into a broader meaning. The body of the sacrificial victim thereby comes to articulate the Law in a moment of brilliant illumination.

Ideally, the individual's body will no longer be his body, but a clear image of Justice Incarnate. At the consummating moment, the temporal inscribing of the text is halted to create a timeless image. The criminal's living body (*Leib*) is destroyed by torture, and violently made to reflect transcendent, imperial power. And it is this supreme moment that reinforces the community: "How we all absorbed the expression of transfiguration from the martyred [*gemarterten*] face, how we held our cheeks in the radiance of this justice, achieved at last and already passing away!"[29] The community is thus grounded in a common,

27. The Hebrew text reads: וְאַחַר עוֹרִי נִקְּפוּ־זֹאת וּמִבְּשָׂרִי אֶחֱזֶה אֱלוֹהַּ. For an extensive consideration of the Book of Job and other Jewish traditions in relation to *In der Strafkolonie*, see Ruth Callahan, *In My Flesh I Shall See God: Franz Kafka's "In der Strafkolonie," the Alphabet, the Covenant, and Isaac Luria's Tikkun Olam* (Ph.D. diss., Cincinnati: Union Institute & University, 2006).

28. Cf. Leonard Glotzer, *Fundamentals of Jewish Mysticism: The Book of Creation and Its Commentaries* (Northvale, NJ: Aronson, [1977] 1992), 18.

29. "Wie nahmen wir alle den Ausdruck der Verklärung von dem gemarterten Gesicht, wie hielten wir unsere Wangen in den Schein dieser endlich erreichten und schon vergehenden Gerechtigkeit!" Kafka, *In der Strafkolonie*, TKTK.

ecstatic moment, in a mystical experience of the common. The spectators participate in this destruction of the condemned man's proper body, celebrating this ceremonious decorporealization. As Georges Bataille would affirm, it is the sacrificial expenditure of private, personal property that allows the emergence of the common.[30] Again, *Eigentümlichkeit* cedes to *Volkstümlichkeit*.

As a man of reason, the Explorer cannot endorse this eradication of the individual and the proper. He distrusts the logic of sacrifice, which he dismisses as crudely illogical, against human reason. At first, his distaste for this ritual expresses itself as mere indifference. He does not attend to the Officer's speech with any great interest; he remains *unbeteiligt*—"nonparticipating," "detached," or "uninvolved" (161). He does, however, pay some attention to his host's corporeal presence, noting how the colonists' "uniforms" are too "heavy" for this climate: *Diese Uniformen sind doch für die Tropen zu schwer* (162/140). By noticing that the colonists are not wearing suitable clothing, the Explorer implicitly alludes to the figure of two foci, so that the arc of the story continues to be determined by two distinct centers: the colonial authority and the authority of the home territory, from where the Explorer presumably traveled. As he observes, the nation's uniforms fail to conform to the colony's conditions. One *form* cannot suit both lives. Every colony, therefore, would appear to constitute an ellipse, governed by two central administrations.

It is, of course, the Explorer's humanism that notices the disparity: he is concerned with men as living, rational beings, not as sacrificial meat. The fact that the Officer must use two "ladies' handkerchiefs" to protect his sweating neck from heat rash, causes him concern over the colonists' well-being. Perhaps the home government has been neglecting them, compelling them to find makeshift solutions. Perhaps the New Commandant has allowed the devotee of the Old Commandant to perish. In any case, it is the Explorer's humanism that gradually instigates his repulsion. He grows ever more appalled by the Officer's fanaticism. He cannot endorse the so-called truth that the Officer has inherited from the Old Commandant, who originally dreamed up this nightmarish practice. In the Explorer's view, this dogmatic tradition barely conceals its ideological violence. He focuses therefore on the deep pit that lies beside the apparatus. For him, what the Officer describes is no sacred ritual but rather a horrific dis-

30. Georges Bataille, "The Notion of Expenditure" [1933], in *Visions of Excess: Selected Writings 1927–1939*, Allen Stoekl, ed. (Minneapolis: University of Minnesota Press, 1985), 116–29.

play of power, a hideous carnival that destroys the body and mercilessly dumps the bloodied corpse into the dark crypt.

Whereas the Explorer believes in the integrity of the human body, the Officer aims to restore the sacred body at the individual's expense. For this lover of the sacred word, writing is not instrumental but rather holy. His most prized possessions are the "handwritten drawings" (*Handzeichnungen*) handed down from the Old Commandant. As the Officer asserts, the Old Commandant was a visionary, having designed the ritual and performing all the functions linked to it—*er hat alles in sich vereinigt* (166/144). The Old Commandant thought of everything and was everything. With eager enthusiasm, the Officer shares the master's precious drawings with the Explorer, but not before he ritually washes his hands. He holds the diagrams up to the Explorer for him to inspect at a close distance, without giving him the right to handle them personally. The sacred pages must be held safe from corruption. Yet, when the Explorer attempts to read them, he sees nothing but "a labyrinthine series of lines, crisscrossing each other in all sorts of ways" (172). Despite the Officer's insistence on their clarity, the Explorer despairingly admits that the writing is impossible to read, impossible to decipher. He has not the eyes to see it.

As a philologist of the body, the Explorer understands the reading process primarily as an act of dematerialization that renders the medium disposable. Yet when the material support of the writing is a human being, then this idea of dispensability is unimaginably cruel and unusual. For the philologist of the body, the book is treated as an instrument for producing sense, as a vehicle of meaning. Yet if the material of production is a singular, unique, enfleshed individual, the instrument of inscription can only be viewed as an instrument of torture. The Officer too believes in legibility; yet he is not willing to dismiss the medium as mere means. In contrast to the Explorer, he is a philologist of the flesh, loving the fleshly medium that is irradiated by the spirit of the Law. Like precious parchment or vellum, the uniqueness of the medium matters. The Officer's philology betrays his bibliophilia. He lovingly holds on to the Old Commandant's drawings in a special leather folio, which is kept in his breast pocket, close to his heart. And his description of the machine's work belies his appreciation for calligraphy: "The actual script runs around the flesh [*Leib*] only in a narrow belt; the rest of the body [*Körper*] is reserved for the embellishments" (172). These embellishments recall the complex illustrations and labyrinthine designs found in illuminated manuscripts, which render the fleshly page more opaque, more difficult to read through, more sacred. Yet, can the carnal body (*Leib*) support the letters? Can the integral body (*Körper*) suffer the elaborate designs? What should be incorporated within a system of inspired legibility may come to be disrupted by material that resists incorporation.

Towards the story's end, when the Officer sets himself down beneath the harrow, the Explorer looks on with horror as the machine begins to break down and fall apart, mangling the body, inscribing nothing, only stabbing the flesh, murderously. Still, his enlightened curiosity draws him to observe the face of the dead man. "Almost against his will, he looked at the face of the corpse. It was as it had been in life. There was no sign of the promised redemption to discover"—*kein Zeichen der versprochenen Erlösung war zu entdecken* (193). As Stanley Corngold comments:

> The fate of an illuminated death is linked to the fate of a medium, which is here consumed by the very signs it is meant to accommodate. The illumination communicated to the cult of the penal colony arises from the prisoner's fleeting grasp of his own body as a medium of communication; but what he actually grasps is that here there is a medium and nothing more—and certainly no message.[31]

The Explorer, indeed, looks explicitly for a "sign," a "sign of the promised redemption," because he regards reading exclusively as a matter of discovering and deciphering signs. In his view, this terrifying machine is but a sick parody of the printing press. The revolution wrought by Johannes Gutenberg contributed greatly to homogenizing reading practices by establishing regularity in the printed word, a regularity that reduced material obstacles and thereby facilitated the passage to verbal meaning. The Officer's machine perverts the printing press by having it function as a torture device, as something that, from the perspective of rationalism, may well be likened to medieval machines of excruciating pain. Although the Officer "promised" redemption—the moment when the individual's flesh would reveal sacred meaning—his own experience beneath the harrow demonstrates how the machine fails to make good on that promise, how we are left only with a bloodied pile of mangled, nonrecuperable flesh. The

31. Stanley Corngold, *Lambent Traces: Franz Kafka* (Princeton: Princeton University Press, 2004), 45.

longing for knowledge dissolves in this blatant display of nonknowledge—an atheological demonstration that is no less religious, if only because it propounds the impossible.[32]

One focal point of Kafka's elliptical parable would seem to have been dispatched. Yet in the story's epilogue, we learn that, although the Officer no longer plays a role, his invisible counterpart, the Old Commandant, continues to steer the plot. Precisely because he has occupied a sovereign, transcendent position to the narrative, he cannot be dismissed as readily as his devoted servant. Presumably in order to follow up on his research, the Explorer has the Soldier and the former Condemned Man take him to the inconspicuous teahouse where the former governor was laid to rest. The New Commandant would not allow his predecessor to be buried in hallowed ground. When a few tables are pushed away to reveal the tombstone, the Explorer has no trouble reading the inscription:

> Here rests the Old Commandant. His followers, who are now not permitted to have a name, buried him in this grave and erected this stone. There exists a prophecy that the Commandant will rise again after a certain number of years and from this house will lead his followers to recapturing the colony. Have faith and wait![33]

The Old Commandant, long dead but still secretly revered, maintains a position of transcendent authority, which, because his power is transcendent, requires authorized interpreters like the Officer. The religious founder needs his Church to promulgate the word, at least until the Second Coming, until the last *judgment*. Yet, the New Commandant is no less transcendent, no less invisible, consistently held beyond the frame of the plot. Two foci, then, come clearer into view—two competing claims of transcendent determination, two

32. The concept of atheology derives from Georges Bataille, who intended to title his collected writings *La somme athéologique*. Paul North brilliantly investigates the atheological core of Kafka's work in *The Yield: Kafka's Atheological Reformation* (Stanford: Stanford University Press, 2015). As North comments, "God is dead already in flesh [. . .] and more than 'dead' in flesh's putrid decay and waste, which makes spirit indeed seem ridiculous" (6).

33. "Hier ruht der alte Kommandant. Seine Anhänger, die jetzt keinen Namen tragen dürfen, haben ihm das Grab gegraben und den Stein gesetzt. Es besteht eine Prophezeiung, daß der Kommandant nach einer bestimmten Anzahl von Jahren auferstehen und aus diesem Hause seine Anhänger zur Wiedereroberung der Kolonie führen wird. Glaubet und wartet!" Kafka, *In der Strafkolonie*, TKTK.

possible sources for legitimate interpretation. Kafka's elliptical parable resists establishing one source as legitimate at the expense of the other. Instead, Kafka the writer—the one who inscribed this harrowing text—allows both sides to come into focus, exposing the power of each, and perhaps therefore exposing power's fundamental meaninglessness.

Readers, like Benjamin, are generally torn between these two philological premises, between the need for signification and the desire for flesh. The human sciences read for meaning but also hold on to some idea that regards literature as a physical manifestation linked to incarnate existence, to the lives of authors and readers, who are fully situated in historical circumstances. Printed books have long cultivated practices that encourage the belief in the writer's presence. Publishers often explicitly promote the conviction that the writers persist in the writing despite their own physical absence. Authors' photographs on the dustcover contribute to this illusion; and the author's personal inscription to the book's recipient provides an even greater reinforcement of some aura of singularity. Accordingly, autograph manuscripts by famous authors are highly coveted and fetch exorbitant prices at auction houses. Even digitization strives to animate the letter by including vivid illustrations, interactive links, multiple hypertexts, and touch-screen technology. These sensual gestures arguably try to compensate for a loss of flesh and can therefore be regarded as vestigial practices that reach back to the era before Gutenberg. Every medieval manuscript differs vastly from the other, even if they contain the selfsame text. Here, individuality is further highlighted by the text's material support, the parchment prepared from animal skin. "We can feel with our fingertips the difference between flesh side and hair side of the leather page; we can see and touch the pores and sometimes old scars; we can even smell the parchment. [. . .] Getting to know a particular manuscript is like getting to know a particular person."[34]

For this reason, medieval book production provides the paradigmatic case for the philology of the flesh, which ultimately proceeds from the idea of incarnation. For medieval Christians, the founding miracle of the incarnate Word is nearly ritually re-created every time someone handled a book produced from vellum, parchment, and leather, that is, from animal flesh that had been scraped, cleaned, tanned, and polished. The religiously institutional act of the divine Word taking on flesh is underscored by the display of text-bearing flesh. Conse-

34. Laura Kendrick, *Animating the Letter: The Figurative Embodiment of Writing from Late Antiquity to the Renaissance* (Columbus: Ohio State University Press, 1999), 12–13.

quently, a specific relation obtains between the initiating miracle of incarnation and the carnal properties of the book. For the enlightened philologist of the body, the book is better—more humanely—regarded as a material vehicle of immaterial meaning. Here, reading serves the quest of discovery; the flesh of the page is made to dissolve into the acquisition of sense, knowledge, and power, incorporated into the rational systems that constitute the modern subject. The philology of the body uses books and ultimately uses them up.

With Kafka, who regarded his life as literature, the writing remains elliptical. *In the Penal Colony*, determined by two distinct foci, indicates crucial omissions in both philological approaches: the enlightened Explorer, driven by instrumental reason, falls short of the sacred and messianic hope; while the mystical Officer falls short of humanity, including his own.

7

The Stillest Night

Midway through his well-known *Meridian* speech, which he delivered on October 22, 1960, on the occasion of accepting the Büchner Prize for Literature, Paul Celan takes the opportunity to address recent public reproaches against the obscurity or opacity of his poetry:

> Ladies and Gentlemen, it is today commonplace, to reproach poetry with its "opacity"—Permit me at this point, abruptly—but hasn't something here suddenly opened up?—permit me, to cite here a word from Pascal, a word that I read some time ago in Leo Schestov: "Ne nous reprochez pas le manque de clarté puisque nous en faisons profession!"—That is, I believe, if not the congenital [obscurity of poetry], then arguably the obscurity attributed to poetry for the sake of an encounter from a—perhaps of its own design—distance or strangeness.[1]

1. Paul Celan, "Der Meridian" in *Meridian. Endfassung – Vorstufen – Materialen*, Bernhard Böschenstein and Heino Schnull, eds. (Frankfurt a. M.: Suhrkamp, 1999). "Meine Damen und Herren, es ist heute gang und gäbe, der Dichtung ihre 'Opazität'

Thus, at the meridian point of *The Meridian*, despite the somewhat convoluted syntax—the starts and stops, the retractions and corrections, the intruding series of citations (quoting Schestov quoting Pascal)—Celan arguably intends to clarify his position. He wants to reveal where he stands in relation to poetry, how he encounters poetry, and thus, presumably, how his own poetry should be encountered. Any contradiction between the discursive form and its content, between Celan's intention to clarify and the tenebrous manner of his prose, may be resolved by observing that the speech strives to elucidate poetic obscurity, not by instructing the audience on how to interpret or comprehend difficult texts, not by pointing the way out of otherwise impassible or impossible passages, but rather by conferring value to obscurity itself. The explanation insists that problems should be retained as problems, as *problemata*, as hindrances or obstacles, or better as *skandala*: as stumbling blocks, which may well impede the reader's arrival to the clear light of meaning, but may therefore, through this very blockage, instigate the "encounter" of which Celan speaks, both here and throughout the speech: a poetic encounter with language itself, a *Begegnung* that strikes "against" (*gegen*), coming from some "distance or strangeness." In citing Pascal ("Ne nous reprochez pas"), Celan encourages the audience to surrender their distance and draw near: to *approach* rather than *reproach*.

The paragraph's opening address to this audience—"Meine Damen und Herren"—already begins to stage this encounter. To be sure, in one regard, the phrase is perfectly ordinary, perhaps the most commonplace of rhetorical gestures, perhaps the emptiest of formulaic expressions, consisting of nothing unexpected within the context of a public lecture. Yet over the full course of Celan's presentation, which repeats the expression no less than seventeen times, the force of this common and somewhat empty vocative, now midway through the speech, has become more provocative. If the very first words of Celan's *Meridian*—"Meine Damen und Herren"—are typical enough to begin any public address, the subsequent repetitions of the phrase, including the one cited here, soon mark a pronounced deviation from standard practice, recurring with increasing frequency, rising to an anaphoric refrain toward the conclusion, before signaling the end: "Meine

vorzuwerfen — Erlauben Sie mir, an dieser Stelle unvermittelt — aber hat sich hier nicht jäh etwas aufgetan? — erlauben Sie mir, hier ein Wort von Pascal zu zitieren, ein Wort, das ich vor einiger Zeit bei Leo Schestow gelesen habe: 'Ne nous reprochez pas le manque de clarté puisque nous en faisons profession!' — Das ist, glaube ich, wenn nicht kongenitale, so doch wohl die der Dichtung um einer Begegnung willen aus einer — vielleicht selbstentworfenen — Ferne oder Fremde zugeordnete Dunkelheit" (7).

Damen und Herren, ich danke Ihnen für Ihre Anwesenheit."[2] Thus, the "ladies and gentlemen" of Darmstadt are the alpha and the omega of Celan's acceptance.

The constant recurrence, together with the concluding reference to the audience's "presence," suggests that Celan does not want simply to describe an encounter but rather to create it or re-create it in the flesh as a present event. He calls upon his listeners to be participants rather than spectators, so that they may serve as incarnate witnesses directly involved in this incarnate event. Celan, the speaking body at the podium, addresses the bodies seated before him. His repeated emphasis on this discursive situation underscores the participants' presence, for which he is grateful: "ich danke Ihnen für Ihre Anwesenheit" (13). The phrase, "Meine Damen und Herren," contributes to the event-like nature of what is present and what is being presented, not despite but precisely because of its commonness and emptiness, precisely because of its emphatic recurrence. In becoming empty and common, in suffering a certain depletion or kenosis, the words of the apostrophe come to appear as mere words and hence as more problems, more stumbling blocks, no longer working simply as a transparent device for addressing a gathering, but rather as a poetic figure in its own right, a word that scandalously prevents total comprehension.[3] Worn out from overuse, the vocative transforms into a nearly silent object, a *Gegenstand* thrown upon the path of communication for the sake of a *Begegnung*.

In this sense, the depleted address is analogous to the "Gegenwort" that Celan singles out in his speech: the "counterword" uttered by Büchner's Lucile, "for whom language is something person-like and tangible [*etwas Personhaftes und Wahrnehmbares*]."[4] At the very end of *Dantons Tod*, the widowed Lucille, aimlessly wandering across the Place de la Révolution, addresses the patrolmen with a senseless "Long live the King!" which brings the play to an abrupt halt. Lucile's pronouncement is senseless, not only because there is no longer any monarchy to salute, but also because this sentence will certainly spell the deranged woman's death sentence.[5] For Celan, this empty address, once a constant refrain during the ancien régime, is now a homage "to the majesty of the absurd which bears witness

2. Celan, *Meridian*, 13.

3. See Kristina Mendicino, who further reflects on the poetic force of Celan's recurring apostrophe: "An Other Rhetoric: Paul Celan's Meridian," *MLN* 126 (2011), 630–50.

4. Celan, *Meridian*, 3.

5. On Celan's engagement with Büchner's *œuvre*, see Michael Levine, "Pendant: Büchner, Celan, and the Terrible Voice of the Meridian," *MLN* 122 (2007), 573–601. I borrow the phrase "death sentence" from Levine, 575.

to human presence" ("Gehuldigt wird hier der für die Gegenwart des Menschlichen zeugenden Majestät des Absurden" [3])—a *Gegenwort* that testifies to the *Gegenwart*, a "waiting" (*Warten*) that is absurd insofar as it runs *counter* to all expectations. Celan identifies Lucile, the bereaved widow, as "often quoted" ("oft Zitierte" [3]), for like a citation, she adduces another, unrecognized authority to bear witness to the present. In her very being, she turns language into "something person-like and tangible." In a similar fashion, Celan turns his repeated address into a palpating, recalcitrant body. Every quotation is essentially a repetition.

Ladies and Gentlemen, it is today commonplace, to reproach poetry with its "opacity." Despite aiming to counter charges of poetic opacity, Celan only perpetuates obfuscation, again, by means of quotation. He allows his person-like and tangible words to be interrupted by a citation in French—"Ne nous reprochez pas le manque de clarté puisque nous en faisons profession!"—"Do not reproach us with a lack of clarity since we openly profess it!" Although Celan's sophisticated West German audience would presumably have little difficulty with the French, the use of foreign language has long been counted as one of the common causes of poetic obscurity, together with rhetorical figures like anacoluthon, asyndeton, ellipsis, hermetic allusiveness, archaisms, private imagery, and esoteric wordplay.[6] To be sure, given this list of devices, Celan is guilty as charged, evident not only in his difficult poetry, but already in the prose passage cited here. In addition to the French intervention, his text freely engages in elliptical syntax, abstruse allusion, and even the kind of vicious word play that anticipates the act of citation (*zitieren*) with the term *Opa-zität*. Whereas in the rhetorical tradition, citations as "witnesses" (*martyres*) should incorporate the intrustion of the diachronic smoothly into the synchronic frame of the discourse at hand, Celan appears to let these two temporalities collide, not because Pascal is not made to serve his general thesis, but rather because his listeners, who have already been shaped into witnesses, are being called upon to bear witness for this witness—a gesture that opens onto the impassibility and impossibility of testimony, which Jacques Derrida has carefully traced in his discussion of Celan's poetics.[7]

6. Cf. J. A. Cuddon, *A Dictionary of Literary Terms*; cited in Päivi Mehtonen, *Obscure Language, Unclear Literature: Theory and Practice from Quintilian to the Enlightenment* (Helsinki: Finnish Academy of Science and Letters, 2003), 9.

7. Jacques Derrida, "Poetics and Politics of Witnessing," in *Sovereignties in Question: The Poetics of Paul Celan*, Thomas Dutroit and Outi Pasanen, eds. (New York: Fordham University Press, 2005), 65–96.

That is to say, in this passage from *The Meridian*'s midpoint, Celan causes a colliding encounter by adducing Pascal's defense. The quote can be read perhaps as an *opacitation*, which exposes the speech to a foreign and distant body, a body inserted into the argument "abruptly" or "suddenly" or "immediately" (*unvermittelt*). Again, whereas rhetorics has consistently stressed the importance of "conveyance" (*Vermittlung*)—relaying an argument, a feeling, or some information—here, we are faced with a conveyance qualified somehow as "not conveyed" (*unvermittelt*). The obscurity that rhetoricians have always reproached is generally this failure to communicate. It is as though Celan wants to bypass the "mediation" (*Vermittlung*) that generally takes place in communicating or conveying something from a source (*vermitteln*). All the same, the citation is explicitly mediated by way of another source, through the work of Leo Schestov, who was brought up in a Jewish family in Kiev and later, under Bolshevik persecution, migrated to Paris, like Celan himself. How, then, to assess the abrupt citation that fills in the gaping wound that opacity itself has opened, if not as the nonmediated eruption of something mediated, as the "conveyance" of something that is nonetheless "not conveyed," as the *Vermittlung* of something that is nonetheless *unvermittelt*?

Celan's quotation of Schestov's quotation of Pascal is at the very least curious. Celan himself was a close reader of Pascal's *Pensées*: he made frequent notations in his edition, beginning around January 1960, and would use this text in his class at the École Normale Supérieure.[8] It would appear somehow important, therefore, that Celan's citation be viewed specifically as a quotation of a quotation, not merely citing a passage from the past, but also citing the act of citation itself. This gesture, of course, is but one example of the extraordinary citational and testimonial energy that organizes and motivates the entire *Meridian* speech, which features countless lines lifted from Büchner—from *Lenz, Dantons Tod, Leonce und Lena*—lines that Büchner himself took mostly verbatim from historical documents.[9] As Celan remarks in *The Meridian*, "Büchner only needs to quote" ("Büchner braucht [. . .] nur zu zitieren" [3]). Throughout his speech, Celan persistently cites Büchner's citations, a practice, more-

8. See A. Richter, P. Alac, and B. Badiou, eds., *Paul Celan: La bibliothèque philosophique* (Paris: ENS, 2004), 685–87.

9. On Celan's citational practices in relation to Büchner's, see Helmut Müller-Sievers, "On the Way to Quotation: Paul Celan's *Meridian* Speech," *New German Critique* 91 (2004), 131–49; and Winfried Menninghaus, "Zum Problem des Zitats bei Celan und in der Celan-Philologie," in *Paul Celan*, W. Hamacher and W. Menninghaus, eds. (Frankfurt a. M.: Suhrkamp, 1988), 170–90.

over, that directly relates to his poetics. In his preparatory notes, Celan tersely defines "the poetic" ("Das Dichterische") as "the quotation marks that blow away in the darkness" ("die im Dunkel verwehenden Anführungsstriche" [63]). The citations, precisely as verbal repetitions, are also events, insofar as they reappear, again, "for the sake of an encounter"—a *philological* encounter, one that maintains a deep and intimate love for words, without necessarily striving for objectivity, without simply appropriating foreign material for the sake of comprehension. On the contrary, this philology would appear to be practiced for the sake of the encounter itself.

As Celan confesses, he lifted the Pascal citation from Leo Schestov, namely from Schestov's 1923 essay, *The Night of Gethsemane*, which was published in German translation in a special number of *Ariadne*, the journal of the Nietzsche-Gesellschaft, edited by Ernst Bertram, Hugo von Hofmannsthal, and Thomas Mann. Reminiscent of phenomenology, Schestov's piece essentially lodges a critique against the kind of philosophical rationalism that divorces the knowing subject from the world to be known. To this end, he presents a figuration of Christ as desperately alone in the Garden of Gethsemane, a man in utter agony, entirely depleted of his divinity. As a god consigned to history and mortality, as a figure pulled down from his sovereign, timeless position, his incarnate being militates against any theory of knowledge that would leave the subject transcendent, detached, invulnerable, and untouchable.

> There is but a single way to avoid all this: to renounce the "veritates aeternae," to renounce the fruits of the Tree of Knowledge—"s'abêtir". To believe nothing of all that reason promises. To abandon the light-filled regions, for the light reveals the lies. To grow fond of darkness: "Qu'on ne nous reproche pas le manque de clarté, car nous en faisons profession!" Inspired by the biblical revelation, Pascal creates an entirely peculiar "theory of cognition", which stands in direct contradiction to our conceptions of the essence of truth.[10]

10. Leo Schestov, *Die Nacht der Gethsemane* (1923), H. Ruoff, trans., *Ariadne: Jahrbuch der Nietzsche-Gesellschaft*, Ernst Bertram, Hugo von Hofmannstahl, and Thomas Mann, eds. (1925), 36–109. "Es gibt nur einen Weg, um alledem zu entgehen: auf die 'veritates aeternae,' auf die Früchte vom Baume der Erkenntnis verzichten—'s'abêtir.' An nichts von alledem glauben, was die Vernunft verheißt. Die lichterfüllten Gegenden verlassen, denn das Licht macht die Lüge offenbar. Die Finsternis lieb gewinnen: 'Qu'on ne nous reproche pas le manque de clarté, car nous en faisons profession!' Von der biblischen Offenbarung inspiriert, schafft Pascal eine ganz

In renouncing the timeless truths, with which reason seduces us, we learn to approach rather than reproach obscurity, to draw near to it, to stumble upon it, to become beastly stupid (*s'abêtir*). Schestov's exemplum for this encounter is the Christian Incarnation—the doctrine that, according to Paul, was greeted "by the Jews as a stumbling block (σκάνδαλον) and by the Greeks as foolishness (μωρίαν)" (1 Corinthians 1:23). Here, the incarnation is moronically scandalous, insofar as it turns everything on its head, pulling divine transcendence down to the pit of mortal immanence. A person who seeks revelation by quitting the light of reason is like Büchner's Lenz, who wished he could walk on his head—a wish, as Celan points out, that would turn the sky above into an abyss.

The poetic theory implicit in Celan's *Meridian* is a philology of the flesh, an approach to obscurity that hinges on the *skandalon* of the Incarnation, whereby the word made flesh is evacuated of transcendent meaning, whereby the vertical axis is cut off. For Celan, Lucile's *Gegenwort* is specifically "the word that cuts the string" ("das Wort, das den 'Draht' zerreißt" [3]); it severs the cord that held up Danton and Camille Desmoulin like puppets. As Celan indicates, Danton and Camille are altogether eloquent, supported by "art," which is "something marionette-like" (*marionettenhaftes*). In contrast, Lucile is "blind to art" ("die Kunstblinde" [3]), someone who fails to use language as an instrument for making clear sense, someone "for whom language is person-like and tangible." Lucile's counterword is analogous to Celan's obscurity, insofar as it resists, for as long as possible, the pull toward a more constative dimension of language, where words ascend to some stability of meaning. Blind to art, including the art of producing sense, Lucile too is a philologist of the flesh whose words have little to do with *Kunst* but everything to do with *Dichtung*. Here, language not only becomes tangible but also remains tangible, without recourse to any subsequent resurrection. For Celan, as for Schestov, the reproachful *noli me tangere* is suspended in favor of a ceaselessly approachable *me tange*. Celan adheres to the Passion of Gethsemane and the Cross and cancels his trip to the empty tomb.

In light of these comments, it is worthwhile to consider the original context of the statement that Schestov cites from Pascal's *Pensées*:

> What do the prophets say of Jesus Christ? That he will be clearly God? No, but that he is a God truly hidden, that he will be slighted, that none will think that

---

eigenartige 'Erkenntnistheorie,' die zu unseren Vorstellungen vom Wesen der Wahrheit im direkten Widerspruch steht" (89).

> it is he, that he will be a stumbling block, upon which many will hit, etc. Let one then reproach us no longer for the lack of clarity, since we openly profess it. But, it is said, there are obscurities and without that no one would have stumbled over Jesus Christ, and this is one of the formal pronouncements of the prophets: *excaeca* . . .[11]

Stumbling upon the Word made flesh may have ultimate religious value, but before any redemptive measure, which for the wagering Pascal may or may not be possible, the incarnate word baffles comprehension. The *logos*-in-the-flesh exceeds every *logos*. Pascal thus engages in an Augustinian tradition, whereby the obscurity of God's revelation humbles human pride and condemns the reprobate to darkness. For this reason, Pascal adduces his own citation, from the Book of Isaiah: a single Latin imperative: *excaeca*, "make blind":

> Blind [*excaeca*] the heart of this people and make their ears heavy and close their eyes, lest they may see with their eyes and hear with their ears and understand with their heart and convert and be healed. (Isaiah 6:10; my translation)[12]

We have already witnessed how Emily Dickinson evokes these lines to illustrate her forced exile from reading. Generally, in rabbinical interpretations, the prophet is here instructed by God to fatten the people's heart—to make them deaf and blind—until they learn to repent; for the ignorance of deafness and blindness contrasts with the understanding that is prerequisite for the healing of God's forgiveness.[13] With eyes shut, they will earnestly pray and thereby be healed. In the Christian reading, which Pascal inherits, the implied ignorance

11. Blaise Pascal, Fondement 5, Laf. 228, Sel. 260 = *Pensées* No. 751. "Que disent les prophètes de Jésus-Christ? qu'il sera évidemment Dieu? non mais qu'il est un Dieu véritablement caché, qu'il sera méconnu, qu'on ne pensera point que ce soit lui, qu'il sera une pierre d'achoppement, à laquelle plusieurs heurteront, etc. Qu'on ne nous reproche donc plus le manque de clarté puisque nous en faisons profession. Mais, dit-on, il y a des obscurités et sans cela on ne serait pas aheurté à Jésus-Christ. Et c'est un des desseins formels des prophètes: *excaeca* . . ."

12. "excaeca cor populi huius et aures eius adgrava et oculos eius claude ne forte videat oculis suis et auribus suis audiat et corde suo intellegat et convertatur et sanem eum" (Vulgate).

13. On historical interpretations of this passage, see Craig Evans, "Isaiah 6:9–10 in Rabbinic and Patristic Writings," *Vigiliae Christianae* 36 (1982), 275–81.

is ascribed to those who neglect to heed the Gospel, to those who do not have the ears to hear. Hence, as we have seen, Jesus himself cites Isaiah 6 to conclude his parable of the sower. With horrific consequences, as early as Justin Martyr in the second century, this text was further used in a polemic against the Jewish people, who were charged with refusing to accept the new covenant.[14] In a similar fashion, Tertullian cites Isaiah's verse to describe a Jewish failure to believe in the resurrection of the flesh—a failure that, for Tertullian, is underscored by the fact of the Jewish diaspora, in which these "exiles from their own soil and sky wander over the world without man or God for their king" (*et soli et caeli sui extorres vagantur per orbem sine homine, sine deo rege*).[15] By remaining blind and deaf to the Christian Resurrection, the Jewish people can pray to no power for safety or salvation. On the contrary, in Tertullian's judgment, by "presuming that Christ is merely a man on the basis of his humility" (*hominem solummodo praesumpserant de humilitate*), the Jewish people had put God in the absurd position of having to pray to them, so that he might be saved from a cruel death by crucifixion.[16]

Three years before accepting the Büchner Prize, Celan gave expression precisely to this scenario, portraying a people whose prayer enjoins a god to pray to them. The poem entitled "Tenebrae" was first published in 1957 in the journal *Jahresring* and subsequently included in Celan's *Sprachgitter* collection of 1959:

Nah sind wir, Herr,
nahe und greifbar.

Gegriffen schon, Herr,
ineinander verkrallt, als wär
der Leib eines jeden von uns
dein Leib, Herr.

Bete, Herr,
bete zu uns,
wir sind nah.

14. Irenaeus, *Dialogus cum Tryphone Iudaeo*, 12.
15. Tertullian, *Liber Apologeticus*, 21.5.
16. Tertullian, *Liber Apologeticus*, 21.17.

Windschief gingen wir hin,
gingen wir hin, uns zu bücken
nach Mulde und Maar.

Zur Tränke gingen wir, Herr.

Es war Blut, es war,
was du vergossen, Herr.

Es glänzte.

Es warf uns dein Bild in die Augen, Herr,
Augen und Mund stehn so offen und leer, Herr.
Wir haben getrunken, Herr.
Das Blut und das Bild, das im Blut war, Herr.

Bete, Herr.
Wir sind nah.[17]

Near are we, Lord,
near and graspable.

Grasped already, Lord,
clawed into one another, as if
the body of each of us were
your body, Lord.

Pray, Lord,
pray to us,
we are near.

Wind-skewed we went there,
we went there to stoop
over pit and crater.

17. Paul Celan, *Die Gedichte: Kommentierte Gesamtausgabe*, Barbara Wiedemann, ed. (Frankfurt a.M.: Suhrkamp, 2005), 97.

To the trough we went, Lord.
It was blood, it was,
what you shed, Lord.

It glistened.

It cast your image into our eyes, Lord,
Eyes and mouth stand so open and empty, Lord.
We have drunk, Lord.
The blood and the image that was in the blood, Lord.

Pray, Lord.
We are near.

Composed with three distinct verb tenses—the preterite, the present perfect, and the present—the poem can be rearranged to reveal a troubling narrative. First, an account of past suffering ("We went there to stoop [. . .] to the trough we went [. . .] It was blood [. . .] It glistened"); then, completed action in the perfect ("Grasped already [. . .] clawed into one another [. . .] we have drunk"), which motivates the prayer, namely that the "Lord" may pray to them in the present. Despite its terseness, the poem's imagery frighteningly conjures the mass murder of the Jews at the hands of Nazis—the countless deaths in the gas chambers (the pile of bodies "clawed into one another") and the rounding up of entire populations, which were subsequently shot (the bodies stooping "over pit and crater," where their blood was mercilessly shed).

In his preliminary sketches, Celan first titled the poem "Psalm," then "Leçons de Ténèbres."[18] The latter most likely alludes to François Couperin's 1714 cantata, *Leçons de Ténèbres*, a powerful setting of the Book of Lamentations, which forms part of the Roman Catholic liturgy during Passion Week (the *officium tenebrarum*), specifically during the Lauds and Matins masses. Here, the candles are extinguished to foreshadow the Crucifixion, when, as the Gospel of Matthew reports: "there was darkness over all the land" (*tenebrae factae sunt super universam terram*, Matt. 27:45 [NKJV]). The poem's depiction of genocide,

18. For a comprehensive account of the secondary literature, see Jean Marcel Vincent, "La figure de l'inversion dans le poème Tenebrae de Paul Celan," *Revue de théologie et de philosophie* 57 (2007), 205–25.

therefore, is somehow brought into relation with the Christian Crucifixion: a bold conjunction of the Passion and the Shoah. This jointure evokes Celan's specific image of a *Sprachgitter*—a "language grid or latticework."[19] With the particular juxtaposition of "Tenebrae," the dual nature of Christ as God and Man is clearly rendered in two, divided between the divine perpetrator of suffering and the human victim of suffering. The Lord's Passion appears to correspond to the suffering of the people who went to the trough, which implies that the prayers of the crucified Christ and the prayers of the Jewish victims have not been heard by the transcendent God; hence, the victims' revised prayer: "Pray to us" because "we are near."

Yet what would these prayers achieve, both the victims' prayer to the human Lord and the Lord's possible prayer to those suffering? Why does the Lord fail to respond in Celan's poem? Is this nonresponse the same as the divinity's failed response? Even if the human Lord answered by praying to them—by approaching them in prayer—what could the victims, as the addressees of this entreaty, possibly offer him? Are the victims, in their suffering, enjoining the Lord to pray for their forgiveness? Should every prayer be expected to elicit a response? Or does praying simply establish the conditions of responsibility, both on the part of the praying subject and on the part of the subject addressed?

The conjunction of the Shoah and the Crucifixion is already operative in the Catholic litrugy, which employs the Hebrew Book of Lamentations as a figure for Christ's abandonment on the Cross. The first four poems of the Lamentations, traditionally attributed to the prophet Jeremiah, consist of twenty-two verses each, composed as an acrostic, with the first word of each verse beginning with a Hebrew letter in alphabetic order. Already on a strictly formal level, Celan's "Tenebrae" mirrors the biblical text, insofar as the poem consists exactly of twenty-two lines. Couperin's *Leçons de Ténèbres* follows the Vulgate translation of Lamentations, which prints the initial Hebrew letter of each verse, even though the acrostic form is not retained in the Latin. The first poem, which provides the text for Couperin's cantata, commemorates the Babylonian destruction of Jerusalem by personifying the city as an inconsolable widow, wallowing

19. Accordingly, Jacques Derrida comments: "there is in [Celan's] writing quite an extraordinary crossing—almost in the genetic sense of the term—of cultures, references, literary memories, always in the mode of extreme condensation, caesura, ellipsis, and interruption." Derrida, "Language Is Never Owned: An Interview," in *Sovereignties in Question*, 97–107, here 100. See also Vincent, "La figure de l'inversion," 212–13.

in despair. The image recalls Büchner's Lucile, drifting across the Place de la Révolution:

> א quomodo sedit sola civitas plena populo facta est quasi vidua
> domina gentium princeps provinciarum facta est sub tributo
>
> ב plorans ploravit in nocte et lacrimae eius in maxillis eius non est
> qui consoletur eam ex omnibus caris eius omnes amici eius
> spreverunt eam et facti sunt ei inimici. (Lam. 1:1)
>
> How lonely sits the city
> *That was* full of people!
> *How* like a widow is she,
> Who *was* great among the nations!
> The princess among the provinces
> Has become a slave!
>
> She weeps bitterly in the night,
> Her tears *are* on her cheeks;
> Among all her lovers
> She has none to console *her*.
> All her friends have dealt treacherously with her;
> They have become her enemies.
>
> NKJV

The Christian appropriation of this ancient document of the Hebrews' Babylonian exile readily engages in the hermeneutic economy of typology, whereby Jerusalem's lament for being abandoned by God serves as a prefiguration of Christ's agonized cry to the God who has deserted him. Jesus's last gasp in Aramaic, "Eli, Eli lama sabachthani" ("My God, my God, why have you forsaken me [με ἐγκατέλιπες]!" [Matt. 27:46, NKJV]), is however but another foreign citation, now from Psalm 22, which underscores divine distance: "My God, my God, why have you forsaken me? Why are you so far from helping me?" (Ps. 22:1). In the Gospel account, the citation not only allows a past text to bear witness to the present, but also transforms the psalmist's word into tortured flesh: a frightening image of God abandoning Himself. In the Septuagint, the Greek verb of forsaking, which translates the Aramaic *sabachthani*, is *enkataleipein*, "to leave (*leipein*) behind (*kata*) and in (*en*)"—a painful *ellipsis* that leaves the divine being "down" (*kata*) and in (*en*) the world, cataleptic and dying.

The Book of Lamentations presents a wrathful God, who plunges the prophet into despair, depolying language that further recalls Celan's poem:

> א ego vir videns paupertatem meam in virga indignationis eius
> א me minavit et adduxit in tenebris et non in lucem
> א tantum in me vertit et convertit manum suam tota die
>
> ב vetustam fecit pellem meam et carnem meam contrivit ossa mea
> ב aedificavit in gyro meo et circumdedit me felle et labore
> ב in tenebrosis conlocavit me quasi mortuos sempiternos
>
> Lam. 3:1–6

> I *am* the man *who* has seen affliction by the rod of His wrath.
> He has led me and made *me* walk
> *In* darkness and not *in* light.
> Surely He has turned His hand against me
> Time and time again throughout the day.
>
> He has aged my flesh and my skin,
> And broken my bones.
> He has besieged me
> And surrounded *me* with bitterness and woe.
> He has set me in dark places
> Like the dead of long ago.
>
> NKJV

In stark contrast to the Psalms, the Lord here shepherds the prophet "in darkness" (*in tenebris*), leaving him to suffer in his aged flesh and broken bones. The description recurs in the setting of Judgment Day in the Christian Book of Revelation (20:11–15), which finds its most powerful liturgical formulation in the hymn *Dies Irae*, composed by the thirteenth-century Franciscan monk, Thomas of Celano—a highly probable source for the pseudonym chosen by Celan (born Paul Antschel). Thomas of Celano's hymn itself cites the Vulgate translation of the Book of Zephaniah, the Hebrew prophet whose own name translates as "Yahweh is hidden."

That day *is* a day of wrath [*Dies irae, dies illa*],
A day of trouble and distress,
A day of devastation and desolation,
A day of darkness [*dies tenebrarum*] and gloominess,
A day of clouds and thick whirlwinds,
A day of trumpet and alarm
Against the fortified cities
And against the high towers.
Zeph. 1:15–16 [NKJV modified]

It is important to note that, in the Hebrew, the phrase "a day of devastation and desolation" reads *yom shoah umshoah* (יוֹם שֹׁאָה וּמְשׁוֹאָה) further brings the Christian Judgment Day into contact with Celan's tenebrous depiction of suffering in the camps.[20]

Celan's poem invokes the figure of the crucified Christ as part of the human race abandoned by God. This humanity, stripped of divine nature, is forcefully expressed through the figure of blood: "It was blood, it was, / what you shed, Lord." Despite the Eucharistic allusion—and despite the syntactical ambiguity: Whose blood was shed? The Lord's or the victims'?—the sacrifice does not serve to redeem mankind, but rather, conversely, calls for God's redemption through mankind, down and in the world. For here, God can no longer pray to Himself; He is instead impelled to pray to those close by, to those who are below and in the world with him. Whereas in the Psalms God's proximity encourages his worshippers to pray heavenward ("Der HERR ist nahe allen, die ihn anrufen" [Luther] ["The Lord is near to all who call upon Him"] [Ps. 145:18; NKJV]), Celan's "Tenebrae" implies God's distance, a divine reproach issued from an inaccessible realm. The "Lord" is still near to those who pray to Him, but this human nearness now translates into divine distance. The poem's collective voice—"we"—continues to pray to the Lord, but now prays that He may pray to them who are near. Transcendence is put out of play. There remains only immanence, an immanence that renders the Lord as "graspable" (*greifbar*) as flesh-and-blood creatures. The Christian condescension is complete, as expressed by Jesus' final word: "Es ist vollbracht!" [Luther] ("It is finished" [John 19:30; NKJV]).

20. On the role of the Book of Zephaniah in Celan's "Tenebrae," see Michael Ossar, "The Malevolent God and Paul Celan's 'Tenebrae,'" *Deutsche Vierteljahrsschrift für Literaturwissenschaft und Geistesgeschichte* 65 (1991), 174–97.

For Hans-Georg Gadamer and others, a Christian interpretation of "Tenebrae," one that insists upon the radically human nature of the Incarnation, points to a poetic expression of universal human existence—an expression of human mortality. Gadamer discerns in the poem a powerful comment on the human condition, an assertion of mankind's ultimate loneliness in facing death. And it is this singular finitude that allows us to affirm our connectedness with each other. For Gadamer, Celan's poem provides a difficult description of a forsaken state that reveals "our unity with the dying Jesus."[21] Slavoj Žižek modulates this atheological premise quite succinctly: "Our radical experience of separation from God is the very feature that unites us with Him. [. . .] Only when I experience the infinite pain of separation from God do I share an experience with God Himself (Christ on the Cross)."[22]

Yet alongside interpretations of Celan's "Tenebrae" as a reflection on the Christian appropriation of a Hebrew lament, one is also invited to read the text as a Jewish appropriation of a Christian episode, or as another quotation of a quotation. John Felstiner, for example, balks at importing any universalizing gesture that would reduce the poem's depiction of pain to general statements on the plight of *all* humans. For Felstiner there is a more *sarcastic* tone in Celan's language, a poetry that literally tears into the flesh (*sarx, sarkos*). Implicitly, for interpreters like Felstiner, a philology of the flesh cannot and should not be subordinated in the Christian system of typology, which invariably proves itself to be spiritualizing and therefore exceedingly carnivorous. Rather than conjure Gethsemane or Golgotha, Felstiner justifiably summons Belzec, Sobibor, and Auschwitz, with allusions to Easter pogroms, anti-Semitic libels, and the inhuman horror of the camps, where victims "clawed into one another."[23]

Of course, as Felstiner himself admits, neither approach necessarily pre-

21. Hans-Georg Gadamer, "Meaning and Concealment of Meaning," in *Gadamer on Celan*, Richard Heinemann, trans. (Albany: SUNY Press, 1997), 173.

22. Žižek, *Puppet and Dwarf*, 91. Žižek's interpretation of the Incarnation rehearses the central claim of the "Death of God" theology exemplified in Thomas J. J. Altizer's *The Gospel of Christian Atheism* (Philadelphia: Westminster, 1966). In brief, Christian Atheism underscores Nietzschean immanence. As Mark C. Taylor explains: "Since this God [i.e., the distant, transcendent God of neo-orthodoxy] is always elsewhere, believers can approach the divine only by withdrawing from the world as we know it. The death of the transcendent neoorthodox God is, therefore, the negation of the negation of life, which allows the true God of Jesus (rather than Christ) to be born anew." Taylor, *After God* (Chicago: University of Chicago Press, 2007), 201.

23. John Felstiner, "'Clawed into Each Other': Jewish vs. Christian Memory in Paul Celan's 'Tenebrae,'" *TriQuarterly* 87 (1993), 193–208.

cludes that Celan's poem is staging a collision of both, for the sake of an encounter. The word *Tenebrae* could be read as iconic in this regard, particularly when one hears by way of paronomasia the *Hebräer* ("Hebrews") in the titular *Ten-Ebrae*. Although the word *Hebräer* is today not common in German usage, it was frequently employed throughout the first half of the twentieth century as a more neutral term for *Juden* ("Jews"), especially in scholarly and pseudoscientific discourses. Given the dual reception of Celan's poem, one could ask whether the title points to the complete absorption of the Hebraic element—for example, as in Gadamer's hermeneutic reading, which attends to a universal-human meaning at the expense of the historical specificity of the Shoah—or to the endurance of this very specificity, which resists incorporation into any hermeneutic scheme: the Hebrew experience that is persistently heard despite obfuscating interpretations. Certainly, in the Christian tradition, the Jewish people are often depicted as those who remain in the dark, insofar as they fail to recognize Jesus as the messianic light. As Jesus claimed to the scribes and the Pharisees of the Temple: "I am the light of the world. He who follows Me shall not walk in darkness [*in tenebris*], but have the light of life" (John 8:12 [NKJV]).

The central motif of grasping (*Greifen*), understood either literally as physical clutching or figuratively as cognitive comprehension (*Begreifen*), addresses the two basic approaches to the poem and may already be heard in the title *Tenebrae*, insofar as the *ten-* could be taken as the root of the Latin verb for having, holding, and grasping: *tenere*. The poem's opening, declarative lines establish the connection between proximity and graspability—"nahe und greifbar"—a connection that subversively rewrites Friedrich Hölderlin's well-known gambit at the head of his hymn "Patmos" (1803):

Nah ist
Und schwer zu fassen der Gott.
Wo aber Gefahr ist, wächst
Das Rettende auch.
"Patmos," lines 1–4[24]

Near and
Difficult to grasp is the God.

24. Friedrich Hölderlin, *Werke*, 4 vols., Friedrich Beißner and Jochen Schmidt, eds. (Frankfurt a. M.: Insel, 1969), 2: 54.

> But where there is danger, grows
> Also that which redeems.

Whereas Hölderlin's lines confound sensuous experience by defining God as difficult to grasp *because of* his proximity, Celan's version reasserts our corporeal knowledge, which understands that nearness entails graspability. Through the force of poetic allusion, Celan essentially defuses Hölderlin's *metaphysics* by shifting to a human focus: Even if, metaphysically, the divine is difficult to grasp despite being close, we are physically near and therefore physically graspable. As the German idiom reminds us: we humans are *zum Greifen nah* ("within reach"). Hölderlin further links the difficulty of grasping divine nearness to "danger" (*Gefahr*), underscored by a close responsion: *Nah ist* [. . .] *Gefahr ist* [. . .]. The idea crops up frequently in Hölderlin's late hymns: close contact with the divine is dangerous without the shield of poetry, which acts as an intermediary, capable of gathering and transmitting the celestial fire to humans without harm. Poetry, which emerges from this dangerous encounter with divine *parousia*, is thereby capable of salvation.[25]

Hölderlin's opening strophe goes on to conjure the darkness where the eagles dwell—"Im Finstern wohnen / Die Adler" (5–6)—a line that recalls the gloom of Celan's "Tenebrae" as well as the talons (*Krallen*); for Celan, not the talons of eagles, but rather the claws of one victim digging into another: *ineinander verkrallt*. The core notion that nearness may hinder grasping is reiterated in the subsequent image that Hölderlin deploys to finish out the first strophe:

> und die Liebsten
> Nah wohnen, ermattend auf
> Getrenntesten Bergen,
> So gieb unschuldig Wasser,
> O Fittige gieb uns, treuesten Sinns
> Hinüberzugehn und wiederzukehren.
> "Patmos," lines 10–15

25. Cf. Jean Bollack, Jean-Marie Winkler, and Werner Wögerbauer, "Tenebrae: Esquisse d'une compréhension," *Revue des Sciences Humaines* 97: 223 (1991), 125–70; here, 126. The intertextual relationship between Celan's "Tenebrae" and Hölderlin's "Patmos" is fully explored in Götz Weinold, "Paul Celans Hölderlin-Widerruf," *Poetica* 2 (1968), 216–28.

and the most loved
Dwell near, languishing on
mountains most separate,
So give us innocent water,
O give us wings, with most faithful sense
To cross over and return.

The poet's prayer is answered and he is carried off to the island of Patmos, where John, whose iconographic emblem is the eagle, received the elaborate vision that is gathered and transmitted in the Christian Book of Revelation.

By inverting Hölderlin's primary conceit—God's ungraspable nearness, the danger it poses, and the poetic redemption that follows—Celan stresses human graspability but also thereby cancels the potential for salvation. Although semantically very similar, Hölderlin's verb for grasping (*fassen*) and Celan's term (*greifen*) indicate the distinction between a transcendent divinity, who is "difficult to grasp" (*schwer zu fassen*) and a human being who died as a Jew: as a reviled sovereign, as the *Rex Iudaeorum*, a physically graspable victim. Jesus as God may be difficult to grasp despite His nearness; yet Jesus as Man is all too readily graspable, precisely because of his nearness. The passage from the poem's first strophe to the second (*greifbar. // Gegriffen*), this striking confrontation of an adjective denoting the potential to be grasped and a perfect participle expressing completed action in the present, further emphasizes the concreteness of the corporeal proximity described. In the following line, this physicality horrifically modulates into an even stronger verb for grasping, *verkrallt*, which immediately calls to mind an animal's *claws* (*Krallen*).[26] Recalling the canonical Aristotelian definition of humankind as the "animal that has or holds *logos*," we find here a dehumanizing, animalistic image of bodies that clutch into each other's flesh or perhaps into the enfleshed word, the *logos* incarnate—"as if / the body of each of us were / your body, Lord."

This human tenaciousness—this grasping (*tenere*) in the darkness (*tenebrae*), this proneness to grasp and to be grasped physically, as distinct from the notion of cognitive grasping—constitutes the basis for praying (*beten*), a verb that is anagrammatically discernible in the *teneb-rae*. Unconventionally, this praying does not bind us to God, but rather the "Lord" (*Herr*) to us. The simple

26. Cf. Magdolna Orosz, "Biblical 'Emblems' in Paul Celan's *Tenebrae*: A Special Case of Intertextuality," *Neohelicon* 22 (1995), 169–88, here 175.

vocative, *Herr*, recurs eleven times in the poem, reminding us of the semantic depletion discerned in the *Meridian*'s repeated "Meine Damen und Herren." Consequently, the *Herr* addressed, over and again, is a princely subject pulled down from his sovereign position, a man emptied of any detached, divine quality. Celan underscores this fatal trait in the shocking rhyme with *leer*: "Augen und Mund stehn so offen und *leer, Herr*" ("Eyes and mouth stand so open and *empty, Lord*.") The only recourse for this word made flesh is to pray to those equally forsaken, as if his body were their body, flesh of their flesh. Yet even this basis of shared suffering is undercut by the rhyming of the unreal subjunctive: "als *wär* / der Leib eines jeden von uns / dein Leib, *Herr*" ("as if / the body of each of us *were* / your body, *Lord*"). If mankind was, indeed, created in the image of God, then this image is now fully desublimated, reflected in a pool of spilled blood.

The chiastic formulation that occurs in the penultimate strophe—*Das* Blut *und das* Bild, *das im* Blut *war, Herr* ("The *blood* and the *image* that was in the *blood*, Lord")—reinforces and also radicalizes the desublimination: *Blut—Bild—Blut,* wherein the "image" occupies the middle, mediating position. The line suggests that it is not so much the image that is being reflected in the blood, but rather the blood that is reflected in and through the image. The poem's fundamental inversion, the conceit of a god praying to humans, is echoed by the equally jarring inversion of this line, which follows upon the sole moment of illumination in the darkness portrayed: "Es glänzte" ("It glistened"). It is a brightness that casts light only on the proximate, palpable darkness of resolutely mortal, blood-soaked flesh.

Yet one could also regard this light as generated by the darkness itself. Here, Celan could draw on a long tradition, primarily among French poets, who have adduced the tenebrous figure of the "black sun of melancholy" as it appears in Albrecht Dürer's well-known engraving, for example in Gérard de Nerval's haunting sonnet, "El Desdichado" (1854):

> Je suis le Ténébreux,—le Veuf,—l'Inconsolé,
> Le Prince d'Aquitaine à la Tour abolie:
> Ma seule Etoile est morte,—et mon luth constellé
> Porte le Soleil noir de la Mélancolie.[27]

27. Gérard de Nerval, *Œuvres*, vol. 1, Henri Lemaitre, ed. (Paris: Garnier, 1966), 693. The figure of the "black sun of melancholy" lies at the heart of Julia Kristeva's study, *Black Sun: De-*

I am the Tenebrous One,—the Widower,—the Unconsoled,
The Prince of Aquitaine at the Tower abolished:
My only Star is dead,—and my constellated lute
Bears the black Sun of Melancholy.

The negative definition of the lyrical subject—presented in the initial line as without light, without spouse, and without solace—suffers, like the figure of the unconsoled widow in Lamentations and like the collective subject of Celan's "Tenebrae," from a death of transcendence: the heavenly Star, otherwise a source of guidance and orientation, is dead. The poet, like the mortal Christ (whom Nerval elsewhere powerfully depicts, namely in his sonnet sequence, "Le Christ aux Oliviers" [1844]), has been abandoned to himself.

Charles Baudelaire, in his sonnet "Les Ténèbres" (1861), likewise describes the poet's state as wallowing in complete darkness, locked within the caverns of his soul. The poem is the first of a brief suite entitled "Un Fantôme" ("A Phantom").

Je suis comme un peintre qu'un Dieu moqueur
Condamne à peindre, hélas! sur les ténèbres;
Où cuisinier aux appétits funèbres,
Je fais bouillir et je mange mon cœur
"Les Ténèbres," 5–8[28]

I am like a painter whom a mocking God
Condemns to paint, alas! on the shadows;
Where, a cook with funereal appetite,
I boil and eat my heart

In this inferno of gloom, the artist-poet must endure a Dantesque punishment: feeding on his own flesh in melancholy solitude, he is forced to paint *on* rather than *in* the darkness, as one would paint on a black canvas, black on black. Yet

pression and Melancholia, Leon S. Roudiez, trans. (New York: Columbia University Press, 1989). Her readings of Nerval and Dostoevsky are particularly pertinent for any philology of the flesh; see esp. 175–217.

28. Charles Baudelaire, *Œuvres complètes* (Bibliothèque de la Pléiade), Claude Pichois, ed. (Paris: Gallimard, 1961), 36. I am grateful to Thomas Fries for alerting me to this network of motifs, both in Baudelaire and in the work of Théophile Gautier that follows.

this sentence ultimately leads to an illumination, reminiscent of Celan's glistening light, which does not dispel the darkness from which it emerges:

> Quand il atteint sa totale grandeur,
> Je reconnais ma belle visiteuse:
> C'est Elle! noire et pourtant lumineuse.
>
> 12–14

> When it attains its total grandeur,
> I recognize my beautiful visitor:
> It is She! black and yet luminous.

This epiphany in the final tercet alludes to the *phantom* of the suite's title—a specter that suddenly comes to the poet's imagination or *phantasia*, a luminous appearance or *phainomenon*, whose brightness is internal, not external. Elsewhere, Baudelaire conjures more explicitly the nature of this divulgement in the dark:

> Mais les ténèbres sont elles-mêmes des toiles
> Où vivent, jaillissant de mon œil par milliers,
> Des êtres disparus aux regards familiers.
>
> "Obsession," 12–14,[29]

> But the shadows are themselves canvases
> Where, leaping from my eye by the thousands,
> Vanished beings live with a familiar gaze.

In the darkened atmosphere of Celan's "Tenebrae," the vanished also reappear, yet by means of inversion: it is the spilt, glistening blood that "cast" the image of the Lord "into our eyes"—*Es glänzte. / Es warf uns dein Bild in die Augen, Herr.* Celan's locution not only inverts Baudelaire's, but also inverts idiomatic usage: Whereas it is common, both in German and English, "to cast an eye on something" (*ein Auge auf etwas werfen*), it is odd to describe something casting something *into* the eye. The violence thereby connoted is not neglible.

29. Baudelaire, *Œuvres complètes*, 71.

A major inspiration for Baudelaire was Théophile Gautier, to whom Baudelaire dedicated his *Fleurs du Mal*. He was particularly taken by Gautier's melancholy, which he judged to be "more positive, more carnal [*charnel*], and more confining sometimes than the sadness of antiquity."[30] Baudelaire's prime example is Gautier's *Ténèbres* (1837), a long poem composed in *terza rima*, which reflects on death, nothingness, and the utter absence of salvation:

> Rien ne sera sauvé, pas même l'innocent.
> Ce sera, cette fois, un Déluge sans arche:
> Les eaux seront les pleurs des hommes et leur sang.
>
> *Ténèbres*, 172–74[31]

> Nothing will be saved, not even the innocent.
> There will be, this time, a deluge without ark:
> The waters will be the tears of men and their blood.

In Gautier's poem, as in Celan's "Tenebrae," this pool of blood subsequently reflects the image of Christ upon the Cross:

> Le Christ, d'un ton railleur, tord l'éponge de fiel
> Sur les lèvres en feu du monde à l'agonie,
> Et Dieu, dans son Delta, rit d'un rire cruel.
>
> 184–86

> The Christ, with a mocking tone, twists the sponge of bile
> Upon his burning lips from the world in the anguish of death,
> And God, in his Delta, laughs a cruel laugh.

Gautier's dying Christ adopts the mocking tone that characterizes God, who laughs malevolently at a distance. Like Baudelaire's *Dieu moqueur*, the transcendent divinity has relegated mankind to perpetual darkness. In the concluding tercet and the final solitary verse, we learn that any hope for a redemptive sacrifice has vanished entirely:

30. Baudelaire, "Théophile Gautier" (1859), in *Œuvres complètes*, 697.

31. Théophile Gautier, *Ténèbres*, in *Poésies complètes*, 3 vols., René Jasinski, ed. (Paris: Nizet, 1970), 2: 56–64.

Voici bien deux mille ans que l'on saigne l'Agneau;
Il est mort à la fin, et sa gorge épuisée
N'a plus assez de sang pour teindre le couteau.

Le Dieu ne viendra pas. L'Eglise est renversée.

196–99

These two thousand years one has bled the Lamb;
He is finally dead, and his exhausted throat
Has not enough blood to stain the blade.

God will not come back. The Church is overthrown.

By interlacing these and countless other allusions from biblical and poetic traditions, Celan's "Tenebrae" disrupts hermeneutic endeavors that strive to sacrifice the poem's language for the sake of redeeming univocal sense. The reflecting blood in Celan's poem is not Eucharistic, not digestible. Rather, it is the blood that has spilled forth from human wounds, wounds that puncture the integrity of the poem's bodies, the body of the crucified Lord as well as the bodies of those who are nearby, "clawed into one another." It is this shared wounding, this shared *vulnerability*, that turns the proximity of the addressers and the addressee into a visceral mirroring: "as if / the body of each us were / your body, Lord"—a mirroring mediated by spilt blood, which "cast your image into our eyes." Apart from the sense of violence, noted already above, this figuration may serve to remind us how the incarnation—the descent into flesh and blood—provided God with an image of Himself. If in the Book of Genesis mankind was created "in the image of God" (Gen. 1:27), in the Gospel of John, God was "born" (*egeneto*) in the image of man (John 1:14).

And the particular image here is one of extreme torture. Following the opening imperatives, the fourth stanza suddenly shifts into the preterite: "Windschief gingen wir hin" ("Wind-skewed we went there"). The adjective *windschief* denotes something that is "skewed" or "crooked" (*schief*) through "contorting," "twisting," or "winding" (*winden*), which would appear to be a concise description of the crucified bodies mirroring, again, the crucified body on the Cross. Moreover, one can also sense the "wind" (*Wind*) that blows against these exposed bodies as well as the painful "wounds" (*Wunden*) heard in the perfect participle of the verb *winden*: *gewunden*—perhaps wounded by the image, glistening in the pool of blood, that is cast into the eyes, the "eyes" and the "mouth" that "stand open and empty" like gaping wounds. The mirroring of the incarnation is here a speculum of pain: wounds wounding the wounded.

The close interplay between the "we" (*wir*) and the "Lord" (*Herr*)—the two components that are announced perfectly contiguously in the poem's first line ("Nah sind *wir, Herr*")—produce a chiasmic structure that recalls Merleau-Ponty's elaboration on flesh. For Merleau-Ponty, the mutual wounding is not the result of violent domination, one subject over against another, but rather a trauma that takes place intimately within each subject. The wounding is therefore telepathic, a suffering from afar that is felt deeply within. As Merleau-Ponty notes: "One feels oneself looked at [. . .] not because something passes from the look to our body to burn it at the point seen, but because to feel one's body is also to feel its aspect for the other."[32] At the core of one's sensuous experience, the point of contact between one's self with itself forms a gap for the encountered other from without, which constitutes the self by decentering it.

> It is that this distance is not the contrary of this proximity, it is deeply consonant with it, it is synonymous with it. It is that thickness of flesh between the seer [*voyant*] and the thing is constitutive for the thing of its visibility as for the seer of his corporeity; it is not an obstacle between them, it is their means of communication.[33]

This kind of reversibility, this consonance of distance and proximity, which Merleau-Ponty discerns in the phenomenology of perception through the "thickness of the flesh," is performed on the level of language in Celan's poem: an entwinement of the *wir* and the *Herr*, "we" praying to the "Lord" to pray to us.

32. Merleau-Ponty, "Working Notes" (posthumous), in *The Visible and the Invisible*, 245. For an extended discussion of Merleau-Ponty's phenomenology of the flesh in relation to Celan's poetry, see James Hatley, "Recursive Incarnation and Chiasmic Flesh: Two Readings of Paul Celan's 'Chymisch,'" in *Chiasms*, Leonard Lawlor, ed. (Albany: SUNY Press, 2000), 237–49.

33. Merleau-Ponty, "L'entrelacs—le chiasme." "C'est que cette distance n'est pas le contraire de cette proximité, elle est profondément accordée avec elle, elle en est synonyme. C'est que l'épaisseur de chair entre le voyant et la chose est constitutive de sa visibilité à elle comme de sa corporéité à lui; ce n'est pas un obstacle entre lui et elle, c'est leur moyen de communication" (1760) [*The Visible and the Invisible*, 135].

The imperative "pray," repeated twice, thus determines the circuit of the perfect chiasmus that frames the entire poem:

Nah sind wir, Herr [. . .] *bete* [. . .] *bete* [. . .] Herr, wir sind nah

This chiasmus, this intertwining or *ineinander* of the encounter, perhaps outlines an ellipse with two foci, as Walter Benjamin described in his essay on Kafka: Here, the Lord's prayer to himself in intimate silence ("bete, Herr") and the prayer to those who are near ("bete zu uns"). Every *apostrophe,* which turns toward the other and thereby, like a citation, invites the other within, implies a *catastrophe,* a turn downward, even a turn to the "abyss."[34] In the *Meridian* speech, Celan lists the many difficulties pertaining to contemporary poetry: "word-choice, the rapid dip [*Gefälle*] of syntax or the alert sense for the ellipsis/ ellipse [*Ellipse*]" (8).

Soon thereafter, Celan's speech moves explicitly to the theme of address, to the need for address and its reversibility, particularly in its most radical form: in *prayer*:

> The poem wants to reach out to another one, it needs this other one, it needs a versus [*Gegenüber*]. It seeks it out, it addresses itself to it.
> Each thing, each person is a form of this other one for the poem, which heads for the other one.
> The attentiveness, which the poem tries to dedicate to everything that encounters it [*allem ihm Begegenden*], its sharp sense for detail, for outline, for structure, for color, but also for the "twitchings" and the "allusions" [. . .] "Attentiveness"—allow me here to cite a word from Malebranche, taken from Walter Benjamin's essay on Kafka—"Attentiveness is the natural prayer of the soul."[35]

34. Cf. Philippe Lacoue-Labarthe's reading of Celan's *Meridian* entitled "Catastrophe" in Lacoue-Labarthe, *Poetry as Experience,* Andrea Tarnowski, trans. (Stanford: Stanford University Press, 1999), 41–70.

35. Celan, *Meridian.* "Das Gedicht will zu einem Anderen, es braucht dieses Andere, es braucht ein Gegenüber. Es sucht es auf, es spricht sich ihm zu. Jedes Ding, jeder Mensch ist dem Gedicht, das auf das Andere zuhält, eine Gestalt dieses Anderen. Die Aufmerksamkeit, die das Gedicht allem ihm Begegenden zu widmen versucht, sein schärferer Sinn für das Detail, für Umriß, für Struktur, für Farbe, aber auch für die 'Zuckungen' und die 'Andeutungen' [. . .]. 'Aufmerksamkeit'—erlauben Sie mir hier, nach dem Kafka-Essay Walter Benjamins, ein Wort von Malebranche zu zitieren—'Aufmerksamkeit ist das natürliche Gebet der Seele'" (9).

Attentiveness or prayer, becoming the form of the poem that you encounter, recognizing the eccentricity that occupies a most intimate place within you—with the flesh of the other wounding you in the flesh—is constituted by the two foci that determine your personhood: one person with two natures. In other words: a citation of a citation.

The elliptical orbit of Celan's *Meridian* speech—"Meine Dame und Herren, ich bin am Ende—ich bin wieder am Anfang" ("Ladies and Gentlemen, I am at the end—I am again at the beginning" [10])—is determined above all, and within all, by the meridian that cuts through it:

> I am finding something—like language—something immaterial yet earthly, terrestrial, something orbital, over both poles turning back into itself and thereby—cheerfully—something crossing through even the tropics/tropes [*Tropen*]—: I am finding . . . a *meridian*.[36]

Celan was able to find many meridians, heavenly and terrestrial, "like language": the fixed longitudes and latitudes that span the circumference of the globe, transforming it into a measurable grid; and the meridional position of the observer on earth, which moves as he wanders.[37] Moreover, there are other meridians that Celan would have encountered, pieces of verbal flesh that could have been ingested into the network of the poet's speech.

For example, there is the "meridian" that Theodor Adorno mentions at the head of an essay on Paul Valéry's prose writings, *Valérys Abweichungen* (*Valéry's Deviations* [1960]), which he dedicated to Celan in gratitude for the story *Gespräch im Gebirg* ("Conversation in the Mountains"). Celan composed this short story in 1959 after a visit to Sils Maria in the Swiss Engandin, where Nietzsche had his epiphany of Eternal Return and where he was to meet Adorno in person for the first time. Celan returned to Paris before Adorno arrived; and it was this failed encounter that produced both Celan's *Gespräch im Gebirg* but also Adorno's essay written "for Paul Celan," which both appeared in *Die Neue Rund-*

36. Celan, *Meridian*. "Ich finde etwas—wie die Sprache—Immaterielles, aber Irdisches, Terrestrisches, etwas Kreisförmiges, über die beiden Pole in sich selbst Zurückkehrendes und dabei—heitererweise —sogar die Tropen Durchkreuzendes—: ich finde . . . einen *Meridian*" (12).

37. This doubling of the meridian, between fixed and transient positions, is the starting point of Thomas Schestag's attentive reading of Celan's *Meridian*, in Schestag, "buk," *MLN* 109 (1994), 399–444.

schau in 1960, the year, of course, when Celan accepted the Büchner Prize.[38] In his essay, Adorno simply points out that the French title of Valéry's prose works, *Rhumbs*, is aptly translated as the German *Windstriche* ("Windstrokes"), a nautical navigational term denoting the imaginary lines that cut through the meridians and thereby chart the ship's course as deviations—an apt image for prose published by a poet.[39] Celan, whose own prose piece, *Gespräch im Gebirg*, marked a deviation from his writing in verse, later alludes to the "missed encounter" toward the end of the *Meridian* speech: "And a year ago, recalling a missed encounter in the Engandin, I wrote a little story in which I had a man 'like Lenz' walk through the mountains [*durchs Gebirg*]."[40] The conversation that never took place "6000 feet beyond mankind" (Nietzsche, *Ecce Homo*) thus situates itself upon the meridian line that separates and thereby connects the two writers.

It is also the line of encounter that connects and separates Celan and Büchner, who, as Celan cites, wrote his own story about Lenz, "who on the 20th of January walked through the mountains [*durchs Gebirg*]"—another apostrophe, and hence another catastrophe. Celan goes on to cite more from Büchner's *Lenz*, introducing the line with ellipsis points: ". . . he sometimes found it unpleasant that he could not walk on his head.' Whoever walks on his head, Ladies and Gentlemen, — whoever walks on his head has the heavens below him as the abyss."[41] The ascent or *anabasis* through the mountains—an ascent rehearsed by Nietzsche and by Nietzsche's Zarathustra—instigates a vision of descent or *katabasis*: the turn downward (*katastrophē*) or *condescension* that results in a forsaken god praying to humans. How much *latency* can be discerned in Büchner's *Lenz*? Or, to impose another ellipsis: How much *Latenz* can be uncovered in *L . . . enz*?

There are, indeed, many more meridians, many more encounters and cross-

38. On the biographical interconnections between Celan's *Gespräch im Gebirg*, Adorno's *Valérys Abschweichungen*, and *Der Meridian*, see Arnd Bohm, "Landscapes of Exile: Celan's 'Gespräch im Gebirg,'" *Germanic Review* 78 (2003), 99–111.

39. Theodor Adorno, "Valéry's Deviations," in *Notes to Literature*, 2 vols., Shierry Weber Nicholsen, trans. (New York: Columbia University Press, 1991), 1: 137–73, here 137.

40. Celan, *Meridian*. "Und vor einem Jahr, in Erinnerung an eine versäumte Begegnung im Engandin, brachte ich eine kleine Geschichte zu Papier, in der ich einen Menschen 'wie Lenz' durchs Gebirg gehen ließ" (11).

41. Celan, *Meridian*. ". . . nur war es ihm manchmal unangenehm, daß er nicht auf dem Kopf gehn konnte.' — Wer auf dem Kopf geht, meine Dame und Herren, — wer auf dem Kopf geht, der hat den Himmel als Abgrund unter sich" (7).

ings, exchanges and intertwinings, that could have informed Celan's *Meridian*. The published conversation between Adorno and Celan is replicated by a prior one that also locates yet another line. It figures in Martin Heidegger's essay, *Zur Seinsfrage* (*On the Question of Being* [1955]), originally titled *Über "die Linie"* ("On 'the Line'") and first appearing in a Festschrift celebrating Ernst Jünger's sixtieth birthday: an appropriate reciprocal gesture in light of Jünger's own contribution in 1949 to the Festschrift in honor of Heidegger's own sixtieth birthday. Ever conscious of the close relationship between "thinking" (*Denken*) and "thanking" (*Danken*), Heidegger responds by offering a critical reading of Jünger's 1951 essay *Über die Linie* ("Crossing the Line"), which attempts to provide a way for overcoming contemporary nihilism. The chiasmic relation, one Festschrift mirroring the other, becomes a citational relation: Heidegger's playful use of quotation marks to distinguish his response (*Über "die Linie"—On "the Line"*) from Jünger's essay (*Über die Linie*). Jünger's evocation of nihilism and his suggestions for its "overcoming" (*Überwindung*) return us again explicitly to Nietzsche's Zarathustra—a "line" that must be crossed. Yet Heidegger regards this line as a "prime meridian" (*Nullmeridian*), which one cannot think *through* or get *across*, because it calls us to think *on* it—not *trans lineam* ("across the line") but rather *de linea* ("on the line").[42]

A year before Jünger published *Über die Linie*, in 1950, Carl Schmitt analyzed the history of the great geopolitical controversies, beginning in the sixteenth century, in establishing lines to divide and thereby colonize what had hitherto been the oceans' free space. In the first chapter, "The First Global Lines," which opens the second part of *Der Nomos der Erde* (*The Nomos of the Earth*), Schmitt refers to these governmental acts as a "catastrophe" and, in a gesture that would have caught Celan's attentive eye, cites Pascal: "A meridian decides the truth" (*Un Méridien décide de la vérité*)—a line that Schmitt, the formidable theorist of sovereignty and decisionism, interprets as "an expression of pain and astonishment" (*Ausspruch des Schmerzes und des Erstaunens*).[43]

Schmitt's reading of Pascal's "meridian" bears a striking resemblance to Heidegger's interpretation of Georg Trakl's poem "Ein Winterabend" ("A Winter Eve-

42. Martin Heidegger, *Zur Seinsfrage* [1955], in *Wegmarken* (Frankfurt a. M.: Klostermann, 1976), 385–426.

43. Carl Schmitt, *Der Nomos der Erde im Völkerrecht des jus publicum Europaeum* (Cologne: Greven, 1950), 63. On this derivation of Celan's "meridian" and others, see Schestag, *buk*, 400–01, n. 3.

ning") in an important public lecture that the philosopher gave in October 1950, the moment when the ban on teaching, imposed by the occupying governments in 1945, was finally lifted. After a few general remarks, Heidegger's lecture, where he crosses the line that hitherto restricted him from the seminar room, opens with the citation from Hamann's letter to Herder, which we have already seen:

> Even if I were as eloquent as Demosthenes I would yet have to do nothing more than repeat one word three times: reason is language, *logos*. I gnaw at this marrow-bone and will gnaw myself to death over it. There still remains a darkness, always, over this depth for me; I am still waiting for an apocalyptic angel with a key to this abyss.[44]

The tautology that goads Hamann ("reason is language" or, "*logos* is *logos*")—the bone that he gnaws on, having eaten through all the verbal *meat* (*Fleisch*)—is for Heidegger the "abyss" (*Abgrund*) that cannot, therefore, serve as the "ground" or "reason" (*Grund*) for anything. The ground for language is language, which is to say, the ground is groundless. Thus Heidegger—like his famous student Gadamer—disrupts the understanding of language as a mere tool or instrument for transmitting ideas. To demonstrate, Heidegger turns to a reading of Trakl's "Winterabend," which describes a lonely wanderer who crosses a threshold to enter into the light of a welcoming house. The line that particularly attracts Heidegger's attention is found in Trakl's third and final stanza:

> Schmerz versteinerte die Schwelle.

"Pain petrifies the threshold," "Pain turns the threshold to stone." For Heidegger, this "pain" is "dif-ference" itself—the *Unter-Schied*—a "cut" or "divorce" (*Scheidung*) that allows an intimate connection "in between" or "among" (*unter*) the two sides.[45] For Pascal as well, the dividing line or "méridien" is that which "decides," that which, for Schmitt, imposes an *Entscheidung* ("decision") expressing "pain" (*Schmerz*) and "astonishment" (*Erstaunen*). If one has ears to hear, one

44. Hamann to Herder, Aug. 10, 1784, cited in Martin Heidegger, *Die Sprache*, in *Unterwegs zur Sprache* (Stuttgart: Neske, 1959), 13 ["Language," in *Poetry, Language, Thought*, Albert Hofstadter, trans. (New York: Harper & Row, 1971), 191].

45. Heidegger, *Die Sprache*, 25 ["Language," 204–5].

might pick up on the *stunning* effect in both *astonishment* and *Erstaunen*—one might even hear a *stoning*.

In any case, in a letter to Celan dated October 28, 1959, the poet Nelly Sachs writes: "Between Paris and Stockholm runs a meridian of pain and of consolation [*Meridian des Schmerzes und des Trostes*]," which Celan in turn cites in his reply to Sachs on May 5, 1960: "You once wrote to me, that between Stockhom and Paris there runs a meridan of pain."[46] The elimination of "consolation"—this profound ellipsis—could not be more striking. Recall the speaker in Nerval's "El Desdichado": "I am the Tenebrous One [. . .] the *Unconsoled*." The "immaterial yet terrestrial" line that Celan finds in varied places marks, immaterially and terrestrially, the circumference between two poles: between two selves or two texts, one reaching out for the other, addressing each other, citing each other—in search of an encounter or *Begegnung*, a *versus* (*Gegenüber*) or a *counterword* (*Gegenwort*), that would connect by separating—but also between high points and low points, between the nadir of pain and the zenith of consolation, at least until the string is cut . . .

As soon as she learned that her eight-year-old nephew Thomas Gilbert was seriously ill, Emily Dickinson visited her older brother's home for the first time in fifteen years, so that she could spend time with the suffering child.[47] Until three in the morning, she stayed with the boy who passed away the next day. A few days later, she managed to write a note to her sister-in-law:

> Dear Sue—
>
> The Vision of Immortal Life has been fulfilled — How simply at the last the Fathom comes! The Passenger and not the Sea, we find surprises us — Gilbert rejoiced in Secrets — His Life was panting with them — [. . .] I see him in the Star, and meet his sweet velocity in everything that flies — His Life was like the Bugle, which winds itself away, his Elegy and Echo — his Requiem Ecstasy — Dawn and Meridian in one.[48]

46. Paul Celan and Nelly Sachs, *Briefwechsel*, Barbara Wiedemann, ed. (Frankfurt a. M.: Suhrkamp, 1993), 25 and 121.

47. See Benjamin Lease, *Emily Dickinson's Readings of Men and Books* (New York: Palgrave, 1990), xvi–xix.

48. Dickinson to Susan Huntington Gilbert Dickinson, [October 8, 1883] (no. 868), in Dickinson, *Letters*, 3: 799.

In the few years between "Tenebrae" and the *Meridian* speech, Celan turned to the work of Emily Dickinson and would eventually translate at least ten of her poems. Scholars have long been puzzled by Celan's decision to translate Dickinson, whose work and biographical context appear to be especially distant and foreign. To be sure, the differences are strikingly pronounced: between a nineteenth-century woman steeped in Christianity, who never left her native Massachusetts, and a man from Eastern Europe, who was raised in a Jewish home and suffered horrifically during the twentieth century's darkest era. All the same, Celan was drawn to this unique American voice, selecting poems that are, moreover, particularly colored by theological matters, mysticism, and the possible meaning or meaninglessness of death.

Dickinson's Amherst, informed as it was by Puritan congregationalism, may not have too much common ground with Celan's Bukovina, yet it does feature many concrete points of contact with the provincial life-world of Büchner's *Lenz*, where questions about communal worship, absolution, salvation, and mystical union are closely tied to issues of language. Consider, for example, Dickinson's poem 1065: "Let down the Bars, Oh Death":

> Let down the Bars, Oh Death—
> The tired Flocks come in
> Whose bleating ceases to repeat
> Whose wandering is done —
>
> Thine is the stillest night
> Thine the securest Fold
> Too near Thou art for seeking Thee
> Too tender, to be told.
> *The Poems*, no. 1117 (1865), 1:750

Celan's translation reads:

> Fort mit der Schranke, Tod!
> Die Herde kommt, es kommt,
> wer blökte und nun nimmer blökt,
> wer nicht mehr wandert, kommt.

Dein ist die stillste Nacht,
der sichre Pferch ist dein.
Zu nah bist du, um noch gesucht,
zu sanft, genannt zu sein.[49]

The poem appears to rehearse the standard Christian plot that portrays worldly life as a long pilgrimage, which finds its merited redemption in a transcendent paradise. In the end, all trials are finished and stillness has been achieved. Dickinson's final line, which points to ineffability, suggests that a truly mystical state has indeed been achieved.

That said, the poem's ominous addressee, "Death," troubles a simple redemptive reading. Although physical death in time could be construed as the prerequisite for entrance into an eternal realm, it could also be regarded as marking an absolute end in itself. Here, it is death that is "too near to be sought." Celan's translation brings Dickinson's language close to "Tenebrae": "zu nah bist du, um noch gesucht [zu sein]." Redemption would be a carnival—a farewell to the flesh—and Dickinson's poem holds off any such celebration. She offers no explicit sign of paradise, but instead stresses mortality, alluding to the time when the bleating of the flock is no longer heard, when language itself vanishes, falling into a darkness "too tender, to be told." Celan's rendering of this finale—"zu sanft, genannt zu sein"—with its marked sibilance, assonance, and nasalization, further insinuates that the poem, despite its religious coloring, is concerned with nothing but language, both its existence in the world and its ultimate barring.[50] Celan's translation insists on the materiality of sound that will "cease to repeat" once life in this world ceases. Tellingly, his rendering *repeats* the poem's key verbs—a repetition that materially doubles what Dickinson expressed as a singular instance: "The tired flocks *come* in" – "Die Herde *kommt*, es *kommt*"; "Whose *bleating* ceases to repeat" – "wer *blökte* und nun nimmer *blökt*." The verbal repetition itself appears to resist the silencing that would come with transcendence. Celan exacerbates this poetic effect by transforming Dickinson's

49. Paul Celan, *Gesammelte Werke*, 5 vols., Beda Allemann and Stefan Reichert, eds. (Frankfurt a. M.: Suhrkamp, 1983), 5: 397.

50. Cf. Shira Wolosky, "The Metaphysics of Language in Emily Dickinson (As Translated by Paul Celan)," in *Trajectories of Mysticism in Theory and Literature*, Phillip Leonard, ed., New York: St. Martin's, 2000, 25–45.

fluid assonant repetition—"Whose bl*ea*ting *cea*ses to rep*ea*t"—as a repetition that stumbles in immanence: "wer *blökte* und nimmer *blökt*," a transformation that perhaps plays with an interlingual pun evoking the very *blockage* to transcendence. The language is scandalous, insofar as it stumbles over itself. Like Büchner's Lucile, Dickinson, particularly Celan's Dickinson, seems to recognize that her counterwords not only sever the transcending strings of the puppeteer, but also can bring meaning to an abrupt halt, where death lets down its bars, where the final curtain drops, mercilessly, like the blade of a guillotine.

A similar challenge to pure transcendence is discernible in another poem selected by Celan for translation:

At Half past Three, a single Bird
Unto a silent Sky
Propounded but a single term
Of cautious melody.

At Half past Four, Experiment
Had subjugated test,
And lo, Her silver Principle
Supplanted all the rest.

At Half past Seven, Element
Nor Implement, be seen—
And Place was where the Presence was
Circumference between.

The Poems, no. 1099 (1865), 1:766

Ein Vogel, einer, um halb vier:
dem Himmel, der da schwieg,
den einen Laut trug er ihm an
sparsamster Melodie.

Das war die Probe. Um halb fünf
gings über sie hinaus,
und sieh: ihr silbernes Zuerst
stach alles andre aus.

Halb sieben: weder Element
noch Werkzeug weit und breit.
Ein Ort hier, dort die Gegenwart,
mit einem Zwischenkreis.[51]

This poem as well stages the emergence of sound and its ultimate silencing. Across three terse stanzas, a birdsong is heard against the marked passage of time, at first cautiously and then with brilliant fullness, before finally evanescing into absence. Again, the "sky," as the site of heavenly transcendence, is merely a quiet foil for the singular event of the bird's song. Even if this avian sound were taken to be a verbal signifier, there is no evidence of a transcendent zone in which to locate the signified. The "single term" is its own termination, unfolding its finitude within the steady march of the hours. Whatever meaning obtains is accomplished by an immanent chain of sounds, whose capacity to represent some fixed idea is severely undermined. Whereas some metaphysical realm, some paradise, could generally be said to give eternal value to temporal experience, here it is mortal time that resolutely measures and delimits eternity.[52]

Celan's version betrays a syntactic form that is much more staggered than Dickinson's: as though it were an attempt to debilitate even further the words' ascent to stable, verifiable sense. Perhaps the clearest evidence of this semantic weakening is Celan's consistent use of inversion, placing Dickinson's first phrase second: for example, "At Half past Three, a single Bird"—"Ein Vogel, einer, um halb vier"; "At Half past Four, Experiment"—"Das war die Probe. Um halb fünf." The feeling of inversion is further underscored by the idiomatic difference between English and German: whereas English marks the half hour *afterward* ("half past three"), German designates it *beforehand* (*halb vier*, "a half hour before four"). In the act of translating, Celan reverses what has been received, allowing language to *turn in* on itself.[53] Consequently, the tentativeness of Dickinson's "cautious melody" rises to a superlative form of parsimony—a "most frugal, the most sparing melody" (*sparsamste Melodie*)—as if the sound—perhaps

51. Celan, *Gesammelte Werke*, 5: 401.

52. Cf. Wolosky, "The Metaphysics of Language."

53. Werner Hamacher has brilliantly demonstrated the poetic significance of figures of inversion in the work of Celan: "The Second of Inversion: Movements of a Figure through Celan's Poetry," in *Premises*, 337–87.

the poem itself—is entirely unwilling to let itself be cashed in for sense. With the adjective *sparsam*, the German translation reveals a poetics that is penny wise and therefore pound foolish, as the English nearly expresses: "Pro*pound*ed but a single term"—a term that is being offered, yet one that, in its singularity, evades any clearcut exchange of word for meaning. Celan thus ignores the *singing* that is sonically evoked by the anaphora of the first stanza: "a *single* bird [. . .] a *single* term." In Celan's rendition, nothing can be carried back. Thus, for the common term "circumference," Celan provides a neologism—*Zwischenkreis*—which is yet another kind of inversion ("Circumference between"—"Zwischenkreis"). Yet in addition to inverting the English phrase, the German composite word closes the poem with an opened interval, an empty space or gap or "circle in between." It insinuates how *reference* is but *circumference*—a verbal "place" that bears itself around and between, inverting, reversing, without ever being borne back. In the end, there is no transcendent meaning apart from the world in which we circulate, stumbling about with stumbling words.

The Earth's circumference is composed of geodesic meridians, which together describe the elliptical surface of the planet: a surface measured by two foci—Bukovina and Amherst, the nineteenth and the twentieth centuries, German and English—convergences premised on distance. The meridian, the line that connects by dividing, calls for a philology of the flesh that suspends a word's vaporization into univocal meaning. Hence, Celan turns his reflections on the meridian to justify poetic obscurity, to convert it from something reproachful to something eminently approachable, even if intransigent, even if frightening. The approach, which brings the distant near and sends what is near into the distance, insists on the palpable tangibility of the words, on their fleshly presence—a verbal potential that will remain singular and distinct and not readily cohere into sure bodies of sense. There are words that, by never ceasing to repeat, block any clear passage to transcendent silence, like Dickinson's citation of the Gospel's expiring word or like Celan's quotation of Schestov quoting Pascal quoting Isaiah. In these cases, a philology of the flesh challenges us to stumble along the difficult, discomforting path of signs, exposing us to unmasterable encounters and obfuscating any secure destination, binding us to the text while blinding us to the already known. Blindness, perhaps, has always been prerequisite for insight.

Acknowledgments

The conception and development of this work owe a significant debt to many friends and colleagues. I am particularly grateful to Susan Bielstein, my editor at the University of Chicago Press, who charitably committed herself to the project after hearing my initial musings on the theme during a conference at Utrecht University: *Book Presence in a Digital Age*, organized by Kiene Brillenburg Wurth in May 2012. Many thanks as well to Michael Koplow for his diligent work in editing the typescript. An earlier version of the chapter on Kafka was given as the Rodig Lecture at Rutgers University in 2013 at the invitation of Martha Helfer and Michael Levine. I presented a first draft of the Dickinson chapter as a Whitney J. Oates Fellow at Princeton University in 2014, hosted by Brooke Holmes and Michael Jennings. The chapter on Kant and Hamann was originally offered as the Sigmund H. Danziger Jr. Distinguished Lecture at the University of Chicago in 2014 at the invitation of Michèle Lowrie and David Wellbery. This talk was subsequently published as "Repetitio Sententiarum, Repetitio Verborum: Kant, Hamann, and the Implications of Citation" in *German Quarterly*. I was also fortunate to discuss part of this work for a 2015 conference held at the Guardini Galerie in Berlin: *We are Meat: Transzendenz, Ästhetik und Technik des Fleisches.*

It was my sincere pleasure to present much of the book's material to participants in a seminar at the ETH-Zürich in December 2016, thanks to a generous invitation from Andreas Kilcher and Sandro Zanetti. I am also altogether grateful to those students who participated in my graduate seminar at Harvard University on "Hermeneutics and the Philology of the Flesh" (2016): Josh Cohen, Corrado Confalonieri, John Dilworth, Adriana Harley, Alice Ju, Ashley Morse, Kathleen Ong, Jahdiel Perez, Robert Roessler, Christian Struck, Colton Valentine, Hudson Vincent, and Etha Williams—their weekly interventions and insights played a crucial role in the formulation of the readings presented here. Moreover, I would especially like to thank those who read and commented on drafts of various chapters: Cecily Cai, Volker Demuth, Thomas Fries, Cécile Guédon, Martin Hägglund, Emily Kanner, Michael Levine, Pablo Maurette, Jennifer Nelson, Lisa Parkes, Katharina Piechocki, Eric Santner, Thomas Schestag, Charles Stang, Lauren Stone, Christian Struck, William Todd, Hudson Vincent, Erica Weitzman, and Antje Wessels; as well as Ashley Morse, who carefully went through the section of Dostoevsky and supplied the Russian text. I have also benefitted deeply from informal conversations with a host of colleagues and friends: Homi Bhabha, Emmanuel Bouju, David Damrosch, Hent de Vries, Paul Fleming, Eckart Goebel, Daniel Hoffman-Schwartz, Dania Hückmann, Carol Jacobs, Racha Kirakosian, Florian Klinger, Michael Levine, Ethel Matala de Mazza, Glenn Most, Helmut Müller-Sievers, Barbara Nagel, Almut-Barbara Renger, Efthymia Rentzou, Jeffrey Schnapp, Richard Sieburth, Adam Stern, Henry Sussman, Nicole Sütterlin, Joseph Vogl, Gernot Waldner, David Wellbery, Christopher Wild, and Svetlana Boym, whom I dearly miss. Heartfelt thanks to everyone for your generosity, encouragement, and vital reassurance! And thanks, as always, to Donna, Jasper, and Henry, who never cease to inspire.

Works Cited

Biblical citations are from the following editions and translations:

Hebrew Bible, 10 vols., David Mendel Harduf, ed. Toronto: Hotsa'at Harduf, 1977.

Greek New Testament, Michael Holmes, ed. Atlanta: Society of Biblical Literature, 2010.

Biblia Sacra: iuxta Vulgatam versionem [Vulgate], Robert Weber, ed. Stuttgart: Deutsche Bibelgesellschaft, 1994.

Die Bibel, oder die ganze Heilige Schrift des Alten und Neuen Testaments [1545], Martin Luther, trans. Stuttgart: Privilegirten Bibel-Anstalt, 1853.

Holy Bible, 1611 edition, King James Version [KJV], Peabody, Mass.: Hendrickson, 2003.

Holy Bible, containing the Old and New Testaments, New King James Version [NKJV], Nashville: Nelson, 1983.

Abel, Günter. *Nietzsche: Die Dynamik der Willen zur Macht und die ewige Wiederkehr*, 2nd ed., Berlin: de Gruyter, 1998.

Adorno, Theodor. *Notes to Literature*, 2 vols., Shierry Weber Nicholsen, trans., New York: Columbia University Press, 1991.

Allman, George J. *Greek Geometry from Thales to Euclid*, Dublin: Hodges, Figgis, & Co., 1889.

Altizer, Thomas J. J. *The Gospel of Christian Atheism*, Philadelphia: Westminster, 1966.

Arendt, Hannah. "Walter Benjamin: 1892–1940" [1968], in Benjamin, *Illuminations: Essays and Reflections*, H. Arendt, ed., New York: Schocken, 1969, 1–58.

Aristotle. *Metaphysica*, Werner Jaeger, ed., Oxford: Clarendon Press, 1957.

Auerbach, Erich. *Mimesis: The Representation of Reality in Western Literature* [1946], Willard Trask, trans., Princeton: Princeton University Press, 2003.

Augustine. *De doctrina christiana*, R. P. H. Green, trans., Oxford: Clarendon Press, 1995.

———. *On the Trinity*, Gareth B. Matthews, ed., Cambridge: Cambridge University Press, 2002.

Bal, Mieke. "Virginity: Toward a Feminist Philology," *Disposito: Revista hispánica de semiótica literaria* 12 (1987), 30–82.

Balzac, Honoré de. *La Peau de chagrin* [1831], in *La Comédie humaine*, vol. 10: *Etudes philosophiques*, Pierre-Georges Castes, ed., Paris: Gallimard, 1979 [*The Wild Ass's Skin*, Herbert Hunt, trans., London: Penguin, 1977].

Barthes, Roland. *De l'œuvre au texte* [1971], in *Œuvres complètes*, vol. 2, E. Marty, ed., Paris: Seuil, 1994, 1211–17 ["From Work to Text," in *The Rustle of Language*, R. Howard, trans., Berkeley: University of California Press, 1989, 56–64].

Bartl, Gerald. *Spuren und Narben: Die Fleischwerdung der Literatur im Zwanzigsten Jahrhundert*, Würzburg: Königshausen & Neumann, 2002.

Bataille, Georges. *Visions of Excess: Selected Writings 1927–1939*, Allen Stoekl, ed., Minneapolis: University of Minnesota Press, 1985.

Baudelaire, Charles. *Œuvres complètes* (Bibliothèque de la Pléiade), Claude Pichois, ed., Paris: Gallimard, 1961.

Bauer, Matthias. "A Word made Flesh: Anmerkungen zum lebendigen Wort bei Emily Dickinson," in *Bibeldichtung*, Volker Kapp and Dorothea Scholl, eds., *Schriften zur Literaturwissenschaft* 26 (2006), 373–92.

Bayer, Oswald, ed., *Johann Georg Hamann: Der hellste Kopf seiner Zeit*, Tübingen: Attempo, 1998.

Benjamin, Walter. *The Arcades Project*, Howard Eiland and Kevin McLaughlin, trans., Cambridge: Harvard University Press, 1999.

———. *Briefe*, 2 vols., Gershom Scholem and Theodor W. Adorno, eds., Frankfurt a. M.: Suhrkamp, 1978. [*The Correspondence of Walter Benjamin*, G. Scholem and T. W. Adorno, eds., M. R. Jacobson and E. M. Jacobson, trans., Chicago: University of Chicago Press, 1994]

———. *Denkbilder*, Frankfurt a. M.: Suhrkamp, 1994.

———. *Illuminations: Essays and Reflections*, Harry Zohn, trans., New York: Schocken, 1969.

———. *Selected Writings*, vol. 2, *1927–1934*, Michael Jennings, ed., Cambridge: Harvard University Press, 1999.

Bentley, Jerry H. *Humanists and Holy Writ: New Testament Scholarship in the Renaissance*, Princeton: Princeton University Press, 1983.

Bergman, Samuel H. *Dialogical Philosophy from Kierkegaard to Buber*, Albany: State University of New York Press, 1991.

Bernstein, Charles. *A Poetics*, Cambridge: Harvard University Press, 1992.

Betz, John R. *After Enlightenment: The Post-Secular Vision of J. G. Hamann*, Oxford: Wiley-Blackwell, 2009.

Blanchard, Donald. "Emily Dickinson's Ophthalmic Consultation with Henry Willard Williams, MD," *Archives of Ophthalmology* 130:12 (2012), 1591–95.

Blanchot, Maurice. *L'entretien infini*, Paris: Gallimard, 1969.

Blumenberg, Hans. *Matthäuspassion*, Frankfurt a. M.: Suhrkamp, 1988.

Bohm, Arnd. "Landscapes of Exile: Celan's 'Gespräch im Gebirg,'" *Germanic Review* 78 (2003), 99–111.

Bollack, Jean, Winkler, Jean-Marie, and Wögerbauer, Werner. "Tenebrae: Esquisse d'une compréhension," *Revue des Sciences Humaines* 97: 223 (1991), 125–70.

Bombaci, Nunzio "Der Prolog des Johannesevangelium als Epiphanie," in *Pneumatologie als Grammatik der Subjektivität: Ferdinand Ebner*, Ermenegildo Bidese, Richard Hörmann, and Silvano Zucal, eds., Vienna: Lit Verlag, 2012, 173–186.

Boyarin, Daniel. *Carnal Israel: Reading Sex in Talmudic Culture*, Berkeley: University of California Press, 1993.

Callahan, Ruth. *In my Flesh I shall see God: Franz Kafka's "In der Strafkolonie," the Alphabet, the Covenant, and Isaac Luria's Tikkun Olam*, Ph.D. diss., Cincinnati: Union Institute & University, 2006.

Camporeale, Salvatore. *Lorenzo Valla: Umanesimo e teologia*, Florence: Instituto nazionale di studi sul Rinascimento, 1972.

Carbone, Mauro. *The Flesh of Images: Merleau-Ponty between Painting and Cinema*, Marta Nijhuis, trans., Albany: SUNY Press, 2015.

Casper, Bernhard. *Das dialogische Denken: Franz Rosenzweig, Ferdinand Ebner und Martin Buber*, Freiburg: Alber, 2002.

Catullus. *C. Valerii Catulli: Carmina*, Roger Aubrey Baskerville Mynors, ed., Oxford: Oxford University Press, 1958.

Cavarero, Adriana. *For More than One Voice: Toward a Philosophy of Vocal Expression*, Paul Kottman, trans., Stanford: Stanford University Press, 2005.

Celan, Paul. *Die Gedichte: Kommentierte Gesamtausgabe*, Barbara Wiedemann, ed., Frankfurt a. M.: Suhrkamp, 2005.

———. *Gesammelte Werke*, 5 vols., Beda Allemann and Stefan Reichert, eds., Frankfurt a. M.: Suhrkamp, 1983.

———. *Meridian. Endfassung – Vorstufen – Materialen*, Bernhard Böschenstein and Heino Schnull, ed., Frankfurt a. M.: Suhrkamp, 1999.

Celan, Paul and Sachs, Nelly. *Briefwechsel*, Barbara Wiedemann, ed., Frankfurt a. M.: Suhrkamp, 1993.

Celenza, Christopher. "Lorenzo Valla and the Traditions and Transmissions of Philosophy," *Journal of the History of Ideas* 66 (2005), 483–506.

———. "Lorenzo Valla's Radical Philology: The Preface to the *Annotations to the New Testament* in Context," *Journal of Medieval and Early Modern Studies* 42 (2012), 365–394.

———. "Renaissance Humanism and the New Testament," *Journal of Medieval and Renaissance Studies* 24 (1994), 33–52.

Christes, Johannes. "Texte im Elementarunterricht als Träger sittlicher Werte in republikanischer Zeit", in *O tempora, o mores! Römische Werte und römische Literatur in den letzten Jahrzehnten der Republik*, Andreas Haltenhoff, Andreas Heil, and Fritz Heiner Mutschler, ed. (Munich: Saur, 2003), 51–68.

Cixous, Hélène. "The Laugh of the Medusa," Keith and Paula Cohen, trans., *Signs* 4 (1976), 875–93.

Coakley, Sarah. "What Does Chalcedon Solve and What Does It Not? Some Reflections on the Status and Meaning of the Chalcedonian 'Definition,'" in *The Incarnation: An Interdisciplinary Symposium on the Incarnation of the Son of God*, Stephen T. Davis, Daniel Kendall, and Gerald O'Collins, eds., Oxford: Oxford University Press, 2002, 143–63.

Cooper, Adam G. *Life in the Flesh: An Anti-Gnostic Spiritual Philosophy*, Oxford: Oxford University Press, 2008.

Compagnon, Antoine. *La seconde main, ou le travail de la citation*, Paris: Seuil, 1979.

Conte, Gian Biagio. *The Rhetoric of Imitation: Genre and Poetic Memory in Vergil and Other Latin Poets*, Charles Segal, ed., Ithaca: Cornell University Press, 1986.

Corngold, Stanley. *Lambent Traces: Franz Kafka*, Princeton: Princeton University Press, 2004.

Cox, Whitney. Review of James Turner, *Philology: The Forgotten Origins of the Modern Humanities, Bryn Mawr Classical Review* (2015), 02.18.

David, Ephraim. "Sparta's *Kosmos* of Silence," in *Sparta: New Perspectives*, Stephen Hodkinson and Anton Powell, eds., 117–46, London: Duckworth, 1999.

Davidson, Cathy N. *Revolution and the World: The Rise of the Novel in America*, Oxford: Oxford University Press, 1986.

Dawson, John David. *Christian Figural Reading and the Fashioning of Identity*, Berkeley: University of California Press, 2002.

Deleuze, Gilles. *Nietzsche and Philosophy*, Hugh Tomlinson, trans., New York: Columbia University Press, 1983.

de Man, Paul. *The Resistance to Theory*, Minneapolis: University of Minnesota Press, 1986.

Demuth, Volker. *Fleisch: Versuch einer Carneologie*, Berlin: Matthes & Seitz, 2016.

Depraz, Natalie. *Transcendance et incarnation: Le statut de l'intersubjectivité comme altérité à soi chez Husserl*, Paris: Vrin, 1995.

Derrida, Jacques. *On Touching—Jean-Luc Nancy*, Christine Irizarry, trans., Stanford: Stanford University Press, 2005.

———. *Sovereignties in Question: The Poetics of Paul Celan*, Thomas Dutroit and Outi Pasanen, eds., New York: Fordham University Press, 2005.

Dickinson, Emily. *Poems*, 3 vols., Thomas H. Johnson, ed., Cambridge: Harvard University Press, 1955.

———. *Letters of Emily Dickinson*, Thomas Johnson and Theodora Ward, eds., Cambridge: Harvard University Press, 1960.

———. *The Poems, Variorum Edition*, 3 vols., Ralph William Franklin, ed., Cambridge: Harvard University Press, 1998.

Dier, Oliver. "Die Verwandlung der Wiederkunft," *Nietzsche-Studien* 30 (2001), 133–74.

Dolar, Mladen. *A Voice and Nothing More*, Cambridge: MIT Press, 2006.

Dostoevsky, Fyodor. *The Brothers Karamazov*, Ignat Avsey, trans., Oxford: Oxford University Press, 1994. [*Brat'ja Karamazovy*, in *Collected Works*, 30 vols. Leningrad: Academy of Sciences, 1972–1990, vol. 14].

Ebner, Ferdinand. *Schriften*, vol. 1, Franz Seyr, ed., Munich: Kösel, 1963–65.

Edwards, Jonathan. *The Works of Jonathan Edwards*, 2 vols., Edward Hickman, ed., London: William Ball, 1839.

Esposito, Roberto. *Bios: Biopolitics and Philosophy*, Timothy Campbell, trans., Minneapolis: University of Minnesota Press, 2008.

———. "Flesh and Body in the Deconstruction of Christianity," Janell Watson, trans., *Minnesota Review* 75 (2010), 89–99.

Evans, Craig. "Isaiah 6:9–10 in Rabbinic and Patristic Writings," *Vigiliae Christianae* 36 (1982), 275–81.

Farr, Judith. *The Passion of Emily Dickinson*, Cambridge: Harvard University Press, 1998.

Felstiner, John. "'Clawed into Each Other': Jewish vs. Christian Memory in Paul Celan's 'Tenebrae,'" *TriQuarterly* 87 (1993), 193–208.

Finnerty, Páraic. *Emily Dickinson's Shakespeare*, Amherst: University of Massachusetts Press, 2006.

Francis, Eric David. "Brachylogia Laconica," *Bulletin of the Institute of Classical Studies* 38: 1 (1991–93): 198–212.

Franck, Dider. *Flesh and Body: On the Phenomenology of Edmund Husserl* [1981], Joseph Rivera and Scott Davidson, trans., New York: Bloomsbury, 2014.

Gadamer, Hans-Georg. *Gadamer on Celan*, Richard Heinemann, trans., Albany: SUNY Press, 1997.

———. *Wahrheit und Methode. Grundzüge einer philosophischen Hermeneutik*, Tübingen: Mohr, 1990. [*Truth and Method*, Garrett Barden and John Cumming, eds., New York: Crossroad, 1982.]

Gautier, Théophile. *Poésies complètes*, 3 vols., René Jasinski, ed. Paris: Nizet, 1970.

Gildenhard, Ingo. *Paideia Romana. Cicero's Tusculan Disputations*, Cambridge: Cambridge University Press, 2007.

Glotzer, Leonard. *Fundamentals of Jewish Mysticism: The Book of Creation and Its Commentaries*, Northvale, NJ: Aronson, [1977] 1992.

Goethe, Johann Wolfgang von. *Aus meinem Leben: Dichtung und Wahrheit. Werke*, Erich Trunz, ed., vol. 9, Munich: Deutscher Taschenbuch Verlag, 1981.

———. *Faust: Der Tragödie erster und zweiter Teil*, Erich Trunz, ed., Munich: Beck, 1987. [*Faust: A Tragedy*, Walter Arndt, trans., New York: Norton, 1976.]

Grafton, Anthony. *Forgers and Critics: Creativity and Duplicity in Western Scholarship*, Princeton: Princeton University Press, 1990.

Graubner, Hans. "Physikotheologie und Kinderphysik: Kants und Hamanns Plan zu einer Physik für Kinder in der physikotheologischen Tradition des 18. Jahrhunderts," in *Johann Georg Hamann und die Krise der Aufklärung, Acta des fünften internationalen Hamann-Kolloquiums*, Bernhard Gajek and Albert Meier, eds., New York: Lang, 1990, 117–45.

Gray, Richard. "Disjunctive Signs: Semiotics, Aesthetics, and Failed Mediation in 'In der Strafkolonie,'" in *A Companion to the Works of Franz Kafka*, James Rolleston, ed., New York: Camden House, 2002, 213–45.

Griffith-Dickson, Gwen. "God, I, and Thou: Hamann and the Personalist Tradition," in *Hamann and the Tradition*, Lisa Marie Anderson, ed., Evanston: Northwestern University Press, 2012, 55–66.

Griswold, Charles L. "Relying on Your Own Voice: An Unsettled Rivalry of Moral Ideas in Plato's *Protagoras*," *Review of Metaphysics* 53: 2 (1999): 283–307.

Guardini, Romano. "The Legend of the Grand Inquisitor," Sally Cunneen, trans., *Cross Currents* 3 (1952), 58–86.

Gumbrecht, Hans Ulrich. *The Powers of Philology: Dynamics of Textual Scholarship*, Urbana: University of Illinois Press, 2003.

Gurd, Sean Alexander. *Iphigenias at Aulis: Textual Multiplicity, Radical Philology*, Ithaca: Cornell University Press, 2005.

Halliwell, Stephen. "The Subjection of Muthos to Logos: Plato's Citation of the Poets," *Classical Quarterly* 50: 1 (2000), 94–112.

Hamacher, Werner. "Für—die Philologie," in *Was ist eine philologische Frage?* J. P. Schwindt, ed., Frankfurt a. M.: Suhrkamp, 2009, 21–60. [*Minima Philologica*, Catherine Diehl and Jason Groves, trans., New York: Fordham University Press, 2015.]

———. *Premises: Essays on Philosophy and Literature from Kant to Celan*, P. Fenves, trans., Cambridge: Harvard University Press, 1996.

Hamann, Johann Georg. *Briefe*, Arthur Henkel, ed. Frankfurt a. M.: Insel, 1988.

———. *Briefwechsel*, 8 vols. Walther Ziesemer and Arthur Henkel, eds., Frankfurt a. M.: Insel, 1955–75.

———. *Sämtliche Werke*, 6 vols., Josef Nadler, ed., Vienna: Herder, 1947–1955.

Hardt, Michael, and Negri, Antonio. *Multitude: War and Democracy in the Age of Empire*, New York: Penguin, 2004.

Harpham, Geoffrey Galt. "Roots, Races, and the Return to Philology," *Representations* 106 (2009), 34–62.

Hatley, James. "Recursive Incarnation and Chiasmic Flesh: Two Readings of Paul Celan's 'Chymisch,'" in *Chiasms*, Leonard Lawlor, ed., Albany: SUNY Press, 2000, 237–49.

Heath, Thomas Little. Introduction to *Apollonius of Perga: Treatise on the Conic Sections*, Cambridge: Cambridge University Press, 1896, xvii–xxx.

Hegel, Georg Wilhelm Friedrich. *Werke*, 20 vols., Eva Moldenhauer and Karl Markus Michel, eds., Frankfurt a. M.: Suhrkamp, 1971.

Heidegger, Martin. *Nietzsche*, vol. 1, Pfullingen: Neske, 1961 [*The Will to Power as Art, Nietzsche*, vol. 1, David Farrell Krell, trans., New York: Harper & Row, 1979].

———. *Unterwegs zur Sprache*, Stuttgart: Neske, 1959 [*Poetry, Language, Thought*, Albert Hofstadter, trans., New York: Harper & Row, 1971].

———. *Zur Seinsfrage* [1955], in *Wegmarken*, Frankfurt a. M.: Klostermann, 1976, 385–426.

Henel, Ingeborg. "Kafkas 'In der Strafkolonie': Form, Sinn und Stellung der Erzählung im Gesamtwerk," *Untersuchungen zur Literatur als Geschichte: Festschrift für Benno von Wiese*, Vincent Günther, Helmut Koopmann, and Joachim Krause, eds., Berlin: Schmidt, 1973, 480–504.

Henry, Michel. *Incarnation: A Philosophy of the Flesh*, Karl Hefty, trans., Evanston: Northwestern University Press, 2015.

Hirschhorn, Norbert and Longsworth, Polly. "'Medicine Posthumous': A New Look at Emily Dickinson's Medical Conditions," *New England Quarterly* 69:2 (1996), 299–316.

Hölderlin, Friedrich. *Werke*, 4 vols., Friedrich Beißner and Jochen Schmidt, eds., Frankfurt a. M.: Insel, 1969.

Horace. *Q. Horati Flacci: Opera*, H. W. Garrod, ed., Oxford: Oxford University Press, 1901.

Horstmann, Axel. "Philologie" in the *Historisches Wörterbuch der Philosophie*, 13 vols., J. Ritter, ed. (Basel: Schwabe, 1971–2007), 7: 552–72.

Husserl, Edmund. *Ideas Pertaining to a Pure Phenomenology and to a Phenomenological Philosophy*, vol. 2: *Studies in the Phenomenology of Constitution* [1913], Richard Rojcewicz and André Schuwer, trans., Dordrecht: Kluwer, 1989, 151–58.

Jachmann, Otto. *Denken wird Wahrnehmung: Die Philosophie von Brentano, Husserl, Heidegger, und Derrida und die Anthroposophie*. Borchen: Möllmann, 2009.

Jacobs, Brian. "Self-incurrence, Incapacity, and Guilt: Kant and Hamann on Enlightenment Guardianship," *Lessing Yearbook* 28 (1996), 147–61.

Janicaud, Dominique, ed., *Phenomenology and the "Theological Turn": The French Debate*, New York: Fordham University Press, 2000.

Jerome, *Liber de optimo genere interpretandi: Epistula 57*, G. J. M. Bartelink, ed., Leiden: Brill, 1980.

Johnson, Kimberly. *Made Flesh: Sacrament and Poetics in Post-Reformation England*, Philadelphia: University of Pennsylvania Press, 2014.

Kafka, Franz. *Briefe 1902-1924*, Max Brod, ed., Frankfurt a. M.: Fischer, 1958.

———. *Gesammelte Werke*, 12 vols., H.-G. Koch, ed., Frankfurt a. M.: Fischer, 1994.

Kant, Immanuel. *Gesammelte Schriften* (Akademie-Ausgabe), 23 vols., Berlin: de Gruyter, 1900–2004.

———. *Political Writings*, H. Reiss, ed., H. B. Nisbet, trans., Cambridge: Cambridge University Press, 1991.

Kantorowicz, Ernst. *The King's Two Bodies: A Study in Mediaeval Political Theology* [1957], Princeton: Princeton University Press, 1997.

Kelber, Werner H. "Die Fleischwerdung des Wortes in der Körperlichkeit des Textes," in Hans Ulrich Gumbrecht and K. Ludwig Pfeiffer, eds., *Materialität der Kommunikation*, Frankfurt a. M.: Suhrkamp, 1995, 31–42.

Kendrick, Laura. *Animating the Letter: The Figurative Embodiment of Writing from Late Antiquity to the Renaissance*, Columbus: Ohio State University Press, 1999.

Kermode, Frank. *The Genesis of Secrecy: On the Interpretation of Narrative*, Cambridge: Harvard University Press, 1979.

Kirk, G. S., Raven, J. E., and Schofield, M., eds. *The Presocratic Philosophers*, Cambridge: Cambridge University Press, 1957.

Kittler, Friedrich, ed., *Austreibung des Geistes aus den Geisteswissenschaften: Programme des Poststrukturalismus*, Paderborn: Schönigh, 1980.

Klossowski, Pierre. *Nietzsche et le cercle vicieux*, Paris: Mercure de France, 1969. [*Nietzsche and the Vicious Circle*, Daniel W. Smith, trans., Chicago: University of Chicago Press, 1997.]

Krell, David Farrell. "Die philosophische Wühlarbeit bei Kant, Hegel und Nietzsche," *boundary 2*, vol. 9 (1981), 155–67.

Kristeva, Julia. *Black Sun: Depression and Melancholia*, Leon S. Roudiez, trans,. New York: Columbia University Press, 1989.

Lacoue-Labarthe, Philippe. *Poetry as Experience*, Andrea Tarnowski, trans., Stanford: Stanford University Press, 1999.

———. *Typography: Mimesis, Philosophy, Politics*, Christopher Fynsk, trans., Cambridge: Harvard University Press, 1989.

Lakoff, George, and Johnson, Mark. *Philosophy in the Flesh: The Embodied Mind and Its Challenge to Western Thought*. New York: Basic Books, 1999.

Lease, Benjamin. *Emily Dickinson's Readings of Men and Books*, New York: Palgrave, 1990.

Leupin, Alexandre. *Fiction and Incarnation: Rhetoric, Theology, and the Middle Ages*, David Laatsch, trans., Minneapolis: University of Minnesota Press, 2003.

Levine, Michael. "Pendant: Büchner, Celan, and the Terrible Voice of the Meridian," *MLN* 122 (2007), 573–601.

Leyda, Jay. *The Years and Hours of Emily Dickinson*, New Haven: Yale University Press, 1960.

Liébert, Georges. *Nietzsche and Music*, David Pellauer and Graham Parkes, trans., Chicago: University of Chicago Press, 2004.

Littau, Karin. *Theories of Reading: Books, Bodies, and Bibliomania*, Cambridge: Polity, 2006.

Liviu, Jitianu. "Dialogisch Denken: Prämissen für eine Theologie der Gegenseitigkeit," *Studia Universitatis Babes-Bolyai – Theologica Catholica Latina* 1 (2003), 47–61.

Loraux, Nicole. *The Mourning Voice: An Essay on Greek Tragedy*, Elizabeth Trapnell Rawlings, trans., Ithaca: Cornell University Press, 2002.

Lubac, Henri de. *Corpus Mysticum: The Eucharist and the Church in the Middle Ages*, Gemma Simonds, trans., Notre Dame: University of Notre Dame Press, 2007.

Lundin, Roger. *Emily Dickinson and the Art of Belief*, 2nd ed., Grand Rapids: Eerdmans, 2004.

Mallarmé, Stéphane. *Œuvres complètes*, 2 vols. (Bibliothèque de la Pléiade), Bertrand Marchal, ed., Paris: Gallimard, 1998.

Mehtonen, Päivi. *Obscure Language, Unclear Literature: Theory and Practice from Quintilian to the Enlightenment*, Helsinki: Finnish Academy of Science and Letters, 2003.

Mendicino, Kristina. "An Other Rhetoric: Paul Celan's Meridian," *MLN* 126 (2011), 630–50.

Menninghaus, Winfried. "Zum Problem des Zitats bei Celan und in der Celan-Philologie," in *Paul Celan*, W. Hamacher and W. Menninghaus, eds., Frankfurt a. M.: Suhrkamp, 1988, 170–90.

Merleau-Ponty, Maurice. *Œuvres*, Claude Lefort, ed., Paris: Quarto Gallimard, 2010.

———. *The Visible and the Invisible*, Alphonso Lingis, trans., Evanston: Northwestern University Press, 1968.

Michaels, Walter Benn. *The Shape of the Signifier: 1967 to the End of History*, Princeton: Princeton University Press, 2006.

Miles, Laura Saetveit. "The Origin and Development of the Virgin Mary's Book at the Annunciation," *Speculum* 89 (2014), 632–69.

Monfasani, John. "Pseudo-Dionysius the Areopagite in Mid-Quattrocento Rome," in *Supplementum Festivum: Studies in Honor of Paul Oskar Kristeller*, James Hankins et al., eds., Binghamton: Medieval and Renaissance Texts and Studies, 1987, 189–219.

Morawski, Stefan. "The Basic Function of Quotation," in *Sign, Language, Culture*, C. H. van Schooneveld, ed., The Hague: Mouton, 1970, 690–705.

Müller-Sievers, Helmut. "On the Way to Quotation: Paul Celan's *Meridian* Speech," *New German Critique* 91 (2004), 131–49.

Nadler, Josef. *Johann Georg Hamann: Der Zeuge des Corpus Mysticum*, Salzburg: Müller, 1949.

Nancy, Jean-Luc. *Corpus*, Richard Rand, trans., New York: Fordham University Press, 2008.

———. *Noli me tangere: On the Raising of the Body*, Sarah Clift, Pascale-Anne Brault, and Michael Naas, trans., New York: Fordham University Press, 2008.

Nerval, Gérard de. *Œuvres*, vol. 1, Henri Lemaitre, ed., Paris: Garnier, 1966.

Nichols, Stephen G. "Introduction: Philology in a Manuscript Culture," *Speculum* 65 (1990), 1–10.

Nietzsche, Friedrich. *Beyond Good and Evil: Prelude to a Philosophy of the Future*, Walter Kaufmann, trans., New York: Vintage, 1966.

———. *The Birth of Tragedy and Other Writings*, Ronald Speirs, trans., Cambridge: Cambridge University Press, 1999.

———. *Briefwechsel: Kritische Gesamtausgabe*, 24 vols., Giorgio Colli and Mazzino Montinari, eds., Berlin: de Gruyter, 1975–2004.

———. *Daybreak: Thoughts on the Prejudices of Morality*, R. J. Hollingdale, trans., Cambridge: Cambridge University Press, 1997.

———. *Homer und die klassische Philologie* (1869), in *Werke in drei Bänden*, Karl Schlechta, ed., Munich: Hanser, 1966, 3: 155–74.

———. *Sämtliche Werke: Kritische Studienausgabe*, 15 vols., Giorgio Colli and Mazzino Montinari, eds., Munich: Deutscher Taschenbuch Verlag, 1980.

Noble, Marianne. "The Sublimity of *Hamlet* in Emily Dickinson's Poem, 'He Fumbles at Your Soul,'" in *Shakespeare and the Culture of Romanticism*, Joseph Ortiz, ed., Surrey: Ashgate, 2013, 121–38.

North, Paul. *The Yield: Kafka's Atheological Reformation*, Stanford: Stanford University Press, 2015.

O'Flaherty, James C. *Hamann's Socratic Memorabilia: A Translation and Commentary*, Baltimore: Johns Hopkins University Press, 1967.

Olender, Maurice. *The Languages of Paradise: Race, Religion, and Philology in the Nineteenth Century*, Arthur Goldhammer, trans. (Cambridge: Harvard University Press, 1992), 88–92.

Orosz, Magdolna. "Biblical 'Emblems' in Paul Celan's *Tenebrae*: A Special Case of Intertextuality," *Neohelicon* 22 (1995), 169–88.

Ossar, Michael. "The Malevolent God and Paul Celan's 'Tenebrae,'" *Deutsche Vierteljahrsschrift für Literaturwissenschaft und Geistesgeschichte* 65 (1991), 174–97.

O'Sullivan, Michael. *The Incarnation of Language: Joyce, Proust, and a Philosophy of the Flesh*, New York: Bloomsbury, 2008.

Peacham, Henry. *The Garden of Eloquence*, London: 1577.

Phillips, Elizabeth. *Emily Dickinson: Personae and Performance*, University Park: Pennsylvania State University Press, 1988.

Phillips, Siobhan. "'Loved Philology': Emily Dickinson's Trinitarian Word," *ESQ: A Journal of the American Renaissance* 51 (2005), 250–75.

Pliny the Elder. *Naturalis Historia* [*Natural History*, vol. 8, *Books 28–32*, W. H. S. Jones, trans., Cambridge: Harvard University Press, 1963].

Plutarch. *Moralia*, vol. 9: *Table-Talk*, Edwin L. Minar, Jr., F. H. Sandbach, and W. C. Helmbold, trans., Cambridge: Harvard University Press, 1961.

Pollock, Sheldon. "Future Philology: The Fate of a Soft Science in a Hard World," *Critical Inquiry* 35 (2009), 931–61.

Polybius. *The Histories: Books 9–15*, W. R. Paton, trans., Cambridge: Harvard University Press, 2011.

Porter, James. *Nietzsche and the Philology of the Future*, Stanford: Stanford University Press, 2000.

Poulet, Georges. "Criticism and the Experience of Interiority," in *The Structuralist Controversy: The Languages of Criticism & the Sciences of Man*, Richard Macksey and Eugenio Donato, eds. [1970], Baltimore: Johns Hopkins University Press, 2007, 56–72.

Proclus, *Proclii Diadochi in primum Euclidis elementorum librum*, G. Friedlein, ed., Leipzig: Teubner, 1873.

Pulver, Max. "Spaziergang mit Franz Kafka," in *Als Kafka mir entgegenkam . . . Erinnerungen an Franz Kafka*, Hans-Gerd Koch, ed., Berlin: Wagenbach, 1995, 130–35.

Puttenham, George. *The Arte of English Poesie*, London: Richard Field, 1589.

Pütz, Peter. "Autorität durch Wiederholung: Von der Herrschaft des Zitats," in *Autorität der/in Sprache: Literatur, Neue Medien*, Jürgen Fohrmann, ed., Bielefeld: Aisthesis, 1999, 694–704.

Quackenbos, John Duncan. *Practical Rhetoric*, New York: American Book Co., 1896.

Quintilian. *Institutio oratoria*, L. Radermacher and V. Buchheit, eds., Leipzig: Teubner, 1971.

Rancière, Jacques. *The Flesh of Words: The Politics of Writing*, Charlotte Mandell, trans., Stanford: Stanford University Press, 2004.

Richter, A., Alac, P., and Badiou, B., eds. *Paul Celan: La bibliothèque philosophique*, Paris: ENS, 2004.

Rine, Abigail. *Irigaray, Incarnation, and Contemporary Women's Fiction*. New York: Bloomsbury, 2013.

Rivera, Mayra. *Poetics of the Flesh*, Durham: Duke University Press, 2015.

Rowe, David. "The Eternal Return of the Same: Nietzsche's 'Value-Free' Revaluation of All Values," *Parrhesia* 15 (2012), 71–86.

Said, Edward. *Humanism and Democratic Criticism*, New York: Columbia University Press, 2004.

St. Armand, Barton Levi. *Emily Dickinson and Her Culture: The Soul's Society*, Cambridge: Cambridge University Press, 1984.

Santner, Eric. *The Royal Remains: The People's Two Bodies and the Endgames of Sovereignty*, Chicago: University of Chicago Press, 2011.

———. *The Weight of All Flesh: On the Subject Matter of Political Economy*, Oxford: Oxford University Press, 2015.

Schestag, Thomas. "buk," *MLN* 109 (1994), 399–444.

———. "Philology, Knowledge," *Telos* 140 (2007), 28–44.

Schestov, Leo. *Die Nacht der Gethsemane* [1923], H. Ruoff, trans., *Ariadne: Jahrbuch der Nietzsche-Gesellschaft*, E. Bertram, H. von Hofmannstahl, and T. Mann, eds, Munich: Nietzsche-Gesellschaft (1925), 36–109.

Schleiermacher, Friedrich. *Pädogogische Schriften*, C. Platz, ed., Langensalza: Beyer, 1902.

Schmitt, Carl. *Der Nomos der Erde im Völkerrecht des jus publicum Europaeum*, Cologne: Greven, 1950.

Scholem, Gershom. "Über Kant," Julia Ng, ed., *MLN* 127 (2012), 440–41.

Schwartz, Regina. *Sacramental Poetics at the Dawn of Secularism: When God Left the World*, Stanford: Stanford University Press, 2008.

Schwindt, Jürgen Paul, ed. *Was ist eine philologische Frage?* Frankfurt a. M.: Suhrkamp, 2009.

Seneca, *Ad Lucilium epistulae morales*, 2 vols., L. D. Reynolds, ed., Oxford: Oxford University Press, 1987–89.

Sewall, Richard. *The Lyman Letters: New Light on Emily Dickinson and Her Family*, Amherst: University of Massachusetts Press, 1965.

Shakespeare, William. *The Complete Pelican Shakespeare*, Stephen Orgel and A. R. Braunmuller, eds., New York: Penguin, 2002.

Shepherd, Melanie. "Affirmation and Mortal Life: Nietzsche's Eternal Return and the Death of Zarathustra," *Philosophy Today* 55 (2011), 22–36.

Simpson, Christopher B. *Merleau-Ponty and Theology*, London: Bloomsbury, 2014.

Slattery, Dennis Patrick. *The Wounded Body: Remembering the Markings of the Flesh*, Albany: SUNY Press, 1999.

Steiner, George. *Real Presences*, Chicago: University of Chicago Press, 1989.

Stierle, Karlheinz. "Der Maulwurf im Bildfeld: Versuch zu einer Metapherngeschichte," *Archiv für Begriffsgeschichte* 26 (1982), 101–43.

Stiewe, Barbara. *Der "Dritte Humanismus": Aspekte deutscher Griechenrezeption vom George-Kreis bis zum Nationalsozialismus*, Berlin: de Gruyter, 2011.

Stockhammer, Robert. *Grammatik: Wissen und Macht in der Geschichte einer sprachlichen Institution*, Frankfurt a. M.: Suhrkamp, 2014.

Suetonius, *Suetonius*, vol. 2, J. C. Rolfe, trans. Cambridge: Harvard University Press, 1914.

Susenbrotus, Johannes. *Epitome troporum ac schematum et grammaticorum & rhetorum*, Zürich: C. Froschouer, 1540.

Szondi, Peter. "Über philologische Erkenntnis," in *Schriften*, 2 vols., J. Bollack et al., eds., Frankfurt a. M.: Suhrkamp, 1978.

Taylor, Mark C. *After God*, Chicago: University of Chicago Press, 2007.

Valla, Lorenzo. *Antidotum Primum: La prima apologia contro Poggio Bracciolini* [ca. 1450], Ari Wesseling, ed., Assen, Germany: Van Gorcum, 1978.

———. *Collatio Novi Testamenti*, Alessandro Perosa, ed., Florence: Sansoni, 1970.

———. *Repastinatio totius dialectice et philosophie*, 2 vols., G. Zippel, ed., Padua: Antenore, 1982.

Vendler, Helen. *Dickinson: Selected Poems and Commentaries*, Cambridge: Harvard University Press, 2010.

Venturi, Franco. "Sapere aude!" *Revista storica italiana* 71 (1959), 119–28.

Vincent, Jean Marcel. "La figure de l'inversion dans le poème Tenebrae de Paul Celan," *Revue de théologie et de philosophie* 57 (2007), 205–25.

Virno, Paolo. *When the Word Becomes Flesh: Language and Human Nature*, Giuseppina Mecchia, trans., South Pasadena: Semiotext(e), 2015.

Wand, Martin and Sewall, Richard. "'Eyes Be Blind, Heart Be Still': A New Perspective on Emily Dickinson's Eye Problem," *New England Quarterly* 52 (1979), 400–06.

Weinold, Götz "Paul Celans Hölderlin-Widerruf," *Poetica* 2 (1968), 216–28.

Wellbery, David. *The Specular Moment: Goethe's Early Lyric and the Beginnings of Romanticism*, Stanford: Stanford University Press, 1996.

Wild, Reiner. "Natur und Offenbarung: Hamanns und Kants gemeinsamer Plan zu einer Physik für Kinder," *Geist und Zeichen: Festschrift für Arthur Henkel zu seinem sechzigsten Geburtstag*, Herbert Anton, Bernhard Gajek, and Peter Pfaff, eds., Heidelberg: Winter, 1977, 452–68.

Willis, Ika. "Philology, or the Art of Befriending the Text," *Postmedieval* 5 (2014), 486–501.

Winchester, James. *Nietzsche's Aesthetic Turn: Reading Nietzsche after Heidegger, Deleuze, and Derrida*, Albany: SUNY Press, 1994.

Wolff, Cynthia Griffin. *Emily Dickinson*, Reading, Mass.: Addison-Wesley, 1988.

Wolff, Kurt. *Briefwechsel eines Verlegers: 1911–1963*, Bernhard Zeller and Ellen Otten, eds., Frankfurt a. M.: Fischer, 1966.

Wolosky, Shira. "The Metaphysics of Language in Emily Dickinson (As Translated by Paul Celan)," in *Trajectories of Mysticism in Theory and Literature*, Phillip Leonard, ed., New York: St. Martin's, 2000, 25–45.

Ziolkowski, Jan. "Metaphilology," *Journal of English and Germanic Philology* 104 (2005), 239–72.

Žižek, Slavoj. *For They Know Not What They Do: Enjoyment as a Political Factor*, 2nd ed. New York: Verso, 2008.

———. *The Puppet and the Dwarf: The Perverse Core of Christianity*, Cambridge: MIT Press, 2003.

Žižek, Slavoj, and Milbank, John. *The Monstrosity of Christ: Paradox or Dialectic?* Cambridge: MIT Press, 2011.

Index of Biblical Verses

General Index